$2.—

WINE MARKETING ONLINE

How to use the newest tools of marketing to boost profits and build brands

Bruce McGechan

Win   uild

WINE MARKETING ONLINE
How to use the newest tools of marketing
to boost profits and build brands

Published by
The Wine Appreciation Guild
360 Swift Avenue
South San Francisco, CA 94080
(650) 866-3020
wineappreciation.com

Text copyright © 2013 by Bruce McGechan

Managing Editor: Bryan Imelli

All rights reserved. No part of this publication may be reproduced, distributed, or transmitted in any form or by any means, including photocopying, recording, or other electronic or mechanical methods, without the prior written permission of by the copyright holder.

Tony's Wine Store and Andrea's Vineyard are the product of the author's imagination and are used in a fictitious and illustrative manner. Any resemblance to actual persons, living or dead, or actual businesses is purely coincidental.

Although all reasonable care has been taken in the preparation of this book, neither the author nor the publisher can accept liability for any consequences arising from the information contained herein or from use thereof. Readers should be aware that internet websites listed in this work may have changed or disappeared between when this work was written and when it is read.

Contents

1 Introduction

1.1 The Wine Store—a burning platform?

The wine retail store and small winery is beset on all sides by supermarket and large liquor chain discounting, wine consumer bargain hunting, aggressive and exclusive liquor distributors, and the spread of wine sale 'flash' websites (super-discounters) not to mention the economic downturn. The original reason for opening a wine store or a winery, passion for wine, can easily be lost in this fight for survival and growth. This book helps provide a path to boosting profits by selling wine using internet and mobile technologies as well as helping you share your wine knowledge and passion with your customers (and avoiding catastrophic discounting practices).

Of course the wine business is not alone in facing aggressive competition. Here's what Stephen Elop, the new CEO of Nokia, wrote in a remarkably frank internal memo[1] to employees in February 2011 that seems equally relevant to wine retailers:

> There is a pertinent story about a man who was working on an oil platform in the North Sea. He woke up one night from a loud explosion, which suddenly set his entire oil platform on fire. In mere moments, he was surrounded by flames. Through the smoke and heat, he barely made his way out of the chaos to the platform's edge. When he looked down over the edge, all he could see were the dark, cold, foreboding Atlantic waters.
>
> As the fire approached him, the man had mere seconds to react. He could stand on the platform, and inevitably be consumed by the burning flames. Or, he could plunge 30 meters in to the freezing waters. The man was standing upon a 'burning platform,' and he needed to make a choice.
>
> He decided to jump. It was unexpected. In ordinary circumstances, the man would never consider plunging

into icy waters. But these were not ordinary times—his platform was on fire. The man survived the fall and the waters. After he was rescued, he noted that a 'burning platform' caused a radical change in his behavior.

We too, are standing on a 'burning platform,' and we must decide how we are going to change our behavior.

A wine retailer's 'platform' is the retail store and website rather than the mobile phone, and unlike Nokia their platform is not burning— it's more like smoldering. But if we don't take that leap into internet waters soon then we may face that burning platform in the near future.

Let's look at some internet research. Forrester Research together with Shop.org surveyed retail businesses and found that 10% of sales were online in 2012. [2] The hype is that retailers will be 'Amazoned' out of business. However I think the evidence is that once you start doing it yourself, selling wine online is about augmenting your brick and mortar sales rather than being cannibalized by online competitors.

Here's an excerpt from The Economist in an article called 'Retail v e-tail in America—Bleak Friday', in 2009 [3] to support this point of view:

> The concept of 'multichannel' shopping, where people can buy the same items from the same retailer in several different ways online, via their mobile phones and in shops, is gaining ground, and retailers are trying to encourage users of one channel to try another. Growing online traffic may actually increase sales in stores too. According to a spokesman for Macys, a department store chain, every dollar a consumer spends online with Macys leads to $5.70 in spending at a Macys store within ten days, because consumers learn about other products online and come into stores to look them over before buying them. Many online retailers offer tools that let people locate the nearest outlet that has a given item in stock.

I think the real concern is when your local customers look to browse for wines before going in-store and can't find your website. So they become customers of competitors that do have websites. You don't lose one bottle of sales per month you lose five bottles per month (as per the Macy's $5.70 ratio above).

However things have become even more complex with the arrival of the iPhone and iPad. These type of smart mobile devices have resulted in people using multiple devices when shopping. A recent Google study[4] found that 67% of us start shopping on one device (a PC/laptop, smartphone, or tablet device) before continuing on to another. Just what device we start on depends on what we're doing and where we are.

On the other hand, some retailers have heard about an (in)famous book called the Four Hour Work Week.[5] Its thesis is supposedly that the internet can allow you to work 4 hours a week and travel the world the rest of the time (though to be fair it's a little more nuanced than this). The internet is full of such incredible stories, some of which may be true, but what you don't see is the other 999 people who gave up when they found that a successful internet business was just a mirage and a hopeful dream.

The truth is in the middle for most of us. An eCommerce site and mobile app is unlikely to make you a millionaire, but it's also unlikely to cannibalize your sales. It's likely to increase your revenue by the industry average, an indication of which is the 4-8% quoted by Planet Retail above. Less if your site is poor and you do no marketing. More if you follow best practice: generate traffic, engage with your online customers, send them to a well-converting shopping cart, provide great customer service, and then develop repeat business.

The Wall Street Journal has said one New York brick and mortar wine store that went online increased sales by 15%.[6] I think that's a reasonable target.

A major theme of the book is that there is not one Single Magic Trick. Rather you will need to create informative and engaging information about wine and put a selling system or process around this system. The Nokia CEO referred to an 'ecosystem' of which his key paragraph was this (a note on jargon, 'devices' mean smartphones like the iPhone):

> The battle of devices has now become a war of ecosystems, where ecosystems include not only the hardware and software of the device, but developers, applications, eCommerce, advertising, search, social applications, location-based services, unified communications, and many other

things. Our competitors aren't taking our market share
with devices; they are taking our market share with an
entire ecosystem. This means we're going to have to decide how we either build, catalyze, or join an ecosystem.

This is an approach I agree with but from a wine store perspective.
Rather than being a wine store, a retailer, a wine expert, a marketing
expert, a capable tech user, and a good sharer of info and knowledge,
in wine forums, wine blogs, and on Facebook and Twitter, a good
wine store is a mixture of all these and more. It sits astride the new
wine ecosystems that are spreading around the world and around the
internet while bringing the best of those back to local customers.

The eCommerce website is a step in the right direction but it's
not enough. Wine consumers are also using various internet services
before deciding where to buy wine. They are using mobile apps, social
media, and local internet-based information to make their choices
about what and where they'll buy wine. *Then* they'll walk into a
wine store (only a few will buy online)—will it be yours?

1.2 Who This Book is For

This book is for primarily small and medium US wine stores and
wineries. Those owned by passionate wine enthusiasts who are being
tossed around in the turbulent wine and retail industries by chain
liquor retailers, supermarkets, liquor distributors, specialist discount
online retailers, and the internet-savvy, small wine store or winery
competitor just down the road. It shows you how to fight back and,
once again, be the natural choice for wine drinkers in your suburb,
city, or region. The aim is to increase your sales by 15% as measured
by online sales and much more in-store depending on how well you
implement the various internet strategies in this book, and how strong
the internet competition is in your region.

It will also be helpful to wine distributor/importers, 'pure play'
online wine retailers, wine bloggers, and wine marketing consultants
as the purpose of all these marketing strategies is to boost sales to
the common end customer—the wine drinker.

This book is written for the US market (and all dollar values are
US dollars); however, it is applicable to the other English-speaking
markets: Canada, UK, Australia, and New Zealand. Note the US

market is different from a legal perspective with its three-tier shipping laws restricting the sale of alcohol across state lines.

I imagine there will be two types of readers: the DIYer and the Delegator. The DIYers, or Do It Yourselfers, find doing things on the internet easy. Perhaps they already use basic Google internet marketing techniques and would like to expand their knowledge. Perhaps they are even experienced users of one area but would like to learn about other forms of wine internet marketing. The DIYer can follow the many step by step instructions in this book as well as access support by fellow wine retailers and the book's wider community in the forums (www.WineMarketingPros.com).

The other reader is the Delegator, who gets someone else to do it for them. They may not be comfortable in using any of the marketing techniques I cover in the following chapters. They are looking to understand how to sell wine online so they can decide how to best do this. The Delegator may then brief a generalist or a specialist wine internet marketing agency. This book would be very helpful for giving the generalist agency a running start.

1.3 Overview

This book is split into five parts, which follow the process of increasing website traffic, turning that into customers, and creating loyal advocates. These parts could be generally considered the strategies in selling wine online with each chapter explaining how a particular tactic achieves that strategy.

- Part I: The 3 Cs. The Customer, the Competitors and your Company, reviews what customers want, what competitors are doing, and how your company can successfully achieve its objectives

- Part II: Traffic. How to increase traffic to your online (and offline) shop. A traditional brand marketer would say this is about building 'awareness'

- Part III: Engagement. How to engage with these wine drinkers in order to build trust and reputation, or 'consideration'

- Part IV: Conversion covers how to convert this traffic into sales

- Part V: Repeat Business covers how to build a loyal customer base and advocates, or 'preference'.

1.3.1 Selling Wine Online—The Process

Successfully selling most products online requires following a similar marketing process:

- Traffic—increase web traffic to your website
- Engagement—build trust, reputation, and rapport with website visitors
- Conversion—convert traffic into sales through copywriting, user shopping experience, and suitable range and market prices
- eCommerce—have an eCommerce website i.e. online catalog, shopping cart, and order administration system
- Repeat Customers—turn new customers into repeat customers and hopefully advocates

Putting this in wine terms:

- Traffic—generate traffic to your site from search, advertising, shopping sites, and social media
- Engagement—interacting with customers on your blog, forums, Facebook, Twitter, and location-based services
- Conversion—convert this traffic into sales through good content, user shopping experience, suitable wine range, and fair prices
- eCommerce—easily administer orders, and comply with liquor age and shipping laws
- Repeat Purchase—turn new customers into repeat customers through follow-up email marketing, and your great customer service.

In essence you are coaxing people to visit, to stay, to become customers, and to become repeat purchasers. Each business will have particular challenges in certain parts of the process, but even the most outstanding online wine retailer constantly will be improving some part of this process.

Exactly where you start depends on your business issues and objectives. For example, many wine businesses have websites that look fantastic ('flash' slides, great vineyard images, trendy artwork) but fail to get any traffic. Their marketing objective is to increase traffic. Their strategy may be to use internet advertising, with a specific tactic being to use Google Adwords to increase new and unique visitor traffic by 20% in 6 months with an ad budget of $1000.

Or they have traffic and an excellent shopping cart but fail to persuade visitors to buy from their store. The problem is possibly engagement. Their marketing objective is to increase trust, interest, and authority with website visitors. Their specific tactic may be to create a blog with short, interesting posts about wine and wine regions. Their measurement of success could be the number of blog comments.

However what usually happens is that the fancy looking website gets few sales, the wine retailer gets frustrated, and then writes the internet off as useless. As mentioned above, research[2] shows that 10% of a retailer's business is now over the internet. My own experience is that some small wine stores already have 15-25% of their sales online.

What's more the phenomenon of people browsing online and buying in-store is now accepted by big retailers all around the world. Here's what Google's latest market research report says,[7]

> If you're not visible online when people are doing that homework, believe me, they'll find others who are. Here's what Brian Dunn, the CEO of Best Buy, told Retail-Geek.com in 2011: 'We know that 60% of our U.S. store sales are influenced by our customers' experience on Best-Buy.com'.
>
> That percentage is not unusual. The numbers are high for beverages, school supplies, and any other goods you normally wouldn't order online.

So let's do some numbers to illustrate this point: see Table 1.1.

Table 1.1: The ZMOT Factor—the internet influences 60% of your business profits

$1,000,000	Store Revenue
$600,000	60% influenced by customer's website experience
$180,000	Gross Margin (30%)

Macy's CEO[8] says that for every $1 of online spending that same customer will then spend $5.70 on in-store purchases. So let's do some numbers to illustrate this point, see Table 1.2.

Table 1.2: The Macy's Factor—the internet drives in-store sales

$1,000,000	Store Revenue
$40,000	4% via the internet
$12,000	Gross Margin (30%)
PLUS	
$228,000	Internet sales $40,000 * later in-store spend $5.70
$68,400	Gross Margin (30%)
LESS	
$6,000	Advertising, web hosting and marketing fees
= $62,400	Additional Profit

A good profit no matter how you look at it (i.e. with the Macy's sales' or not). Now it could be a lot more or a lot less than that. One thing is for certain, eCommerce is increasing and driving in-store purchase.

That's where this book helps. This book follows this process of increasing website traffic, turning that into customers, and creating loyal advocates. In the following section we introduce some specifics and see how important each part of the process is.

1.3.2 The Process in More Detail

1. Traffic—generate traffic to your site via:

- Search Engine Optimization (SEO): high quality and relevant external links and in-page optimization
- Pay Per Click advertising (PPC): Google Adwords, Facebook Ads, Yahoo / Bing PPC
- Social Media (& SEO): unique and compelling product descriptions, reviews, posts, articles, images, and videos
- Shopping Comparison Site Integration: with the likes of Google Product Search, Snooth, and Wine-Searcher.

How important it is for sales: VERY IMPORTANT to have leads but still need to turn them into revenue.

2. Engagement—build trust and reputation through:

- Social Media: Blog, Facebook, Twitter, Google+, Pinterest, other blogs and forums where your customers hang out
- Social Media: Reviews, Ratings, and Recommendations (from you, your staff, customers, and wine experts).

How important it is for sales: VERY IMPORTANT to have leads but still need to turn them into revenue.

3. Conversion—convert this traffic into sales by:

- User Experience: easy to understand navigation; advanced search capabilities; unique and compelling copywriting.

How important it is for sales: HUGELY IMPORTANT to funnel your leads into sales through great content and easy navigation.

- Catalog: category and product management with custom fields (e.g. brand or appellation); bulk product and inventory upload/download; unique product descriptions.

How important it is for sales: SOMEWHAT IMPORTANT, still no revenue, most eCommerce software can do this.

- Shopping Cart: upfront shipping cost estimation; guest checkout (no registration required); easy one-page-checkout process; discounts and coupons, gift messages and wrapping; payment methods: credit card, PayPal etc, internet banking, purchase order; security: SSL (i.e. the 's' in https://) and PCI (a tough credit card security standard).

How important it is for sales: HUGELY IMPORTANT as 30-70% of shopping carts are abandoned!

- Order Management: pre set-up shipping services; good invoice/credit process; legal compliance: minimum age and shipping laws.

How important it is for sales: IMPORTANT for your everyday use but does not directly increase revenue.

- Set up: graphic design; ease to set up; simple to maintain (through 'cloud computing'); third party/other software integration ('API').

How important it is for sales: IMPORTANT but it's spending money not making it.

- Reporting: Analytics, Adwords and Conversion reporting; Best-sellers, Search, and Top Customers reporting.

How important it is for sales: VERY IMPORTANT, need to continuously improve by analyzing what works and what doesn't.

4. Repeat Purchase—turn new customers into repeat customers with:

- Email Marketing (i.e. a pro service with 'double opt-in' and auto unsubscribe)
- Social Media engagement with customers (blog comments, tweeting, forum discussions)
- Testing and Analysis.

How important it is for sales: HUGELY IMPORTANT it's your list and your existing customers, that will provide 80% of your profit (if set up correctly).

Note that social media can fall into each part of the process though I mainly cover it in the Engagement part of the book.

1.4 An Example Wine Store

In the Company chapter we'll introduce Tony, the owner of Tony's Wine Store a hypothetical small wine retail business. We'll go through his problems and how we'll resolve them using internet marketing strategies. By using an example business we can directly tie internet marketing strategies to business objectives and financial performance. We will show how Tony's Wine Store went from a financial loss to a financial profit.

1.5 Sister Website and the Internet

Given the breakneck speed of internet development a book will only paint a picture of internet marketing at a point in time. Therefore this book has a sister website, `www.WineMarketingPros.com`, to allow revision and updates to each chapter. WineMarketingPros is a community of wine marketers that ask questions, discuss and debate wine internet marketing topics. It also has videos, blog posts and other resources about wine marketing online. The relevant website addresses are given at the end of each chapter in the Resources section.

While reading this book it will be helpful to have a computer with an internet connection to hand in order to fully maximize your understanding of the various internet strategies.

1.6 Summary

Wine stores and wineries, like most other businesses, are facing increasing technological challenges. The internet has become a vital part of a retailer's marketing and sales strategy yet internet marketing is poorly understood in the wine retail industry. The sales process is one of traffic, engagement, conversion, and repeat business. Each part is important though some parts more important than others. Throughout this book an example wine store is used to illustrate internet marketing strategies. This book has a sister website with more resources readers can use.

1.7 Resources

- The first point under each chapter's Resource section will be a website address to discuss, debate, and clarify the chapter's wine internet marketing strategy. To get an overview of this website go to www.WineMarketingPros.com.

Part I

The 3Cs—Customers, Competitors, Company

One framework for establishing a comprehensive view of your business is the 3C approach. You look at what your Customers want, what your Competitors are doing, and how your Company can offer something unique and compelling in a profitable way.

In the chapters in Part II: The 3Cs, I use this approach to outline various research studies into the wine drinkers, the potpourri of wine competitors a wine store and winery faces, your point of difference versus these competitors that appeals to consumers, and a resulting business plan to achieve your financial and lifestyle objectives. I provide a comprehensive brand management process specifically for wineries. I also introduce Tony's Wine Store, my hypothetical and illustrative wine store.

2 Customers

2.1 Who Are the Wine Consumers

According to the Wine Market Council[9] 20% of US adults drink wine at least once a week, 14% drink it less often, 26% drink beer and spirits, and 39% do not drink alcoholic beverages. The first group are rightly called the 'Core Wine Drinker' as they consume 91% of wine by volume. Two-thirds of Core Wine Drinkers drink more than once a week and are drinking more wine than they did five years ago; indeed the percent of Core Wine Drinkers has doubled since 2000 from 10% to 20%. Wine drinkers in their twenties, thirties and forties are certainly drinking more wine—this is a growth market!

The same study said 64% used the internet to get information about wine. Not surprisingly, about half to two-thirds wanted information about types of wine, specific wines, wine prices, and wineries. About one-third wanted information about a wine region, critics wine ratings, and retail stores that carry wine.

2.1.1 Wine Consumers and the Internet

There are many internet tools that you can use to research wine. The data they produce is immense—you can see who, when, what, and how consumers buy wine. You can use very sophisticated tools, such as the free Google Analytics and Webmaster Tools to analyze this quantitative data. However, this data can only take you so far. At some stage you need to put digital pen to digital paper and persuade wine consumers to buy from your store. The best way to do this is to know why your customers buy wine. That way you can write in ways that appeal to them. This is where research comes in—it helps you with 'copywriting'—and most of the day to day tasks of internet marketing require creating relevant and interesting content.

You need to be able to get into the consumer's head. Ideally you would be able to know each of your customers in the same way an old green grocer used to know each of his customers back in the 50s. Mrs.

Brown is busy and likes convenience food, Mrs. Smith pretends she likes fresh produce but really wants any excuse to buy chocolate, Mrs. Lee has just had a baby ... a local wine retailer has the advantage of having personal relationships with its customers. But it's hard to do that for large groups of faceless consumers like those on the internet whom you have not met. Because we don't meet them in-store we cannot build a personal relationship with them as easily.

To get around this issue what marketers do is build profiles of typical customers—then 'talk' to a particular profile. Through research we know that there are groups of people who are similar to Mrs. Brown, Mrs. Smith, and Mrs. Lee so we communicate to each group differently—chocolate to Mrs. Smith, canned food to Mrs. Brown, diapers to Mrs. Lee. Or, to take a more sophisticated approach, we know Mrs. Lee wears fashionable clothes, likes to come across as a sophisticated and attractive women, and wants to lose weight post birth. So you communicate healthy weight loss messages to her showing sophisticated, attractive, and fashionable women buying at your store.

It's called 'segmentation'. If we can understand why people buy and consume wine then we can create better website content, social media posts, ad copy, and emails. We'd love to be able to customize our various messages to particular individuals based on their particular motivations. But that's plainly impossible so what professional marketers do is create wine consumer groups, or 'segments'.

These segments are workable groups of similar wine consumers. It is usually done through focus group research to identify key purchase motivators and surveys to gather enough data to make statistically valid conclusions. In the following section I outline three wine market research studies. With the use of the internet now widespread there are other ways to conduct market research so I also cover two more ways: one is in the new field of netnography and the second is my own analysis of amazon.com wine book reviews.

But first let's talk about price.

2.2 What is the Most Important to Consumers?

A Vintage Wines[10] LinkedIn forum had a very active discussion about this question:

What is most important to wine consumers? Is it selection or price or both?

Commenters were split among the usual contributors: drinkers, wineries, retailers, other pros, and an interesting comment by a wine researcher, called Isabelle Lesschaeve[11]. She gave a great summary of wine consumer research in only a few paragraphs (I paraphrase by using square brackets):

> We don't make the purchasing experience easy for consumers. There is an overwhelming number of SKUs to choose from, many labels look the same, the classification by wine origins is not obvious for everyone. For most consumers, it's intimidating. It has been established that on average, consumers make a wine selection in 40 seconds, [so wine labels] being visible is important. [But I do] admit there is not one consumer, but a diversity of consumers. There are few differences in purchase decisions that can be explained by gender, although females seem to become the primary shoppers.
>
> Researchers like segmenting consumers according to different criteria, Lifestyle is one of them. Another criterion that was found critical to explain behavior differences is the consumer involvement with wine. High involved consumers are these enthusiasts who like to learn more about wine, read magazines, belong to wine clubs: they will select wine based on origin, appellation, varietals or style. Low involved consumers are the confused ones (about 2/3 of the population) and yes they use strategies to reduce the risk of making the wrong choice.
>
> Although you all seem very keen to assist your consumers on the floor, low involved consumers are intimidated and afraid to ask, because they don't want to look like idiots (nobody likes that). So they use price, awards, cool labels as risk reducing strategies.
>
> What I found fascinating and upsetting at the same time is that the sensory experience consumers have when tasting the wine can be influenced by those extrinsic cues (label, award, price, etc.). As it was mentioned before some consumers drink labels not wine. Several experiments have demonstrated that wines tasted blind were

usually not appreciated the same way as wines tasted with all these cues. And this was found for all types of consumers, including highly involved people and wine professionals.

So what is the most important to consumers? It depends but I would say a good match between the imagery (brand, labels, story etc.) and the taste of wine. How do we accomplish that? Not easy. By recognizing maybe that we—wine professionals—represent only a small % of the wine drinker population. Most of consumers like fruity and sweet wines and some marketers got it right by making their labels very visible so that in 40sec they can be seen and bought.

How do we take these consumers to the next level? May I suggest by 'involving them'. The professional talk might not be the right strategy or the glamorous image of wine might not be so appealing to these consumers. The good news: the coming generation of wine drinkers (Gen Y, Millennials) does drink wine and likes to experiment. However, they don't recognize themselves in the wine culture and wine advertising currently proposed. One of the challenges that wine professionals will face is to adapt their communication and customer relations differently to make wine accessible and understandable.

Consumers do not just want selection and lower prices. This is the rational and sensible answer they'll give when asked directly, but it's not necessarily the reason why they purchase particular wines— which is where research helps.

2.3 Market Research: Lifestyle Segments

2.3.1 Wine-Related Lifestyle Segments

I believe the best academic research on wine drinkers is an Australian study by Johnson and Bruwer.[12] I also believe it's very applicable to the US (UK, Canada and New Zealand) as you see when you read another US study below.

The Segments are:

1. Conservative, Wine Knowledgeable Wine Drinkers (20.9% of wine drinkers)
2. Image Oriented, Knowledge Seeking, Wine Drinkers (22.3%)
3. Basic Wine Drinkers (16.8%)
4. Experimenter, Highly Knowledgeable Wine Drinkers (19.0%)
5. Enjoyment Oriented, Social Wine Drinkers (20.9%)

Conservative, Wine Knowledgeable Wine Drinkers (20.9%)

The consumers are likely to:

- be tertiary educated males (63%) working in a professional capacity middle to high incomes
- enjoy drinking wine with about 40% of them drinking wine every day
- store wine appropriately, including having a cellar, and serve with correct glassware, decant, and check for spoilage
- display a good knowledge of wine and wine-related matters
- be influenced in what wine is purchased by the wine drinking occasion
- be very interested in wine information but not seek information or advice when purchasing wine
- be somewhat reluctant to purchase wines that they have not tried before, preferring to rely on their own knowledge, and be uninterested in experimenting. They have a wide selection of brands from which to choose
- prefer retailers which are fine wine stores.

Image Oriented, Knowledge Seeking, Wine Drinkers (22.3%)

Consumers in this segment share many of the characteristics of the previous segment. They are likely to:

- be tertiary educated males (65%), middle to high incomes
- enjoy drinking wine with about 40% of them drinking wine every day
- enjoy drinking wine and like the image that this portrays
- store wine appropriately, including having a cellar and serving with correct glassware, decanting, and checking for spoilage
- have some knowledge about wine and are actively seeking to further their existing knowledge, including wine-related media

- seek information about their wine in the wine store, and be guided by others' recommendations including wine writers and other opinion leaders. Partly because they are averse to risk
- be aware of wine prices but tend to have the view that the more expensive the wine, the better it is
- have been drinking wine for some time, probably since their university days, but now have the income to buy the wines recommended by others
- prefer retailers which are fine wine stores.

Basic Wine Drinkers (16.8%)

The consumers in this segment of the Australian wine market are likely to:

- be secondary and sometimes tertiary educated males and females with low to middle incomes
- enjoy drinking wine but have little interest in wine information or the image
- treat the occasion as not mattering, spend relatively little, drink relatively less, and have a few safe brands
- prefer retailers which are national wine chain stores.

Experimenter, Highly Knowledgeable Wine Drinkers (19.0%)

The consumers in this segment of the Australian wine market are likely to:

- be tertiary educated males (61%), middle to high incomes
- enjoy drinking wine with about 40% of them drinking wine every day
- really enjoy drinking wine and be less aware of the image that this portrays
- store wine appropriately, including having a cellar and serving with correct glassware, decanting, and check for spoilage
- be separated (in part) from those other segments by their very detailed knowledge of wine and wine-related subjects
- still have the desire to learn more, ask for advice and information, and take recommendations based on this information
- like to take a risk and be keen to drink wine that they have not tried before—'be experimenters', the main distinguishing factor

- not have a safe set of brands
- prefer retailers which are fine wine stores.

Enjoyment Oriented, Social Wine Drinkers (20.9%)

The consumers in this segment of the Australian wine market are likely to:

- be secondary and tertiary educated females, younger, low to middle incomes
- enjoy drinking wine possibly having a little interest in wine information
- be occasional drinkers, sometimes trying a variety of wines
- be influenced by packaging and labeling of a bottle
- prefer retailers which are national wine chain stores.

2.3.2 Risk and Confusion

Having looked at the different wine segments Johnson and Bruwer[13] then analyzed how they made their choices about wines.

As seen by the research, most wine drinkers are often confused about wine. They need to make a decision about what wine to purchase and yet often the quality and taste profile is uncertain—or risky.

They take certain measures to reduce that risk including seeking information, tasting, relying on well known brands, and relying on price as an indicator of quality. Here's a short summary of what they found using Experimenters as an example.

Experimenters used the following strategies to reduce risks depending on the wine price point:

Low price:

- Rely on favorite brands
- Price
- Rely on well known brands

Medium price:

- Opportunity to try before buying
- Seek information before buying
- Price

High price:

- Seek information before buying

- Opportunity to try before buying
- Price.

'Seeking information before buying' is either the first or second risk reduction strategy an Experimenter has for the higher price ranges. In comparison,

- the Conservative segment would rely on favorite brands for the middle price point then look to have an opportunity to try for the other two price points
- the Image Oriented segment would look to try before buying, except for the bottom price point where it would rely on brands

Wine retailer relevance?

- A website or mobile app provides the information that two of the three target segments are looking for to reduce the risk of making a bad choice
- Well-known brands are an important part of the range
- In-store wine tasting is a winning strategy.

Tony Spawton[14] is a well known wine researcher. In the same LinkedIn discussion[10] group mentioned at the start of this chapter, he made the following contribution in reference to the above risk reduction research. The edits are in square brackets are mine.

> I know from my research that Jono [Bruwer] is on the money. The expectations of the consumer varies with the occasion for which the wine is purchased. The wine consumer is promiscuous in brand, price, region and style so to suggest that the consumer is stuck in one category is a fallacy. Consumers are most influenced by the advice of others 'people drink other peoples wines' a phrase I coined in the late 1980's. Brand is important as a choice factor and variety is a given. At last the French have woken up to this and now variety to be included in their labeling. Another phrase of mine is, 'the package sells the first bottle the wine maker the second'. The extrinsic attributes need to be distinctive to break though the clutter and jog the consumer memory whether in the retail store or the restaurant.
>
> Consumers generally fall into 3 purchase motivation categories:
> Monday to Thursday wines—drink and enjoy at home,

known brand that is suited to the buyers experience—
safe brand—low price and easily dispensed and stored (
a big plus for screw cap).
Lifestyle Wines—shared with peers—high psychological
risk—as a poorly selected wine reflects on the purchaser's
lack of wine knowledge. (this purchase is strongly influenced by WOM) [word of mouth].
And the treat—the luxury purchase—to celebrate, to honor.
The buyer may not personally like this particular wine or
can ill afford the price—but the 'loss of face' would be
considered very damaging.
The lifestyle wine is a 'social lubricant'—the luxury wine
is the 'topic of the conversation'.

So having looked at some Australian academic research let's look
at some American corporate research.

2.4 Market Research: Project Genome

In the last few years Constellation Wines has conducted a comprehensive and impressive wine drinker study in the US called Project
Genome[15]. The most insightful finding for me is that 32% of consumers make up 54% of industry profits, see Figure 4.8. Indeed one
segment called Luxury Enthusiasts make up 3% of drinkers but 16%
of profits.

Obviously there are 4-5 segments that will buy lots of high margin
wine driving your financial result. Indeed in late 2010 Constellation
Wines sold its Australian and South African wine businesses[16]. My
speculation is that these brands were not profitable as they were
servicing low price / low margin segments, whereas the other brands
were servicing segments that were willing to pay a little more and
were therefore profitable. So Constellation changed its business and
focused on profits rather than being the largest wine company in the
world. I think the same lesson applies to fine wine stores—use wine
(internet) marketing strategies to focus on customer segments that
are profitable and ignore the rest.

Here are some more details from Constellation Wines' Project
Genome presentation:[15]

Figure 2.1: Project Genome Home and Habits Study: Consumer and Profit Share. [15]

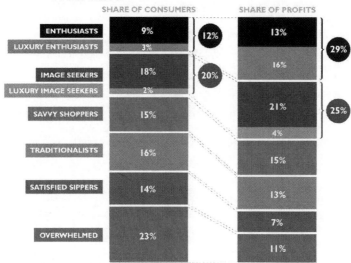

Enthusiast (9%)

Who I Am

- I consider myself knowledgeable about wine. Because of my wine knowledge, I know that I don't have to spend a lot of money to get a great bottle of wine.
- We entertain at home often and enjoy wine with friends.

How to Connect With Me

- I love to spend time browsing in the wine section. I like to refer to wine publications, and I'm influenced by wine ratings and reviews.
- I like to be offered a well-known as well as unique wine selections. I appreciate and understand sophisticated wine information.
- On-Premise: I use my knowledge of wine to make smart buying decisions. I typically buy wine by the bottle.

Enthusiasts are great at using their knowledge to make smart buying decisions.

- 96% of Enthusiasts buy wine over $6 and it accounts for 39% of what they buy on a volume basis
- 48% of Enthusiasts buy wine in a 1.5L size—not too surprising considering that they need an 'everyday wine' along with their 'weekend wine'

Luxury Enthusiast (3%)

Who I Am

- I have a wine cellar at home and enjoy shopping for wine to enjoy everyday as well as adding to my collection.
- I have a personal passion for wine and food; they are a key part of my everyday life.

How to Connect With Me

- I usually have a personal relationship with the wine steward/buyer in my favorite store. I like it when they call me when special items arrive and track down unique wines for me.
- I entertain often because I enjoy spending time creating food and wine pairings that elevate the epicurean experience.
- For me, wine is a global experience. I constantly seek additional knowledge. At retail, I read labels, appreciate detailed winemaking notes, and enjoy lingering in the wine section.
- On-Premise: I order off the reserve wine list. I also keep a few bottles at my favorite restaurant and spend time talking with the Sommelier.

What we know about Pinot Noir—Luxury Enthusiasts are in to it big time.

- Luxury Enthusiasts who appreciate the artistry behind this hard-to-craft wine bought nearly 50% more than Image Seekers and Luxury Image Seekers.

Image Seeker (18%)

Who I Am

- For me, wine is a status symbol. Discovering wine is new to me. I only have a basic knowledge of wine, which is driven by my awareness of the latest trends.
- I like to be the first to try a new wine.

How to Connect With Me

- I use the internet as a key source of information, and I like 'sound bites' and 'factoids'.
- At retail, new item shelf-talkers attract me. I also like it when stores have tags that give you unusual facts and lifestyle messaging.
- When I'm going out to a nice restaurant, I typically check out the wine list ahead of time on-line so I can impress my friends.

This segment is one of the youngest. Currently they do a lot of their socializing (and drinking) On Premise.

- As the economy continues to be uncertain, we're expecting these consumers to shift some of their On-Premise purchasing to Off-Premise purchasing
- Off Premise: Can you turn your wine section into 'the place' to go after work?
- On Premise: How can you keep them coming to your restaurant?

Luxury Image Seeker (2%)

Who I Am

- For me, wine is a status symbol and I don't mind spending the money to buy luxury-priced wine. I have a wine refrigerator with a few of the latest wines for when my friends drop by.
- After work, I'll meet my friends at a bar for happy hour which often leads to eating dinner at the latest spot.

How to Connect With Me

- I use technology to get information, so I'm open to in-store kiosks and receiving wine information on my cell phone.
- I like to try new wines, so I prefer a fresh selection.
- Because I like to experiment, I'm open to innovative packages. When I buy wine, I include screw cap wines, 3L boxes, and tetra packs.
- When I'm not sure what to buy, I typically go for the one that's more expensive. I'm influenced by unusual facts and lifestyle messaging.
- On Premise: I like a 'By the Glass' wine list with a lot of unusual offerings. For me, price isn't a key concern. I will order off the reserve list.

Luxury Image Seekers like others to think that they drink a lot of different varietals.

- Contrary to what the 'Sideways' movie might have you think, the number one varietal for this group is Merlot.
- This varietal accounts for 32% of their wine volume.
- Remember to have a good selection of the top varietals for this segment.

Savvy Shopper (15%)

Who I Am

- I enjoy shopping for wine and discovering new brands and varietals on my own. I get a lot of personal satisfaction when I buy a great $15 bottle of wine and only pay $10.
- I like discovering new wines but have a group of favorites. I get most of my information from the TV, newspaper, and the internet. I never go to the store without a stack of coupons.

How to Connect With Me

- I shop in a variety of stores each week to find the best deals so I like to be offered a variety of wine specials and discounts. I am a heavy user of coupons and rebates and know what is on sale even before I walk into the store.
- I'm willing to buy 6 bottles at once so that I get an additional discount and spend time looking at the close-out wines.
- When I'm On premise: I typically buy a glass of the house wine since I think it's a better value for the money.

Savvy Shoppers are second only to Luxury Enthusiasts in the amount of wine they buy.

- On average, Savvy Shoppers have bought 67 bottles (750mL eq) of wine at retail in the last 18 months!
- Off Premise: Make it easy for this consumer to find your items on sale both the well known brands as well as unusual finds.
- On Premise: Make sure your house wine is up to par for this group.

Traditionalist (16%)

Who I Am

- Since I was raised on traditional values, I enjoy wines from established wineries. I feel like they have perfected the art of winemaking.
- I think that wine makes an occasion more formal; so, when I entertain, I use my grandmother's silver and serve a nice bottle of wine with dinner. I prefer to stay home and entertain friends and family rather than going out.

How to Connect With Me

- I like to be offered a wide variety of well-known national brands, especially those that spend money on advertising to me. I dont try new brands very often. I want to shop at a retail location that makes it easy for me to find the brands I want to buy.
- On Premise: I always order wine brands with which I'm familiar. I won't order wine if I don't recognize any of the brands on the list.

For the Traditionalist, wine $8+ accounts for 25% of their wine volume.

- Just because they like well known brands, it doesn't mean that they don't spend money to buy a good wine.
- Make sure you have a good assortment of Super Premium and above priced well-known brands.

Do you want to increase your wine sales by 5%?

- Off Premise: Make sure you always have a few well-known brands on display and in your promotions.
- On Premise: If your current wine list doesn't have a few well-known, nationally advertised brands, the Traditionalist won't order any wine.

Satisfied Sipper (14%)

Who I Am

- I don't know much about wine; I just know what I like to drink. I usually buy the same brand, preferably a domestic wine.
- To me, wine is an everyday beverage, so I don't think much about it.

How to Connect With Me

- I don't enjoy the experience of buying wine, so I like to buy the 1.5L bottles. Since I usually buy the same brand, I shop at

places that make it easy to find the wine that I want to buy.
I don't care about shelf-talkers or signs; I'm not interested in
learning more about wine.

- On the rare occasions when I'm dining out, I typically order
the house wine and don't worry too much about wine and food
pairing.

Satisfied Sippers aren't into the whole wine mystique.

- Satisfied Sippers just drink what they like, so make sure you
dont run out of their favorite wine.

Overwhelmed (23%)

Who I Am

- There are so many wines on the shelves. Sometimes I select a
wine based on the label, but it's confusing since I can't always
tell from the label how the wine is going to taste.
- I like to drink wine, but I don't know what kind to buy.

How to Connect With Me

- I'm looking for wine information at retail that's simple and easy
to understand. I am very open to advice, so it's frustrating
when I go to a store and there is no one in the wine section to
help me.
- If it's too confusing or there's not any information, I won't buy
anything.
- On Premise: I'm easily intimidated. Sometimes it's safer not
to order wine in case I get stuck with something that doesn't
taste good.

The Overwhelmed consumers buy more than just White Zinfandel.

- In the first Project Genome study, it looked like about half of
what this segment purchased was White Zinfandel. However,
we now know that the Overwhelmed consumers just had a hard
time remembering what they purchased.
- 80% have bought White Wine (43% of volume)
- 77% have bought Red Wine (26% of volume)
- 36% have bought Blush/White Zinfandel (31% of volume)

Constellation Wines

The above study was reprinted with the kind permission of Constellation Wines (note I have no commercial relationship with Constellation Wines). They do offer to tie in your wine retailer sales data with their segmentation and other category management assistance which may be helpful. Please ask your local Constellations Wines sales rep for more information.

2.5 Wine Social Media Market Research: Avatar Hybrid Bodies

The above Constellation Wines research is immensely helpful in writing wine internet marketing copy but with the explosion of social media a new form of research has been developed—it's called netnography.

In the movie 'Avatar' you probably remember Sigourney Weaver was an anthropologist who was studying another community by becoming immersed in it (a research method called 'ethnography'). Netnography is something similar—immersing yourself in internet communities. The difference is we don't use Na'vi-human hybrid bodies to interact with the natives of Pandora, rather we use the internet to get involved with other humans in their own internet environment. A little easier I think.

Netnography uses the burgeoning area of social networks to monitor and engage with consumers. Not only are there lots of consumers in one place but they are less inhibited about saying what they really think. So, like the star of Avatar ex-marine Jake Sully, you get to learn their 'warrior dreamwalker ways', ...I mean what they really think about, and how they use the brands you are researching. They are in their natural environment, in front their PC at home, and like Jake you are immersed in this environment (and abide by ethical research principles).

A few academics started to cotton on to internet based ethnography in the nineties including Dr Robert Kozinets.[17] Usually what a researcher like Dr Kozinets used to do is immerse himself in a target community. In the case of business research it might be a middle class family to see how they use coffee throughout the day or, in the case of academic anthropology it may be a tribe in Africa. It's called ethnography, and is a very accepted market research method.

But Western communities started to move online in the nineties with email, forums, user groups, and of course by 2010 social media has become a huge area of our life with Facebook, blogs, Twitter etc etc. So some researchers have moved online with the various communities.

What Dr Kozinets and his colleagues have done is to bring the rigor of professional research to the internet. So rather than simply summarize what is being said, researchers study, query, and analyze what these communities are saying.

However the issue is that there are billions of web pages and a human is unable to find, analyze, and notate all relevant conversations easily. You can use Google blogsearch, Facebook, and Twitter search to sift through screeds of discussion threads to find the customer insight nuggets. Or you can use some social media research software. My favorite is Netbase and in the Competitor Chapter we'll look at the results of some research they did for wine stores. But first let's look at champagne as it illustrates how powerful social media and the internet have become.

2.5.1 Passion, Champagne and, er, Supermarkets

NetBase has posted about Champagne Brands, 'Piper's Bubbles Burst with Love'.[18] They use a graph called the Brand Passion Index to show social media sentiment and size, see Figure 2.2. The amount of chatter about a brand is indicated by the size of the bubble, while the placement of the bubble shows the intensity of passion.

Given these are well known French champagne brands I guess it's no surprise that they are liked (top half of the graph). But only a few are passionately loved. In particular, Piper-Heidsieck. Here's how NetBase puts it,[18]

> Piper-Heidsieck who generated the most amount of love chatter. Metrics in NetBase showed that consumers love the extravagance, the romance of it being a favorite of Marie-Antoinette, combined with its affordability. Piper is a champagne with a long history of 225 years.

Remember that's from a consumer point of view and reminds me of the adage that a brand only exists in a consumers mind. Everything else is just graphic design.

Figure 2.2: Champagne Brand Passion Index (courtesy of NetBase)

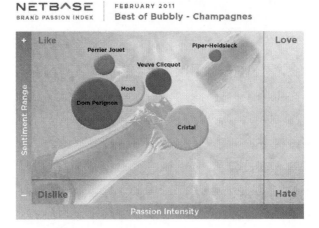

Other insights that stand out is that Dom Perignon is regarded as boring and a social media disaster for Cristal.

Cristal's boss apparently made a controversial remark which accounts for the poor net sentiment. Jay-Z (hip hop artist whose rap includes, 'Let's sip the Cris and get pissy-pissy') apparently heard that his attention was unwelcome, did not appreciate it, and made a controversial remark in return leading to a social media disaster for Cristal. The fact that it hasn't bottomed out in the Hate section of the Brand Passion Index is probably due to the wording of the comments.

The key to me is the importance of the wine story. I can see someone trading up from a cheap sparkling wine to Piper-Heidsieck based on a yarn about Marie-Antoinette. They could take that story to a dinner table. It would be a brave or foolish person who took a bottle of Cristal when Jay-Z was making damaging remarks about the brand.

2.6 Wine Segments—from Amazon Wine Book Reviews

This last study is one done myself. I was looking to see what wine consumers liked to read so I could use this for ideas for selling wine online. Here's what I found.

Wine books can be categorized into the following:

- Wine Tasting Methods
- Ratings and Reviews
- Pocket Guides
- Travelogues
- Atlases
- General Compendia
- Encyclopedia

Tasting Methods

How to drink it. Written versions of a wine tasting course covering the various senses (eye, nose, mouth), storage, glassware, cellaring.

Reviews and Ratings

What to buy. Carefully indexed and organized books that cover very specific wines often from a particular region. Now slowly being superseded by websites.

Pocket Guide

What to buy. As per above but smaller and shorter so you can take it to a store. Now slowly being replaced by iPhone and mobile apps.

Travelogue

Good stories. To quote one review, 'a wine lovers guide to places to dream about and wines to drink while doing so'. Full of maps, personal stories, vineyard stories, tend to be old world.

Atlas

About Wine. Full of maps, diagrams, and descriptions of geography in a graphical format.

General Compendium

About Wine. Description of regional AOCs, DOCs, and some maps.

Encyclopedia

About Wine. Information on varietals, winemaking, maps, regions, chemistry, viticulture, history, data, old vs new world...everything really.

How this is relevant to a wine retailer

Obviously the Reviews and Ratings. If your business is about a particular niche you could use the other books as prompters to write attractive content for search engines. For example 'the rock star who owns a vineyard in Sonoma valley', 'helping the harvest in rural France', '100 clones of Pinot Noir', 'the Burgundy AOC'. Including photos, maps, diagrams will certainly appeal to some segments.

2.7 How Many Premium Wine Drinkers are in Your Area?

In the Company chapter I outline a financial model for a wine store and analyze what the most important financial factors were. Some of the most important factors are the segment sizes in the local store's catchment area. In this section I outline how to conduct local market research to help you estimate this. It's an easy and cheap, but statistically valid, way of doing research.

In the Company chapter section 4.3 I identify these as the most sensitive financial factors:

- Store Penetration in Year 3 and Year 2
- Image Seeker Segment Size, Market Share, and Volume Purchased
- Enthusiast Segment Size and Market Share
- Luxury Enthusiast Segment Size
- Conversion rate from internet marketing campaigns

I'll be using a mailbox drop with a letter (no envelope) from me asking people to go online to complete a survey. Here is how to create the online survey.

Create Questions

I want to find out how many bottles they buy, from where, and what their likely price range is. Here are the questions and answers.

Q1. In the LAST MONTH where and how many bottles of wine have you purchased? (Please enter bottle numbers in as many options as apply below):

- Store A
- Store B
- Store C
- Internet Wine Store
- Vineyard Direct
- Liquor Chain A (outside of town)
- Other

Q2. Would you basically describe your views on wine as (please select one option below):

- There are so many wines on the shelves—it's confusing since I can't always tell from the label how the wine is going to taste. I like to drink wine, but I don't know what kind to buy.
- I have some knowledge about wine and am actively seeking to further my wine knowledge. I look to wine writers and other experts for guidance. Buying a wine my friends don't like is very disappointing.
- I enjoy wines from established wineries. I feel like they have perfected the art of winemaking. I like to be offered a wide variety of well-known wine brands.
- I shop in a variety of stores each week to find the best deals so I like to be offered a variety of wine specials and discounts. I am a heavy user of coupons and rebates and know what is on sale even before I walk into the store.
- I don't know much about wine, I just know what I like to drink. I usually buy the same brand, preferably a domestic wine. To me, wine is an everyday beverage, so I don't think much about it.
- I love to spend time browsing in the wine section. I'm a confident wine buyer. I like to refer to wine publications and I'm influenced by wine ratings and reviews. I appreciate and understand sophisticated wine information.

Q3. How much do you spend on a bottle of wine for:

- After work, everyday wine
- Weekend BBQ with friends
- Formal Dinner at your place with some good friends
- A special occasion—your loved one has a big birthday
- I'll give them these price point options in columns along the top: n/a, Less than \$4, \$5-10 \$10-15 \$15+

For the full survey questions see the Resources section at the end of this chapter.

Sign up for a free account at Survey Gizmo. They provide an easy way to create a survey on the internet (not your computer), they publish it via their servers, and provide reports you can use. You get up to 250 responses when using a free account. Which is about how many I need for a statistically valid sample. They give you a website address and this address I put into the mail drop letter.

Results

Once I have enough results I redo my financial model estimates. If the survey suggests there are a large group of 'Enthusiasts ', who are buying lots of wine from a boring Liquor Chain Store, at high prices then a premium wine store may be very successful.

If there are mainly 'Satisfied Sippers', who are buying little wine, at cheap prices then the store is doomed.

No doubt the results will be somewhere in between.

The Math: how many do I need?

Now I hate math and statistics as much as most people, but there are some great tools and methods to keep this simple. First let's make sure we get a representative sample of the population. Use the online calculator from Custom Insight.[19] The best way to explain this is by using an example.

I want to see how many people have wine cellars in the local area. This is an indication that they are a high price/ high volume wine drinker.

If the 50% of the population has a wine cellar then I'm ecstatic. If 5% has a wine cellar then I may be in trouble. In fact I don't care if 20% or 26% of the population has a wine cellar, only that it is about that figure. I'm after big differences here so I'm willing to tolerate rough figures:

- My tolerance for error is high, and I'll choose 6% margin of error in the field: How much error are you willing to tolerate?

- How many people are in your population? 25,000

- Confidence refers to how likely the figure is going to be correct. I'm happy with a 90% Confidence level

Clicking Calculate tells me I need 188 respondents. So if I did this survey 100 times, then 90 of those times the survey would show results that are within a 6% range (between say 20 and 26% as in the example above). However 10 of those times the figures would be outside of that range. Which is pretty loose but I'm a businessman not an academic, I need the results fast and cheaply.

How many surveys to send out? I believe that I'll get a 20% response rate because I'm a local person asking sweetly, not some faceless corporate. To increase response I could offer a prize but I don't feel I need to, yet. So for the next field in the calculator I'll put in 20%. The calculator tells me I need to send the survey to 940 people.

Random Sample and Delivery

Let's make sure the sample is not biased by choosing random houses. I could just get a student to deliver 940 surveys to the first 940 letter boxes he comes across. The problem is the sample will be biased towards those streets. They may be in a poor part of town, or a rich part. They may be closer to the shop, have lots of vacant houses ...all sorts of things could skew the sample.

I handle this as follows. Let's say I know there are 7000 households: 7000 households divided by 940 delivered surveys = 7. So I'll ask him to go to every street and post a survey request in every 7th letter box. At no time are they to decide whether the house is worthwhile or not as that will ruin the randomness of the sample.

The Survey Request

I'm just going to print out or photocopy the following:

> Hello, my name is [your name], and I'm researching whether I should open a fine wine store in [town]. It would be great if I could, but I just don't have enough information to make that decision so I thought I'd ask you :).

Your answers will be immensely helpful to me in either opening a great wine store that suits you or ... helping me avoid making a financial mistake! I'll ask a few questions about your preferred wines, your recent purchases, and what factors influenced these. It should only take about five minutes. It is an online survey, so please use your internet browser to go here: [website address from survey gizmo] Your answers will be anonymous, and are for my own use to create the best store I possibly can. Please only complete this survey if you are 21 years or older. Kind regards [your full name] [full contact details] The Online Survey is here: [website address from survey gizmo]

Note you can shorten the SurveyGizmo website address by using a free url shortening service like bit.ly.

Pilot Survey

Sometimes everything just goes wrong, so it's best to have a trial run yourself first. Print out 100, deliver yourself, and see what happens. You may need to adjust the questions or offer an incentive. By finding out with a small group first you check your process.

The Results

You can monitor your surveys day by day as well as run reports and download them. Once you have enough completed surveys then put the results into the Financial Model I'll outline in the Company chapter.

2.8 Summary

We've looked at five wine consumer studies to discover how wine consumers think and therefore how we should communicate with them. The Luxury Enthusiast, Enthusiast, Image Seeker and Luxury Image Seeker segments based on Constellation Wines' study; and Experimenter, Image Oriented, and Conservative segments based on Johnson and Bruwer' studies. Each is interested in different topics and ways to reduce risks. Keep these segments in mind as you read the rest of this book.

2.9 Resources

- How well did you understand? Visit my website to discuss or ask questions about Wine and Customers: `www.WineMarketingPros.com/custchap/`
- For the full survey questions go to the above website page.
- *Wine Marketing and Sales* Wagner, Olsen, and Thach. Wine Appreciation Guild. 2007.
- *Wine Brands: success strategies for new markets, new consumers, and new trends* E. Resnick Palgrave MacMillan. 2008.

3 Competitors

3.1 Online Wine Competitors

The US national online wine market has many players. In Figure 3.1 I've shown a representative sample for illustrative purposes.

Figure 3.1: The US Online Wine Market

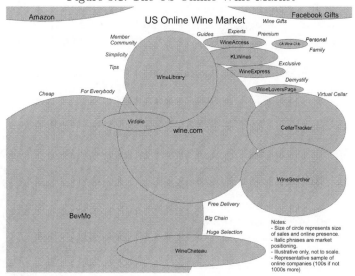

The larger the circle the greater the online presence and/or sales in the US online wine market. The closer a competitor is to a word in italics the more likely it is positioned that way. For example WineLibrary is close to Member Community reflecting its active 'Vayniacs'.

It's not from a market research 'Usage and Attitude' study with carefully calculated multivariate cluster segmentation—which is what market researchers use to create this sort of model in a more scientific way. Just my own in-depth analysis using tools such as Alexa,

Quantcast, ispionage, and various Google tools.

In late 2012 the wine internet industry was shaken up by two of the internet industry giants—Amazon and Facebook. They have been depicted in the above graph as larger players slowly sinking in from above. Just how far they'll penetrate the wine internet industry is a matter of diverse opinion. They are both shipping wine from wineries themselves to avoid shipping compliance and marketing agent legal issues. Certainly the Facebook Gift button could have huge ramifications for the wine gift industry given the prominence that this button has on a Facebook user's page.

Of course wineries may see the players above as sometimes channels to market and sometimes competitors. My rule of thumb is that the closer to home the more competitive wineries from the same region are. So when customers are in Napa then all Napa wineries are competitors. When Napa wineries go to a tasting event in New York then they are competitors and partners in promoting their region. When they go to London then they are partners promoting greater awareness and trial of a less well-known appellation.

If we apply that thinking to the internet world then it all depends on where the person is browsing. In Northern California it will likely be Napa wineries, other Northern Californian wineries and indeed retailers as everyone has similar freight costs. Unless the internet browser can go and pick up an order nearby in which case the local wine retailer has a significant advantage in freight cost and 'delivery time'. Note I also discuss winery competitors as part of brand management in the Company—Winery chapter.

Large Online Wine Competitors and Wine Websites

Let's go through the wine retailer's large internet competitors, with the last few being possibly more partners rather than competitors.

BevMo. Arguably the largest in the market because of its offline chain of stores in western US. It boasts a huge selection of wines at cheap prices that can be picked up at the local BevMo.

Wine.com. Others might argue that wine.com is the largest, and they do have warehouses across the country. They also have the biggest presence in wine drinkers minds if not on Google. They offer large range, ratings, reviews, shipping deals, virtual cellars, recommendations, and wine guides. An impressive site backed up by deep pockets.

WineLibrary. Gary Vaynerchuk owns it. Do I need to say more. Such a big advantage to have the king of wine social media (indirectly) drive sales to his own online wine store. Good store with most of the features and a passionate younger community of wine drinkers. He has since moved from the free website model to a paid subscription model, 'the Daily Grape'. It will be interesting to see whether this does as well.

WineAccess. Related to Stephen Tanzer, this is much more traditional (compared to Gary V). An acknowledged expert providing sound advice on 10,000+ wines, care of a network of wine stores. This makes it a bit of a shopping comparison site like Snooth. Great reviews and ratings.

WineChateau. Offers a huge range of 17,000+ wines coupled with discounts. Owned by a youngish entrepreneur who leverages his father's wine shop (like Gary V) to offer a comprehensive online store. Big presence on the web.

Snooth. More of a Comparison Shopping Engine (CSE) than a direct competitor. It offers the wine drinker the ability to get ratings and reviews from stores and drinkers all round the world. You can compare prices and get recommendations. They charge the wine store 10% of any sale to be a featured wine store (an 'affiliate' model) and offer advertising. They could be the classic 'coopetition': you compete and cooperate with them.

Wine-Searcher. A bit of software that allows wine drinkers to search for particular wines from wine retailers around the world. Similar to Snooth in that it is a wine shopping comparison website though they use Facebook for their social media component.

CellarTracker. A virtual cellar tracking system that allows members to track their cellar online and share reviews. Has serious kudos in the wine industry.

Wineloverspage. A large passionate community of wine lovers with some good guides to wine. The revenue stream is from affiliate sales and advertising.

The following are perhaps more similar to the websites that wine stores generally launch and therefore directly competitive.

Direct Online Wine Competitors

Their (unique) selling proposition is in quotation marks. I usually take this from the 'meta description' or 'title' in the invisible header section of their home page (see the Search Engine Optimization chapter for more about these technical terms).

Vinfolio. 'Above and beyond typical wine store, Vinfolio sells fine wine and services to wine collectors and enthusiasts.' A comprehensive fine and rare wine retailer for the knowledgeable wine drinker. Superb website, community, and reviews together with a collector marketplace and virtual cellar. If MyWinesDirect are expert at marketing these guys are experts at the eCommerce and mobile side of the game.

WineExpress. 'Exclusive Wines at Great Value. Everyday take 15% off case prices.' The Wine Enthusiast people. They seem to do well with with the wealthier in-crowd and their marketing programs reflect this. Smart operators.

KLWines. or K&L Wine Merchants, '1000s of Rare and Collectable Wines from around the globe ... ' Californian, 3 large stores, switched on state player, almost a chain wine store operator. Some really good reviews on Yelp and Google Places, sharp website.

CA Wine Club. 'We personally hand select and deliver great tasting, limited production California wines and introduce our members to the winemaking families handcrafting each wine.' More precisely a Wine Club than a normal wine retailer, included because of the way they have targeted a niche (California wines) and made it very personal. Perhaps a good model for a local wine retailer. Not much of an online presence. I'm guessing these guys are very good at Direct Marketing or are just small players.

Your local wine store competitors. The most direct competitors will be the local wine stores near your store that have an online presence—probably an eCommerce website, but also possibly a blog or Facebook Page. If they have followed many of the strategies outlined in this book then they could well be the largest competitor of all.

A Very Competitive Market

It's a very competitive market place with some very capable players especially: wine.com, BevMo, Vinfolio, WineExpress, K&L Wines, and WineLibrary. Each has one or all of these:

- a point of difference
- great search engine optimization and internet advertising
- ratings, reviews, and recommendations

- a community through social media
- range and price

However I still think there is a large gap in the market, I cover that in the next chapter about your *Company*. First let's look at competitors from a search engine optimization perspective.

3.1.1 Competitors on Search Engines

We go into a great deal of detail in how search engines rank websites in the SEO chapter. In short when a Google user searches for a particular keyword phrase Google will rank web pages mainly on the basis of how many, and how authoritative, the links from other websites are. There are many other factors but external links still make up a large part of the web page rank on search engine results pages.

Online Wine Retailers

In late 2012 the highest ranking online wine retailers (as of, 21 January 2013 and having no more than one store to be classified as predominantly online) for the phrase *buy wine online* were in order: www.wine.com, winelibrary.com, and www.marketviewliquor.com. This is an extremely competitive word to rank well on. Wine.com ranked the highest because it had 2360 websites with pages linking to it (based off SEOmoz Pro tools), ten times more than the nearest competitor. It also had 4381 websites with pages linking to any page on wine.com. When Google sees this number of links it takes note. However the quantity of links is just one factor the other is quality and wine.com has done a spectacular job with many high authority websites linking to it.

Wine Retailers

The highest ranking 'brick and clicks' wine retailers (any number of stores) for the phrase *buy wine* were in order: www.grandwinecellar.com, Bottle King's www.thewinebuyer.com, and www.winex.com. Again it is very competitive. Grandwinecellar.com does well partly because of some top quality links from Huffington Post and Martha Stewart.

Napa Merlot Wineries

Wineries will be looking to rank well in search engines for their varietal and region. Generally the most talented internet marketing
wineries are those nearest Silicon Valley i.e Napa so we'll use Napa
and the most popular varietal Merlot as the example. The highest
ranking web pages for the phrase *napa merlot* were in order: Yahoo
Shopping Napa Merlot page, www.hallwines.com/hall-napa-valley-
merlot, and www.swansonvineyards.com. They shared the top spots
with Wine Library, Wine Spectator and Gayot. Well done to Hall
Wines and Swanson Vineyards, they have done a superb job with
SEO to rank so highly.

3.1.2 Competitors on Facebook

We look at Social Media in detail in Part III: Engagement. Currently
there is no independent company that can provide good information
on how well companies do on Facebook, the biggest of the social media services, due to poor publicly available Facebook data. In short,
only two measurements are publicly available number of 'Likes' and
people 'Talking About This'. Both these are problematic engagement measurements, read the Social Media and Facebook chapters
for more about engagement, in particular I cannot isolate the paid-for
promoted posts from regular posts. However VinTank, a wine social
media technology company, has made the best attempt to provide a
ranking of winery social media, called the Top 50 Winery Social Index. This takes Facebook and Twitter publicly available data, puts
it through an algorithm to try and measure fan growth and engagement levels. Generally the top performers in late 2012 were Wine
Sisterhood, Cornerstone Cellars, V.Sattui Winery, La Crema, Jordan Vineyard and Winery, Sutter Home, and Kendall-Jackson with
many more coming and going on a weekly basis.

3.1.3 Competitors on Twitter

If we take three of those top Social Media wineries: Wine Sisterhood,
Cornerstone Cellars, and Jordan Vineyard and Winery we can use
some software called Followerwonk to compare the three. Jordan
does very well, it has more retweets, mentions, and influence than
the other two. Digging into its followers shows it influence is based
on some high profile TV reporters and wine celebs.

3.1.4 Internet Advertising Competitors

We look at advertising in the Internet Advertising chapter. In terms of Google ads, there are about 1000 advertisers competing for ad space with many of the big names such as wine.com, grandwinecellar.com, winechateau.com, marketviewliquor.com, amazon.com, totalwine.com, target.com, and wineaccess.com. The most competitive keyword by far is *wine gifts online* with other keywords like *napa wine, barbera wine, wine retailers, bordeaux wines, california cabernet sauvignon,* and similar varietal-region combinations being also competitive (we look at keywords in the SEO chapter).

3.2 America's Most Popular Wine Store

Social Research suggest wine consumers want a wide selection of wine most of all. BevMo has it and, crucially, has the numbers according to social media research from NetBase. NetBase kindly gave me the data and a demo of their software to analyze some of America's most popular wine stores (plus a distributor):

- BevMo
- Total Wine and More
- K&L Wine Merchants
- The Wine Club
- National Wine & Spirits

It is compiled using NetBase's ConsumerBase [20] product. One of the things this tool does is find, understand, and automatically analyze social media conversations about a brand or topic, and then generate graphs and reports on the emotions, behaviors, and levels of passion surrounding that brand.

The Brand Passion Index Graph is one example of the output, see Figure 3.2 for what it said about wine stores. Note the choice of stores was by NetBase not myself.

On the vertical axis is 'Sentiment and Chatter Volume', negative at the bottom going up to positive at the top. The horizontal axis is 'Passion Intensity', weak to the left, strong to the right. The amount of sentiment and chatter is indicated by the size of the bubble. So it's best to be large and in the top right.

The key insight is how well BevMo is regarded. Total Wine and More does best with position but is drowned out by BevMo which also

Figure 3.2: Wine Store Brand Passion Index (courtesy of NetBase)

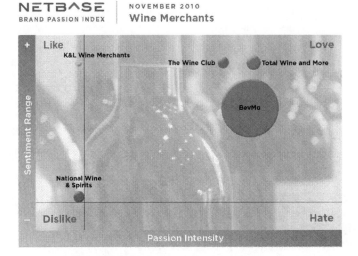

does well though without the same percentage of positive sentiment. The Wine Club also does very well but is squeezed out by Total Wine. K & L Wine Merchants is well liked but does not evoke passion among its customers. Let's dig into the report.

Likes and Dislikes. For these wine stores the most popular phrases were 'great selection' and 'not have it' for Like and Dislike respectively. So range seems to be the biggest issue in social media chatter. Of course price was mentioned in various ways, mainly positively. Service was mentioned negatively. Otherwise the phrases are general likes and dislikes. From this I'd say that consumers are after range, at the right prices, with good service. Frankly that's not terribly insightful to industry insiders though it probably confirms the accuracy of the software.

I'd prefer to dig into the data over a period of days or weeks to assess exactly what range, but the demo suggests there were sufficient posts to work this out.

What is very interesting are the domains. Here are the Top 10:

- twitter.com

- yelp.com
- cellartracker.com
- chow.com
- facebook.com
- chowbound.chow.com
- bigsoccer.com
- almanacnews.com
- santabarbaraview.com
- wineberserkers.com

This for me is probably the biggest insight of all. Yelp and Cellar-tracker are very powerful—but Chow and Wineberserkers are much bigger than I expected. Twitter is as important as ever, and Facebook is only ranked five (perhaps because NetBase cannot access private personal pages, only business 'fan' pages). Bigsoccer is about soccer, but it does have other forum topics including wine. And almanac-news.com and santabarbaraview.com are reporting on the plans of Bevmo to open stores in their area (mainly negative articles).

3.3 Summary

Bevmo and Wine.com are serious competitors with strong internet presence in social media and search engines respectively. There are a myriad of other competitors many with very professional websites and search engine marketing practices. Many of them have found a good point of difference in this competitive market.

3.4 Resources

- How well did you understand? Visit my website to discuss or ask questions about Wine and Competitors: `www.WineMarketingPros.com/compchap/`
- SEOmoz `seomoz.org`

4 Company—Wine Retailer

The last couple of chapters have looked at how complex wine customers are and how competitive the market is. Don't get depressed, in this chapter we look at the very significant advantages of being a local wine retailer.

There are all sorts of advantages a local retailer has compared to a national online retailer. But the key advantage is simply the lower freight cost of shipping relatively heavy physical products. There is some concern about Amazon entering the wine market. Some of this paranoia is warranted but much of it isn't.

Amazon and other internet retailers do well with products that are cheap to ship or can be downloaded via the internet. Distribution of physical products requires packing and freight, the greater the product weight and/or size the higher the freight cost. I disagree with people who talk of the inevitability of the internet taking over the physical retail sector, as the obvious cost advantages in distribution are just not there (unlike with digital distribution e.g. music, movies, kindle-type books).

Let's take the wine industry. The winery and national wholesalers deal with pallets, layers, and cases of wine. It costs about the same to send one bottle of wine across the States as it does to send one case. In fact if you have to break a case from a pallet and then take a bottle from the case then it arguably costs a large operation even more to sell a single bottle than a case when you take (un)packing into account.

Here's what The Economist magazine said in an eCommerce special report [21],

> ...two things soon became clear. One was that shipping costs were (and remain) one of the biggest deterrents for consumers considering online purchases of physical products. The second was that traditional warehouse and distribution centers were not well suited to the business of eCommerce fulfillment: if it is to work properly, it needs newly designed systems.

Both these things have combined to undermine some of
the economic advantages of online shopping. Perhaps this
should not have come as a surprise. Physical shoppers,
after all, handle their own order fulfillment, by choosing
the goods and paying for them at the check-out, as well
as their own delivery, by personally taking them home.
And they do all this at their own expense, in both time
and money. Merely to replicate this system efficiently,
down to the individual consumer, is demanding enough;
financing it, whether by absorbing the cost or by adding
it to the bill, makes it even harder. It might have been
better had eCommerce firms given more attention to this
end of their business first. Ironically, the delivery problems encountered by pure plays were one of the things
that led many traditional retailers to assume that they
could do better. Ironically because, here as elsewhere,
many quickly found that their own distribution systems,
geared to moving goods on pallets from warehouses to
shops, proved a disadvantage, not a benefit.

Wal-Mart, for example, has the most highly praised
distribution system in the world: even the tyre pressures
of its lorries are calibrated so that, when fully laden with
pallets, the vehicles will be at exactly the right height
for the unloading docks at Wal-Mart stores. But such a
system is unable to cope with individual orders that have
to be delivered to people's homes. So Wal-Mart has had
to outsource its website distribution to two rivals...

The Lesson from Online Grocery

A year later The Economist [22] reports on a UK supermarket's entry
into the States using internet retailing in an article called 'The Lesson
from Online Grocery',

Tesco's chief executive, Terry Leahy, says that by using
his company's distribution model he expects the American joint venture to be operating profitably by the end of
next year. While Tesco's distribution methods may, with
hindsight, be seen as a clever way to enter a small and
uncertain new market, dedicated warehouses may ulti-
mately be more efficient. But it depends on the numbers

and geography. Tesco officials have said that before it makes commercial sense, a dedicated warehouse needs to receive about 10,000 online grocery orders a week from its delivery area. At present, there are rarely enough people in one area ordering their groceries by computer to justify that. But in time there might be. So, as with many dotcom ideas, the pioneers of online grocery may simply have been way ahead of their time.

Actually they weren't. Peapod struggled, Webvan went bankrupt, and Tesco sold out of the above operation in 2006.

I wonder about Wine.com's profitability as it faces a similar conundrum. It probably needs about 10,000 online orders per week from its delivery area to justify a dedicated warehouse (I believe they have a good number of warehouses across the country).

Wine.com and the national online retailers assume that their most accessible population is the US population less children, teetotalers etc. In fact its accessible population are those within 15-25 miles from their warehouse, based off the online grocery model. Perhaps 1 million people if they're lucky, more likely about 50,000 (2500 to 5,000+ people per square mile) depending on the county.

So if you're going to only sell locally, and the population isn't numerous enough to justify a dedicated warehouse, what do you do? Open up a retail store of course. The Economist[23] again, in an article called 'Santa's Helpers',

> Lots of consumers clearly see useful connections between the online and offline worlds. Many of the big retailers with websites, such as Circuit City and Sears, offer the option of picking up the goods in their shops. This may seem old-fashioned, but it is surprisingly popular. That could be because people can't or don't want to wait for a delivery van to show up, or they are in a hurry, or they don't want to bother with a salesperson, or they know they can return what they buy if it goes wrong, or they just want to save on the delivery charge, especially if it is something heavy. At Sears, 40% of online sales (excluding garments) are now picked up in store.

In the introduction I mentioned Macy's CEO saying *$1 of online sales drives $5.70 of offline sales.* Most consumers want the convenience and information of a website but don't want to wait for delivery and do want the trust of a local store. So let's go over the pros and cons of online eCommerce in the wine retail industry.

Advantages of Selling Wine Online

- You can sell all over the world at any time of the day.
- It's more convenient for time-poor consumers who don't want to drive, find a parking place, walk to the store, ask for product information, or wait in a checkout line.
- The internet and retailer websites can provide a vast array of content (reviews, ratings, recommendations) as well as advanced sorting and screening and even virtual wine cellars.
- Websites accumulate large amounts of data that can be used in sophisticated internet marketing campaigns.
- For some industries there are lower distribution costs e.g. music, newspapers, DVDs. Sometimes a wholesaler can be avoided by shipping direct to consumers. With wine in the US this advantage is not as apparent.

Disadvantages of Selling Wine Online[24]

- Consumers do not have the instant gratification of possessing (and drinking) the wine. The mail order industry has been limited to about 3% of total retail sales in the US. Internet only, or pure play retailers, probably face the same issue.
- Sending single bottles of wine can be very expensive from an order processing, packing, and shipping perspective. When a consumer 'picks up' they are in effect using packing and shipping themselves at their cost of time and petrol. So retail stores may actually be the most cost effective way to get a wine from the winery on one side of the world to a wine drinker in the middle of New York.
- Some people enjoy going out to shop. Men often joke about women being addicted to shopping when in fact they can be just as bad in a fine wine store. The actual purchase of shoes (or wine) is only one part of the shopping experience; whereas, diversion from the routine of daily life, exploring the latest trends etc. can be more important. Many like the ambience of a fine wine store and find it integral to the shopping experience.
- Search engine results pages and poor websites can be confusing and frustrating rather than the seamless simple process that

they should be.

- Some consumers still have concerns about using their credit card (which they shouldn't) and giving their personal details online (which is perhaps more reasonable).

If you're selling a digital product, such as music, or have a low mail and handling cost product then an internet-only business could well be very profitable (just look at Apple with music and Amazon with books). If freight and handling are a significant cost then the internet will be a means to pre-sell the product with the actual sale more likely being made in-store rather than online.

The exception is with case lots of wine which have sufficient margin to cover freight costs and lower handling costs—but still suffer many of the disadvantages listed above.

So I am a strong advocate of local wine retailers selling wine online because $1 of online sales drives $5.70 of offline sales. You can provide the most profitable customers the information they want, and you can use sophisticated internet marketing to drive sales. Note that Amazon seriously considered selling wine online but backed out at the last moment.[25]

4.1 The Advantage with Local Customers Shopping Online

Twenty-four percent of searches across Google[26] are local and this number doubles to 50% for mobile searches.[27] What's more there is a Location War that is going on to become the de facto directory for local businesses on the Web. It's between the likes of Yelp, Foursquare, Twitter, Yahoo, Apple, and Google. Indeed Google has launched local services such as Places, Maps, Hotpot, Boost, local search, and Adwords location extension which are now incorporated into Google+ Local.

Google+ Local is trying to become the de facto local business directory that helps local consumers find the best place for a cup of coffee, a book...or a bottle of wine. It's not completely altruistic of course as what they really want to do is sell paid advertising in the directory for heavily searched terms.

The difference between Google+ Local and the other armies of 'geo start ups' is that Google is coming from the search angle; whereas, the others are coming from a social media angle. In short, Yelp relies on people writing reviews and 'checking in' to offer an informative directory of local businesses. Whereas Google uses its search algorithms to rank local search results.

It's closely tied into Google Maps. It accepts user reviews from Google Maps but also from third party providers. How the listings and the reviews are ranked is dependent on the relevance of the search terms, geographical distance and the usual Google algorithmic secret sauce.

This is a very interesting battle, one that will have a big effect on small businesses for years to come. Will Google be able to offer more of the social aspects that the others have? If so, they could dominate the local advertising sector one more time (the first time being local Adwords).

4.2 Your Point of Difference

Here are the opportunities I see for a local retailer in the internet based market.

4.2.1 Your Point of Difference vs. Price of Entry

First let's distinguish between the 'point of difference' and 'price of entry' for an online wine retailer.

The Price of Entry. Most good online wine retailers already offer what could be called the 'price of entry'. In other words if you don't have these, your sales will be limited. However if you do have these then you're simply 'in the game', but not enough to be 'winning the game'. These include:

- wide wine range
- prices at market values
- tasting notes and preferably photos
- ratings and reviews, ideally with customer reviews
- eCommerce
- newsletter and email subscription

An online customer can visit six shops in one minute. With shopping comparison websites they can visit the whole country (and indeed the world) in 10 seconds. It's as though they can go to a wine shop with a shelf that goes all the way down Main Street with retailers hawking their wines every couple of yards. You need to stand out—you need a point of difference.

Points of Difference. Here's a possible list with examples in brackets:

- Pick up, on your way home
- 30 minutes delivery (the Dominos of wine)
- Personalized recommendations based on computer algorithms (Wine.com, Snooth)
- Discussion forums (WineLoversPage)
- 18,000 wines to choose from (BevMo, WineChateau)
- Expert tasting panel recommendations (WineExpress)
- Cheapest (BevMo, WineChateau)
- Exclusive small vineyard wines (CA Wine Club, WineAccess)
- In-depth articles (WineLovers)
- Cellar Management (Vinfolio, CellarTracker)
- Maps, showing wineries and terroir
- Mobile store
- Outrageous, highly-entertaining video reviews and fan commenting (WineLibrary)

If you can find something you can do well that is a point of difference in the market, and crucially, valued by wine drinkers, then position your wine store online in that way.

WSJ.com on Great Wine Stores

The WSJ wine writers[28] also have an interesting view on this and have written a Wall Street Journal review of 'wine stores with shtick'.

In summary they suggest you do some of the following:

- Smaller selection
- Wines by weight or taste profile
- Keeping cool
- Food pairings
- Do one thing well
- Kids' areas
- Tasting notes
- Remember me (greet me on entry by name)
- 'Handpicked' wines
- 'Enomatic' machines
- Meeting, tasting or lounge space
- Quiet wine education

Great starter for finding your brick and mortar point of difference some of which can be applied to the internet.

4.2.2 Two Possibilities: Local or Niche

I see two clear gaps depending on your particular interests:

- the Local Market (within 1-20 miles of your store, depending on population density)
- a Small Niche (e.g. Californian Pinot Noir, or Bordeaux)

The Local Market

As sophisticated as the national competitors are they cannot offer the ability to provide pick up or quick delivery. Nor can they offer the face to face trusted personal service a local retailer can. Even Wine.com, with all its warehouses is going to be restricted in just how fast it can deliver to your local customers. Even BevMo doesn't have stores in every township in California. Most wine drinkers[29] will drink their wine the same day or weekend they get it so they're reluctant to wait for next day or 3-day delivery.

This is the gap in the market for most local wine retailers. It can be supported by very specific 'local' internet marketing techniques. By staying local you also avoid the interstate shipping legal compliance issues in the US.

A Niche

If you have lots of knowledge about a specific wine niche then this strategy is another possibility (indeed you could do both).

For instance, I know the New Zealand wine region Central Otago extremely well. There are over 100 wineries, 6 subregions in different mountain valleys, different soil types, different micro climates, fascinating winery personalities, and some great and not so great wines. In fact I lived there and helped create a specialist Central Otago internet wine store with a local retailer. So I'm immensely proud and not a little bit biased about Central Otago pinot noir and could write about it all day. Which is the key.

You have to create unique and compelling content for the niche and for the wine brands. If you can write, or do videos/podcasts about a niche—we're talking 15-30 minutes a day, 3 days a week, 40 weeks a year—then this is a good possibility. If you can't find the time then you're going to struggle getting enough unique and compelling content to keep your customers engaged as well as the search engine benefits of 'non-duplicate' content (see the SEO chapter). You're also going to struggle to stand out in a competitive market.

My recommendation is you start with your Local Market. If you find you have the enthusiasm and the time to comment and review a niche then go for it. In fact I think this is a good way to build knowledge of various wine niches and explore the worldwide wine industry.

Let's now pull together the chapters on Customers, and Competitors, and how to position your Company, into the start of a business plan—firstly some financials.

4.3 A Wine Store Financial Model

I've created a hypothetical financial model for opening a *new* wine store based on a local area I know well. We will also look at an existing wine store financial model later in this chapter. The financial model is split into two sections—Input and Calculations. I suggest you download this now so you can work through the figures while you read by doing the following:

- Go to www.WineMarketingPros.com/cmychap/, the Resources webpage for this chapter which will give you a link to a Google Docs spreadsheet
- Go to the bottom of the page and click *Edit this page (if you have permission)*. This will open a new page
- Under the Google Docs brand, click *File >Download as >Excel*
- Then open the spreadsheet up in Excel and start changing the Input section cells (and the Calculation cells if you're comfortable with spreadsheets) which we'll go over below

Input, see Figures 4.1 and 4.2:

- The input section is all the variables
- You change these to see how they affect cash flow at the bottom of the spreadsheet
- There are no formulas in these cells—feel free to change them as much as you want and see how it affects Net Cash Flow (i.e. profit)

Figure 4.1: Wine Shop Financial Model: Input Section (1 of 2)

Wine Store Financial Feasibility Model				
Input section				
Description				Notes, Sources, Formulas
Buyer Numbers:				
Population of Geographical Area	25,000			look for local stats
Annual population growth rate (%)	1.0%			look for local stats
Adult Population	60.0%			look for local stats
Wine Drinkers as a % of adult population	32.6%			core (13.7) plus marginal (18.9) wine drinkers (Wagner, Olson, Thach, p.30)
Year	1	2	3	constant
Store Penetration %	25.0%	50.0%	75.0%	Estimate: occasional customer, x% buys at least 1 bottle pa. (not market share)
Segment:	% of drinkers			Project Genome: US Constellation Wine Study
Enthusiasts	9.00%			Project Genome
Luxury Enthusiasts	3.00%			Project Genome
Image Seekers	18.00%			Project Genome
Luxury Image Seekers	2.00%			Project Genome
Savvy Shoppers	15.00%			Project Genome
Traditionalists	16.00%			Project Genome
Satisfied Sippers	14.00%			Project Genome
Overwhelmed	23.00%			Project Genome
My Market Share of Segment:	market share %			Eg. Half of purchases reflects everyday wine bought from discounter, 3 other stores.
Enthusiasts	25.00%			Like the range
Luxury Enthusiasts	50.00%			Love the range
Image Seekers	25.00%			Like the descriptions and ratings
Luxury Image Seekers	50.00%			Love the descriptions and ratings, and higher prices
Savvy Shoppers	5.00%			Too expensive, only on impulse
Traditionalists	15.00%			Find reputable wine brands
Satisfied Sippers	5.00%			Too expensive, only on impulse
Overwhelmed	5.00%			Too expensive, only on impulse
Price / bottle (USD ex tax):				Price categories, rounded to nearest $5 price point (p.41 Wine Mktg Sales)
Enthusiasts	$15.00			Super Premium
Luxury Enthusiasts	$25.00			Ultra Premium
Image Seekers	$15.00			Super Premium
Luxury Image Seekers	$25.00			Ultra Premium
Savvy Shoppers	$5.00			Sub Premium
Traditionalists	$10.00			Premium
Satisfied Sippers	$5.00			Super Value Wine
Overwhelmed	$5.00			Super Value Wine

Figure 4.2: Wine Shop Financial Model: Input Section (2 of 2)

Quantity pa (bottles):				Based off Aussie Johnson and Bruwer study. Checked against US average.
Enthusiasts	104			Estimate 2 bottles pw
Luxury Enthusiasts	104			Estimate 2 bottles pw
Image Seekers	104			Estimate 2 bottles pw
Luxury Image Seekers	104			Estimate 2 bottles pw
Savvy Shoppers	52			Estimate 1 bottles pw
Traditionalists	52			Estimate 1 bottles pw
Satisfied Sippers	52			Estimate 1 bottles pw
Overwhelmed	52			Estimate 1 bottles pw
Margin:				
Retailer Gross margin (%)	30.0%			Industry standard
Expenses:				
Store Lease per period ($)	$30,000			1000 ft2 @ $30 / ft2 pa
Manager's required income per year ($)	$45,000			Employed or Owner Manager
Staff Salary	$35,000			estimate
Number of Staff (exc Manager)	1			estimate
Administration ($ pa)	$20,000			Accounting and legal, insurance, utilities, security
Capital:				
Inventory	$25,000			estimate
Store Fit out	$20,000			estimate includes IT
Promotion:				
Year	1	2	3	constant
Internet Marketing activity	1	1	1	Dummy variable. 1 = active, 0 = inactive.
Tastings Activity	1	1	1	Dummy variable. 1 = active, 0 = inactive.
Tastings Vending Machine activity	0	0	0	Dummy variable. 1 = active, 0 = inactive.
Concept Store PR activity	0	0	0	Dummy variable. 1 = active, 0 = inactive.
Price promotions activity	0	0	0	Dummy variable. 1 = active, 0 = inactive.
Local newspaper advertising activity	0	0	0	Dummy variable. 1 = active, 0 = inactive.
Internet Marketing Visitors	6000			estimate 500pm
Internet Marketing Conversion Rate	0.5%			estimate
Post Store Purchase (Macys Factor)	5			Macys $5.70 factor, i.e. for every $1 bought online $5.70 bought in-store
Impact on Sales of Tastings	5%			estimate
Impact on Sales of Tastings Vending Machine	10%			estimate
Impact on Sales of Concept Store PR	10%			estimate
Price Elasticity	1			estimate (eg 1=same % increase in buyers as discount, or 1.5= 50% increase)
Dollars newspaper advertising per customer ($)	100			estimate: every $100 of advertising brings 1 customer
Cost of internet marketing / year ($)	5000			estimate
Cost of tastings	500			estimate
Cost of Tasting Vending Machines	10000			Estimate: 8 slot www.enomaticusa.com
Cost of Concept Store extras	5000			estimate: mainly computer equipment
Price Promotion Discount (%)	20.0%			variable
Cost of local print advertising/year ($)	$5,000			estimate

Calculations, see Figures 4.3 and 4.4:

- There are four calculation sections Revenue, Variable Costs, Fixed Costs, and Cashflow
- Do not change these cells (unless you want to change how the spreadsheet works of course)
- The key figure is 'Cumulative cash flow periods 1-3'
- The store will be cash negative in Year 1 (fit out costs and inventory) but expect to be profitable after that

Figure 4.3: Wine Shop Financial Model: Calculation Section (Revenue)

Revenue Calculations				
Description	1	2	3	Notes
Total population	25,000	25,250	25,503	Population * growth rate
Available population	4,890	4,939	4,988	Total population *Adult% * Wine Drinkers %
Store Penetration	1,223	2,469	3,741	Available Population * Store Penetration %
				% of popn that uses store at least once pa.
Store Penetration By Segment:				Store customers look like this:
Enthusiasts	110	222	337	Store Penetration * Segment % of drinkers
Luxury Enthusiasts	37	74	112	Store Penetration * Segment % of drinkers
Image Seekers	220	445	673	Store Penetration * Segment % of drinkers
Luxury Image Seekers	24	49	75	Store Penetration * Segment % of drinkers
Savvy Shoppers	183	370	561	Store Penetration * Segment % of drinkers
Traditionalists	196	395	599	Store Penetration * Segment % of drinkers
Satisfied Sippers	171	346	524	Store Penetration * Segment % of drinkers
Overwhelmed	281	568	860	Store Penetration * Segment % of drinkers
Buyers # (without marketing)	1,223	2,469	3,741	Sum of Store Penetration
Store's Annual Wine Revenue by Segment Customer:				Each customer purchases this amount from My store pa
Enthusiasts	$390			Segment's Price * Quantity * My Market Share
Luxury Enthusiasts	$1,300			Segment's Price * Quantity * My Market Share
Image Seekers	$390			Segment's Price * Quantity * My Market Share
Luxury Image Seekers	$1,300			Segment's Price * Quantity * My Market Share
Savvy Shoppers	$13			Segment's Price * Quantity * My Market Share
Traditionalists	$78			Segment's Price * Quantity * My Market Share
Satisfied Sippers	$13			Segment's Price * Quantity * My Market Share
Overwhelmed	$13			Segment's Price * Quantity * My Market Share
Revenue by Segment:				I then multiply this by Store Penetration customers
Enthusiasts	$42,910	$86,678	$131,317	Segment Store Penetration * Store's Annual Wine Revenue by Segment Customer
Luxury Enthusiasts	$47,678	$96,309	$145,907	Segment Store Penetration * Store's Annual Wine Revenue by Segment Customer
Image Seekers	$85,820	$173,355	$262,633	Segment Store Penetration * Store's Annual Wine Revenue by Segment Customer
Luxury Image Seekers	$31,785	$64,206	$97,272	Segment Store Penetration * Store's Annual Wine Revenue by Segment Customer
Savvy Shoppers	$2,384	$4,815	$7,295	Segment Store Penetration * Store's Annual Wine Revenue by Segment Customer
Traditionalists	$15,257	$30,819	$46,690	Segment Store Penetration * Store's Annual Wine Revenue by Segment Customer
Satisfied Sippers	$2,225	$4,494	$6,809	Segment Store Penetration * Store's Annual Wine Revenue by Segment Customer
Overwhelmed	$3,655	$7,384	$11,186	Segment Store Penetration * Store's Annual Wine Revenue by Segment Customer
Revenue without marketing	$231,713	$468,060	$709,110	Sum of Revenue by Segment
Buyers from Marketing:				
Internet Marketing	150	150	150	(Visitors * Macy's Factor) * Conversion Rate * on/off
Tastings	61	123	187	Buyers # (without marketing) * impact of tastings * on/off
Tastings Vending Machine	0	0	0	Buyers # (without marketing) * impact of vending machines * on/off
Concept Store PR	0	0	0	Buyers # (without marketing) * impact of concept store PR * on/off
Price promotions	0	0	0	Price Promotion % * Price elasticity * Buyers # (without marketing) * on/off
Local newspaper advertising	0	0	0	Cost of print advertising / Dollars per customer * on/off
Sum of Incremental Buyers	211	273	337	Sum of buyers from marketing
Weighted Average Revenue per non marketing buyer	$190	$190	$190	Revenue without marketing / Buyers # (without marketing)
Revenue from Marketing	$40,017	$51,834	$63,887	Buyers from marketing * Weighted Average Revenue per non marketing buyer
Revenue	$271,729	$519,894	$772,997	Price * Number of purchases per year

Model notes:

- Ignores all taxes (sales, company)
- Note this is for illustrative purposes only. Before starting a business you need professional accounting and legal advice
- Capital costs may be understated due to the small store size and DIY fit-out

Figure 4.4: Wine Shop Financial Model: Calculation Section (Costs and Profit)

Variable cost calculations				
Year	1	2	3	Notes
COGS	$190,210	$363,925	$541,098	Revenue * (1 – Gross Margin)
Cost of Price Promotion Discount	$0	$0	$0	Revenue * Discount % * on/off
Variable costs	$190,210	$363,925	$541,098	Sum of variable costs above
Fixed cost calculations				
Year	1	2	3	Notes
Lease	$30,000	$30,000	$30,000	Store Lease per period ($)
Salaries	$80,000	$80,000	$80,000	Manager's salary + (staff salary * staff #)
Administration	$20,000	$20,000	$20,000	Administration
Internet Marketing	$5,000	$5,000	$5,000	Cost of internet marketing / year ($)
Tastings Activity	$500	$500	$500	Cost of tastings
Tastings Vending Machine	$0	$0	$0	Cost of Tasting Vending Machines
Concept Store PR activity	$0	$0	$0	Cost of Concept Store extras
Local newspaper advertising activity	$0	$0	$0	Cost of local print advertising/year ($)
Inventory	$25,000			Inventory
Store Fit out	$20,000			Store Fit out
Fixed costs	$180,500	$135,500	$135,500	Sum of fixed costs above
Worksheet 5 - Cashflow calculations				
Year	1	2	3	Notes
Net Cash flow	($98,981)	$20,468	$96,399	Revenue per year -(Variable costs per year+Fixed costs per year)
Cumulative cash flow periods 1 -3			$17,886	Sum of cash flows of periods 1, 2 & 3

- The town in mind is seasonal. This model ignores tourism purchases during summer but may overstate the number of permanent residents during winter
- The figures have been changed.
- References: Financial Modeling[30] and Wine Drinkers[31]

Usually I'd have a much higher expectation of profit but I'm willing to make less return on investment for this venture. Note that we are simply looking at feasibility. If I end up taking this to the next step I will complete a full monthly cashflow analysis for 36 months (companies fail because they run out of cash, not necessarily because they are unprofitable). It's a pretty standard feasibility model, apart from the way I treat Segments and Promotion.

Segments. I'm a bit of a fan of Project Genome market research so I've split customer numbers into the segments each with different market share, price points, and bottle purchase volume. I've done this because the revenue estimation is the most difficult, yet the most profit-sensitive input variable. Costs are reasonably certain and controllable.

Promotion. I have outlined six marketing activities:

- Internet Marketing (i.e. the topic of this book!)
- In-store tastings (regular tastings every week)
- Tasting Vending Machines i.e. machine-based, nitrogen-pumped, bottles (I had enomatic machines in mind)

- Concept Store (mainly PR of new retail and internet technology aimed at a nearby large city)
- Price Promotions—a discount off everything
- Local newspaper adverts

To turn the marketing activity on and see its effect on Net Cashflow, enter 1 in the relevant cell, in range C68 to E73. To turn it off enter 0. Do not use any other value than 1 or 0 or your results will be nonsensical. We will focus just on the Internet Marketing strategies in the next section.

Change a variable, see how it affects cashflow, write it down, go back to the base case, change another variable... you'll see which variables are the most important and sensitive. You can then spend more time on researching these than the other less important variables.

When doing this 'Sensitivity Analysis' the most sensitive variables are almost always price, gross margin ($), and volume related. Here's what I found to be the most sensitive in this case:

- Store Penetration in Y3 and Y2
- Image Seeker Segment Size, Market Share, and Volume purchased
- Enthusiast Segment Size and Market Share
- Luxury Enthusiast Segment Size
- Conversion Rate from Internet Marketing Campaigns

In my case I'm not looking at discounting so margins (price and cost) are not as important. Instead it all comes down to the volume. How big is the market and what share will I get? By splitting out the segments I can be a lot more accurate in my estimates than if I were to just use a simple wine drinker average. In this case I need to research just how large the higher margin segments are in the local area.

It also shows the craziness of competing on price (unless you're Wal-Mart). Assuming a price elasticity of 1 (i.e. if I drop prices by 20% I'll get a 20% increase in volume), I'll make a massive loss of about $280,000 on the promotion (i.e. 3-year cashflow comparison with price Promotion turned on for all 3 years vs. turned off for all 3 years). If price elasticity is 1.5 that drops to $270,000. If it's 3 it drops to $228,000, if it's 11 then I break-even, if price elasticity is 0.5 then I lose almost $300,000.

Now I appreciate that you could limit the discount to a few bottles. So you advertise a special and hopefully the greater store traffic makes up for the lower average price. However the numbers will most likely work against you—time to find another way to promote your wines, frankly, for the good of your own business and the industry.

4.3.1 Business Plan

Here's an outline or sketch of a wine store business plan. The plan is based on an old Deloittes[32] small business plan template but then altered based on my marketing experience, for a wine shop, and other various business plans and templates I've seen over the last couple of decades.

You'd use it to plan and monitor your business of course—the e-Myth[33] idea of working on your business not in your business. It is also the sections of a plan that a bank or equity investors would want to see if you needed to raise cash.

There is a lot of disagreement over the meaning of the words: Goal, Objective, Strategy, and Tactics. Here's how I use them.

Objective: The most important outcomes for the business e.g. profit. When I use it for marketing it is usually around revenue or volume. A General would say 'win the war', we say 'make profits'—perhaps not quite as motivating. An Objective example: To increase revenue by 20% while maintaining Gross Margins for the period 2013 vs. 2012.

Strategy: A concept or idea on how to achieve the objective. I use the 4Ps+S (Product, Price, Place, Promotion, Service) as a more robust way to come up with strategies. A Strategy example: Competing wine outlets tend to be cheap and nasty, with discounting, clueless staff, and poor product range. 'Image Seekers' want advice and a wide range of premium wine in a sophisticated setting. We will attract more of the 'Image Seeker' segment into store by having a premium store fit-out, staffed with knowledgeable and helpful wine experts.

Tactics: The action points on how to implement the strategy. A Tactics example: Premium fit-out. I will brief an interior designer by Month 2, consulting budget is $5000, timeline for designer plan is 2 months with weekly meetings in Month 4. Then you may list other key action points to do with builders etc. Tactics tend to be more short term—a list of SMART (Specific Measurable Attainable Relevant Timely) action points. Strategies by comparison, tend to be more ideas and longer term.

Wine Retailer Business Plan

Here's the plan with a bit of commentary and a few examples to bring it to life.

Executive Summary. Succinctly cover the key parts of your business plan—probably the store, key financial figures, and key marketing strategies. This is all most people will read—I kid you not! It should be one page. Do this last.

The Customers. Describe your customers, their wants and needs:

- General demographics for local area: population, % adults, % wine drinkers (see financial model)
- Extent of seasonality (around holiday periods)
- Segments e.g. see Project Genome and chart below

Figure 4.5: Project Genome Home and Habits Study: Consumer and Profit Share. (Graph printed with the permission of Constellation Wines)

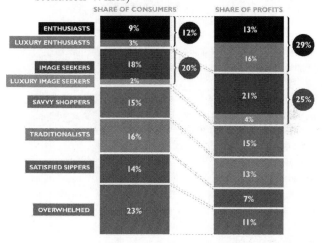

Choose your target segment(s). As this book is all about small wine retailers I'd suggest you want to target the customers who often buy premium wines: Luxury Enthusiasts, Enthusiasts , Image Seekers, Luxury Image Seekers and/or perhaps Traditionalists.

It is arguably a good idea to choose just one primary segment as it allows you to focus on just that segment's needs and wants. I usually have a primary segment and then 1-2 secondary segments.

I would suggest you don't bother targeting Savvy Shoppers, Overwhelmed, or Satisfied Sippers as they are likely to purchase from the cheapest place possible and/or only buy budget wines. You're likely to pick up a small percentage share of these segments regardless (due to convenience or special occasion).

The Competition Describe the competition within 2, 5, or 20 miles. Also look at:

- Their estimated share of each segment
- Type: Grocery, Big Liquor Chain Store, Small Liquor Store, Fine Wine Store, Internet
- Their points of difference

The Company. Describe the company and what you think its 'mission' or overall aim is. Write a brief summary of:

- Financials
- Location
- Fit-Out
- Range
- Staff
- Point of Difference

So, for example, Financials may read: e.g. profit after drawings of $100,000 in the next financial year, revenue increased by 20%, at a 30% GM, overheads increase by 2%, and owner is only working five days per week eight hours per day.

Do you have a Point of Difference? Why will your target customers buy from your store, versus the competition? Review the above for points of difference from your competitors. If you're just a 'me too' store then you'll rely on price and convenience. Both of these strategies are fraught with problems. If you rely on relationships then what happens if competitors also develop relationships with your customers.

You may want to review your Point of Difference regularly as you write this business plan.

Major Issues and Business Objectives. What are your major issues? From this will come your business objectives. I suggest you just write all the issues down then work out what are the most important by using your financial model and 'gut feel'. There should only be a few. You are trying to get to the heart of what drives your business and then focus on the most important issues.

Business issues and objective examples. Usually at least one business issue is a financial one—you're not achieving the profit that you'd like to. So the objective might be 'make a net profit after tax of $200,000 in the next year'. Your strategies to do this could be growing sales by 25% (Marketing strategy) while maintaining gross margins (Marketing) and keeping fixed costs steady (Operations). Another objective may be to increase growth rather than profits with the view to sell the business in a few years time. Or you may be facing unprecedented losses and need to stop hemorrhaging cash by reducing Fixed and Variable Costs while adjusting suppliers' terms of trade.

Other business issues may include:

- Very high fixed cost—perhaps your lease is too expensive (Operations— Lease Cost)
- Cash flow issues—due to poor trade debtors (Finance—Accounts)
- Customer Service—perhaps your staff are just plain rude (Operations— HR)

From this commentary you'll probably identify many issues. The idea is to concentrate your effort on the most important issue to the business—what is having the biggest effect on the bottom line? A good financial model helps identify these, as seen with the segment market share, margin, and volume in the wine store financial model above.

Here are some examples of marketing related issues and objectives:

- No one knows your store because you have little natural foot traffic. So your objective is to increase your store awareness.
- You have a large liquor chain store close to your store which is sucking all the wine drinkers to their discount campaigns. So your objective is to recover market share without decreasing overall margins.
- You have lots of foot traffic and great exterior signage so people know your store—but they aren't giving you a try. Your objective is to encourage them to trial your store at least once.
- People seem to buy from you once but never again. Your objective is to boost repeat purchase.

Note that internet marketing has to meet business objectives not be merely justified on it's hype alone.

Marketing Strategies. Once you have decided on your top few issues and corresponding objectives (about 2-5) then you can start your marketing plan. It cascades out like this:

Figure 4.6: Business Plan Structure

Objective
    Primary Segment
        Marketing Strategy 1 with KPIs
            Marketing and Sales Tactic 1
            Marketing and Sales Tactic 2
        Marketing Strategy 2 with KPIs
            Marketing and Sales Tactic 3
            Marketing and Sales Tactic 4
    Secondary Segments ...

Using this method you're forced to start with the customer. You get into his/her head first before you think of how you can help them. I start off each segment section by quickly reviewing the relevant segment e.g. Enthusiasts—like to browse the wine section, publications, and are influenced by wine ratings and reviews. What they want is different from Savvy Shoppers who like to shop in a variety of stores each week to find the best deals, and like specials and discounts. Enthusiasts want information. Savvy Shoppers want discounts—leave them to the low-cost, big liquor chains.

So you're now completely absorbed into the segment's world? Great, start to come up with strategies for the Product, price, Place, Promotion and Service. The *Market Strategy with KPIs* above.

Strategies around: Service
Tactic suggestions:

- Staff expertise
- Formal vs. Friendly
- Tastings
- Information in-store
- Info/eCommerce on website

Strategies around: Product
Tactic suggestions:

- Varietals, Regions by price Points
- Range extent and stock holding

Strategies around: Price
Tactic suggestions:

- Pricing at normal GM%/above/below
- Discounting: always/occasional/never

Strategies around: Place

Tactic suggestions:

- Foot traffic
- Parking
- Fit-out

Strategies around: Promotion

Tactic suggestions:

- Tastings
- Clubs
- Internet: SEO, PPC, LPO, SM etc (i.e. The major parts of this book!)
- Newspaper, Magazine and Radio Advertising
- Discount Campaigns
- Holiday Campaigns: Gift with Purchase, Prizes

KPIs, Benchmarks or Measurements of Success. In Objectives above we had a specific objective about profit. We need to do the same for each of our Strategies and Tactics. If they're not successful we need to know so we can change or drop them. We'll cover this more in each chapter as well as below.

So that's the marketing. Let's move onto the other parts of the business.

Operations

Staff

- Your Management Ability or HR Consultant: staff numbers, salaries, conditions, training
- KPIs: Customer Satisfaction, Qualified Staff, Staff Turnover

IT Systems

- Point of Sale, Register, Inventory System, Accounting System
- KPIs: No downtime, accurate timely inventory, and accounting

Risks

- Negative cash flow, Unexpected Events (bad debt, sickness, IT failure), Liquor license issues (prosecution), Insurance
- KPIs: can weather potential future disasters and stay in business

Financials

- Cash Flow budget/actual/forecast; P & L, Balance Sheet; Cost-Volume-Point and Break-even analysis; Access to Financing (overdraft, loans, owner or third party equity); Large outlays (e.g. fit-out, computers)
- KPIs: various

It's time to introduce Tony from Tony's Wine Store, the illustrative wine store we are using throughout this book.

4.4 Tony's Wine Store

In this book we're going to follow Tony, the owner of a hypothetical small wine retail business Tony's Wine Store. We'll go through his problems and how we'll resolve them using internet marketing strategies.

Tony owns a small wine store in Notown, an average sized town (or perhaps a suburb or a few blocks in larger city) somewhere in the US. He employs a couple of sales assistants and has a wide range of wines (this book ignores spirits and beer). Tony is comfortable with using a computer to browse the internet, has a simple wine store website, and sometimes uses Facebook to catch up with friends. He uses Microsoft Outlook to send newsletters, nowadays really just price promos, to his customer base but has seen little interest. So far the internet hasn't done anything for his business. With all the media hoopla about the internet he feels like he's missing out on something, but quickly dismisses this as plain old tech industry hype.

He started the business because he wanted to share his passion about wine with fellow wine enthusiasts as well as making a living out of something he loved. But now he is increasingly disillusioned as his profits disappear and losses accumulate.

Tony's problems

A large liquor chain store has opened up nearby and has started to offer price promotions and cheaper wine at most price points. He immediately noticed a significant drop in customer numbers. He has tried discounting as well but has watched profit levels plummet and losses accumulate. As a result he has reduced his part time staff and started to work longer hours. He feels he is losing customers to the discounting competitor, but if he discounts enough he sometimes pulls them back.

Although he is picking up cheaper customers he seems to see those regular premium customers less. He is worried that these premium customers, whom he used to spend a lot of time with but now can't (as he has fewer staff), are going across town to a new wine specialist store.

Tony is wondering how to rebuild profits and once again enjoy his business.

Current Profit and Loss Statement

See Figure 4.7 for this year's forecast Profit and Loss Statement.

Tony is in financial trouble, but luckily he had read this book, talked to a consultant (with a hard to pronounce Scottish name), and has created a plan that is outlined below and will unfold in the following chapters of this book.

4.5 Tony's Wine Store Business Plan

4.5.1 Executive Summary

The market is made up of 10,000 wine drinkers, 880 of whom are regular customers of Tony's Wine Store. Split as per normal markets across the Project Genome segments. There are four competitors of which the large discounter and the new specialist wine store are the most worrisome. The company is forecast to make a financial loss for the current year. Recent discounting has resulted in a poor retail environment, a poor product mix, and poorer value customers. Sales staff are low cost but have little wine knowledge.

The two major issues the business faces are the margin destruction of discounting, and the poorer margins of a poorer customer mix. The business's key objectives are to boost margins by stopping promotional discounting and moving his customer mix to a higher value mix.

Tony's Wine Store primarily will be focused on the Luxury Enthusiast customer segment as well as Enthusiasts, Luxury Image Seekers, and Image Seekers.

The business will help these target customers experience the delights of wine by extending their palate and building their knowledge, whilst helping them explore the world of wine.

Figure 4.7: Tony's Wine Store Year 1 Profit and Loss Statement

Revenue Calculations	
Year	**1**
Segment sizes:	
Enthusiasts	880
Luxury Enthusiasts	293
Image Seekers	1,760
Luxury Image Seekers	196
Savvy Shoppers	1,467
Traditionalists	1,565
Satisfied Sippers	1,369
Overwhelmed	2,249
Wine Drinker Market Size	**9,780**
Customers:	
Enthusiasts	132
Luxury Enthusiasts	44
Image Seekers	264
Luxury Image Seekers	29
Savvy Shoppers	220
Traditionalists	235
Satisfied Sippers	205
Overwhelmed	337
Total Customers	**1,467**
Tony's Volume by Segment (bottles):	
Enthusiasts	13,731
Luxury Enthusiasts	4,577
Image Seekers	27,462
Luxury Image Seekers	3,051
Savvy Shoppers	11,443
Traditionalists	12,205
Satisfied Sippers	10,680
Overwhelmed	17,545
Total Volume (bottles)	**100,695**
Tony's Revenue by Segment ($):	
Enthusiasts	$205,967
Luxury Enthusiasts	$114,426
Image Seekers	$411,934
Luxury Image Seekers	$76,284
Savvy Shoppers	$114,426
Traditionalists	$122,054
Satisfied Sippers	$53,399
Overwhelmed	$87,727
Total Revenue	**$1,186,216**
Variable cost calculations:	
Year	1
COGS	$830,351
Cost of Price Promotion Discount	$237,243
Variable costs	**$1,067,595**
Sales Contribution	**$118,622**
Fixed cost calculations:	
Year	1
Lease	$30,000
Salaries	$115,000
Administration	$20,000
Internet Marketing Cost	$0
Fixed costs	**$165,000**
Profit & Cashflow	
Year	1
Profit (Loss) or Net Cash flow	**($46,378)**

Tony's Wine Store will reorient its store to focus on these segments by stopping discounting, offering more wines at higher price point ranges, and stocking more artisan wines. The business will reemploy highly knowledgeable staff, provide wine factoids in-store, refurbish the fit-out, and remove all price promotional material. The business will move to non-price promotions such as traditional 'Gift with Purchase' and 'Enter to Win' promotions as well as regular tastings.

Tony's Wine Store will extensively use internet marketing to promote to the target consumers given their strong desire for wine information and extensive use of the internet.

In the following two years Tony's Wine Store profits will increase to $160,000 and $300,000 as a result of stopping discounting and changing the customer mix from low-value customers to high-value customers.

4.5.2 The Customers

- Notown has a local population of 50,000 people, of which about 10,000 are wine drinkers of an adult age. This is the total accessible market.
- Seasonality is around all major holidays but especially the Christmas and New Year period.
- There is no reason to believe that the market is split any way other than per the Project Genome segmentation.

Primary Segment: Luxury Enthusiasts (see Marketing Strategies for a description)
Secondary Segment: Enthusiasts, Luxury Image Seekers, Image Seekers (in that order). Note much of the Image Seekers purchased from bars and restaurants rather than wine stores.

4.5.3 The Competition

- Large Liquor Discounter, Small Specialist Wine Store, two Average Liquor stores, two online wine retailers, and a large discount mail order wine club that now uses the internet
- the discounters offer regular heavy discounts on value, sub premium and premium wines—their point of difference is price
- the other small specialist wine store has a premium wine range, regular tasting and has great relationships with customers—

Figure 4.8: Project Genome Home and Habits Study: Consumer and Profit Share. (Graph printed with the permission of Constellation Wines)

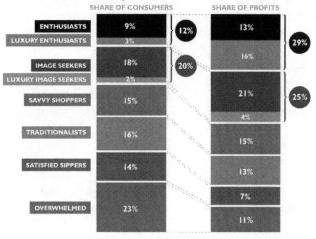

their point of difference is unclear but may be the regular tastings

- the other liquor stores compete purely based on location and always feature beer, liquor, and wine distributors' promotions no matter how crass—they have no point of difference
- the online wine stores offer lots of information, reviews, and ratings of wines as well as being able to offer a wide range however they suffer a price and delivery penalty from being out of state—their point of difference is presenting lots of wine information from themselves and others in their website communities

4.5.4 The Company

This Financial Year (outlined for comparison and context):

- is forecast to make a loss of $46,000. This is on revenue of about $1 million less Cost of Goods Sold of $830,000 and discounting 'cost' of $237,000. This leaves a sales contribution of $118,000 to cover $165,000 of fixed cost. Tony is currently dipping into his mortgage to fund these losses

- the wine store is in a desirable location on Main St used by the surrounding wealthy households as its prime shopping destination. However there is also a large liquor discounter nearby
- fit-out was originally tasteful dark wood cabinet and shelving with few other distractions other than the wine itself. Currently the store is covered in discount shelf talkers and posters with cases of value wine stacked at the aisle end on 'Super Special'
- range has moved from an even split of Ultra and Super Premium Wines: Premium and Sub Premium Wines: Value Wines, to a preponderance of Sub Premium and Value Wines
- the store used to have passionate, excited, and knowledgeable wine staff but has since had to employ cheaper staff with less knowledge to keep costs down
- Tony originally thought there was no need for a point of difference as business is all about relationships. He thought once you have built a good relationship with a customer they keep coming back for life

4.5.5 Point of Difference

The point of difference is the provision of wine information in a format that the Enthusiast consumer segment wants—on the internet as well as in-store. Tony, his staff, his in-store factoids, and his informative wine website are guides to understanding and buying wine. Proposition:

> *Tony's Wine Store helps you experience the delights of wine by extending your palate and building your knowledge, whilst exploring the world of wine.*

4.5.6 Major Issues and Business Objectives.

Issue 1: Discounter.

A large liquor chain discounter is offering much lower prices. This has led to a loss of customers, even those Tony had great relationships with. Tony has tried to pull them back by discounting himself but is simply unable to match the discounter's prices. Discounting has cost him $190,000 which the business cannot afford.

>*Business Objective 1. Boost Margins.* Stop discounting while maintaining or growing the customer base.

Issue 2: Customer and Product Mix.

The average order value has decreased which is due to discounting as per the previous issue. But it has also decreased due to attracting more customers who purchase lower priced wine, and these customers are purchasing fewer bottles. There are fewer customers who purchase higher priced wine and purchase many bottles of high-priced wine. It seems many premium customers are now going across town to a new wine specialist store or shopping on the internet.

>*Business Objective 2. Boost Margins and Volume.* Change to a Higher Value Customer Mix.

4.5.7 Marketing Strategies

A short review of the Primary Target market.

Luxury Enthusiast Segment Review

Who I Am[15]

- I have a wine cellar at home and enjoy shopping for wine to enjoy everyday as well as adding to my collection.
- I have a personal passion for wine and food; they are a key part of my everyday life.

How to Connect With Me

- I usually have a personal relationship with the wine steward/buyer in my favorite store. I like it when they call me when special items arrive and track down unique wines for me.
- I entertain often because I enjoy spending time creating food and wine pairings that elevate the epicurean experience.
- For me, wine is a global experience. I constantly seek additional knowledge. At retail, I read labels, appreciate detailed winemaking notes, and enjoy lingering in the wine section.
- On-Premise: I order off the reserve wine list. I also keep a few bottles at my favorite restaurant and spend time talking with the Sommelier.

What we know about Pinot Noir—Luxury Enthusiasts are in to it big time.

- Luxury Enthusiasts who appreciate the artistry behind this hard-to-craft wine bought nearly 50% more than Image Seekers and Luxury Image Seekers.

The Luxury Enthusiast has detailed knowledge about wine but always desires to learn more. They are also very comfortable asking for advice and seeking information. They're open to any recommendations especially from people they trust. They like taking risks when buying wine and trying new wine regions and varietals but try to mitigate the risk of poor wines by seeking information and tasting if possible.[13] They like to experiment so are not loyal to particular wine brands but rather loyal to people and stores that help them discover new ones.[12]

The segment differences:

- The Enthusiast is just as keen and knowledgeable about wine as the Luxury Enthusiast, but has less income and so makes smart buying decisions that give the best wine at the price point.
- The Image Seeker is also very interested in wine information but is less knowledgeable and is guided a lot more by wine experts than the Enthusiasts. Quick summaries of information are appreciated as are wine ratings. They are risk adverse so would rather not experiment and would really prefer to taste wines before buying. They are younger and drink more On-Premise. They love the image of Status that drinking wine portrays.
- Luxury Image Seekers are like Image Seekers except they have more money to spend and drink more at home than at bars and restaurants.
- The Traditionalists are interested in information about the wine they drink but do not seek any advice or information. They tend to have a good knowledge about these wines but do not wish to drink other wines or even know much about them. They have favorite brands and believe these represent the perfected art of winemaking.
- Savvy Shoppers enjoy shopping for wines and are heavy users of coupons. They have favorite brands and buy a lot of wine from many stores based off the best deal they can possibly get.
- Overwhelmed enjoy drinking wines, seek simple to understand information about wine, and often rely on wine labels. They find wine purchase risky.
- Satisfied Sippers do not care about the background of wines they just enjoy drinking low-priced, safe brands. They tend to be lower income.

Customer Interview: Larry, a Luxury Enthusiast. Based off a (hypothetical) interview with Larry (by the aforementioned marketing consultant).

Larry loves wine, loves talking about it, tasting it, reading about it, and exploring it. Larry is a well-off Dentist. Sure the economy has hurt his business a little but he's still doing well enough to keep buying interesting wines. He has an iPhone and a laptop for work and play. Play is often using Google to browse the internet looking for interesting wine and wine stories. Facebook has helped him to catch up with all his buddies from high school and university as well as new friends from his work life. LinkedIn is proving to be a great networking tool for his business. He is experimenting with Twitter and wine mobile apps but is not a regular user, yet.

For the past five years Larry has regularly come to Tony's Wine Store. Tony really supported him in his love and extended learning of wine, and generously helped him to find gems on his in-store 'trips around the wine world'. These days Tony has seemed rather busy so Larry hasn't felt so good about tying him up with his questions or conversation—he has just found his wine and left. He misses the discussions about wine and the new wine regions. He has found that Tony's Wine Store is more difficult to find his way around these days, and thinks that it is possibly because of the new bright color scheme, and discount signs that distract his search on every corner. He says that what he really wants to buy is a case of hand-picked intriguing wines, and unfortunately these days Tony's just doesn't seem to stock an interesting enough variety, or perhaps he just can't find it anymore. He thinks nostalgically and gratefully about Tony's Wine Store, but over the past six months has started to just shop where he can find a wide range of wine, or if he's on the other side of town he'll drop in to see an interesting new small wine shop, where the young owner there has time to share stories about vineyards, winemakers, regions, and varietals over a tasting of the latest Pinot from California.

Larry sadly says that he feels that Tony's Wine Store is just not for him any longer, but wishes Tony all the best.

>Business Objective 1: Boost Margins by stopping discounting while maintaining or growing the customer base

All strategies below are the responsibility of Tony unless otherwise stated.

Price

- Range will be 30% Ultra and Super Premium Wines, 50% Premium and Sub Premium Wines, and 20% Sub Premium Wines. Value Wines will no longer be stocked. All attempts will be made to not stock the same brands as the Discounter (though customer demand may restrict this). Range Renewal will be completed by Q2 with excess wine sold off to out-of-state trade customers if possible.
- Discounting will be reduced and then eliminated by Q1 as the new strategies are launched.
- The removal of discounts will be cushioned by the promotions below.
- Volume discounts (1 case or more) and trade discounts (restaurants and bars) will still be offered though at affordable levels.

>Business Objective 2: Boost Margins and Volume by changing to a Higher Value Customer Mix

Service

- The store will employ the passionate excited and knowledgeable wine staff (Enthusiasts) by end of Q1
- Create individual wine shelf cards with wine factoids and integrate into new wine website by using QR codes. Seven per week on the shelves, every week throughout the year.

Product

- New range will be purchased based off the price points below, the Enthusiast's desire for a wide selection of varietals and regions, and the Luxury Enthusiast's desire for an artisan crafted wine range. Range Renewal will be completed by Q2 with excess wine sold off to out-of-state trade customers if possible.

Place

- Remain at current premises as it's a good location near high-income households who regularly shop on the store's street.
- Fit-out will be taken back to the original tasteful dark wood cabinetry and shelving with few distractions other than the wine itself. All price promotion related shelf talkers and posters will be taken down. New, fixed shelf talkers will be added with key information and a QR code for more information about specific wines. Any new promotions will be tastefully designed using photos of beautiful vineyards etc. Fit-out to be stripped of old promo material and professionally cleaned/refurbished by week 1 of the new financial year. QR codes as per Service strategy above.

Promotion

- Renew Weekly Tasting Evenings with Local experts and visiting winemakers by end of Month 1.
- Holiday Campaigns: premium promotions that help establish the store's reputation as a premium store e.g. buy a case of wine and win a trip to Bordeaux, buy a case of Pinot Noir and get a Reidel Burgundy glass, a Christmas promo where the wooden gift boxes are free. Each promo requires a small number of high quality posters and shelf talkers. Have one promo leading up to each major holiday period organized three months before the holiday with all materials arriving 2 weeks before the promo period.
- Internet marketing: driving traffic through search engine optimization, internet advertising, and comparison shopping engines; building relationships and engaging with customers by creating great content on blogs, interacting with customers on Facebook and Twitter, encouraging in-store visits with mobile websites, apps and the new Location Based Services; boosting conversions through better eCommerce, social commerce, landing page optimization, and email marketing.

The following chapters outline the internet marketing strategies which you can use to offer high value customers what they value, information and assistance, while ignoring those who shop just on price.

4.5.8 Financial Analysis

In the following two years Tony's Wine Store profits will increase to $160,000 and $300,000 as a result of stopping discounting and changing the customer mix from low-value customers to high-value customers.

Back to the Business Plan's Financial Analysis section. It uses the same type of financial model that we used earlier in the chapter for opening a new wine store. It has an Input section for all the variables and a Calculation section for calculating the components of a Profit and Loss Statement. See Figures 4.9 and 4.10 for Financial Model Inputs. See Figure 4.11 for this year's (Year 1) and future years' (Years 2 and 3) forecast Profit and Loss Statement. See the Resources section at the end of this chapter for where these can be downloaded.

Model Notes

To most effectively see how this model works you'll need to get your hands dirty and change the Inputs to see how it affects the Calculations. The notes on the right hand side help explain exactly what is going on. Given book width limitations, the notes on the right hand side of the model may be cut off, please download the spreadsheet.

The key difference in this model versus the earlier financial model, for Opening a Wine Store, is that I'm now only using internet marketing for promotion—not tastings, tasting machines, and newspaper ads.

The increase in customer numbers is driven by estimated market share. To change how effective internet marketing is as a whole simply change the variables under *Store Market Share of Segment*. For example the model says that of the 880 Enthusiast wine drinkers in the market, Tony's Wine Store's internet marketing will increase it's share of enthusiasts from 15% to 25% in Year 2, and 35% in Year 3 (due to providing detailed information). However your Savvy Shoppers will decrease from 15% to 5% as you will no longer be providing them what they want, the lowest prices possible. Note that the sum of the segments does not need to equal 100% as we are talking about the store's market share of the segment, not the segment share of the market.

The outcome in Years 2 and 3 is to make substantially more profit because discounting has stopped and the customer mix has changed

Figure 4.9: Tony's Wine Store Years 1-3 Financial Model Inputs Page 1

Wine Store Financial Feasibility Model				
Input section				
Description				Notes, Sources, Formulas
Buyer Numbers:				
Population of Geographical Area	50,000			look for local stats (e.g. 2500-5000 per people per square mile)
Adult Population	60%			look for local stats (e.g. Census)
Wine Drinkers as a % of adult population	32.6%			core (13.7) plus marginal (18.9) wine drinkers (p.30, Wagner et al)
Segment % of drinker:				Project Genome: US Constellation Wine Study
Enthusiasts	9%			Project Genome
Luxury Enthusiasts	3%			Project Genome
Image Seekers	18%			Project Genome
Luxury Image Seekers	2%			Project Genome
Savvy Shoppers	15%			Project Genome
Traditionalists	16%			Project Genome
Satisfied Sippers	14%			Project Genome
Overwhelmed	23%			Project Genome
Store Market Share of Segment:	Y1	Y2	Y3	Y1 based on 4 other stores including a big discounter
Enthusiasts	15%	25%	35%	Estimate based off Targeted internet marketing
Luxury Enthusiasts	15%	30%	50%	Estimate based off Targeted internet marketing
Image Seekers	15%	25%	35%	Estimate based off Targeted internet marketing
Luxury Image Seekers	15%	30%	50%	Estimate based off Targeted internet marketing
Savvy Shoppers	15%	5%	5%	Estimate based off Targeted internet marketing
Traditionalists	15%	15%	15%	Estimate based off Targeted internet marketing
Satisfied Sippers	15%	5%	5%	Estimate based off Targeted internet marketing
Overwhelmed	15%	5%	5%	Estimate based off Targeted internet marketing
Price / bottle (USD ex tax):				Price categories, rounded to nearest $5 price point (p.41 Wagner et al)
Enthusiasts	$15			Super Premium
Luxury Enthusiasts	$25			Ultra Premium
Image Seekers	$15			Super Premium
Luxury Image Seekers	$25			Ultra Premium
Savvy Shoppers	$10			Sub Premium
Traditionalists	$10			Premium
Satisfied Sippers	$5			Super Value Wine
Overwhelmed	$5			Super Value Wine
Quantity pa (bottles):				Based off Aussie Johnson and Bruwer study. Checked against US average.
Enthusiasts	104			Estimate 2 bottles pw
Luxury Enthusiasts	104			Estimate 2 bottles pw
Image Seekers	104			Estimate 2 bottles pw
Luxury Image Seekers	104			Estimate 2 bottles pw
Savvy Shoppers	52			Estimate 1 bottles pw
Traditionalists	52			Estimate 1 bottles pw
Satisfied Sippers	52			Estimate 1 bottles pw
Overwhelmed	52			Estimate 1 bottles pw
Margin:				
Retailer Gross margin (%)	30%			Industry standard
Expenses:				
Store Lease per period ($)	$30,000			1000 ft2 @ $30 / ft2 pa
Manager's required income per year ($)	$45,000			Employed or Owner Manager
Staff Salary	$35,000			estimate
Number of Staff (FTE exc Manager)	2			estimate
Administration ($ pa)	$20,000			Accounting and legal, insurance, utilities, security
Internet Marketing Cost	$65,000			Internet marketing manager employed, Agency, Contractors, and/or Owner's tir

Figure 4.10: Tony's Wine Store Years 1-3 Financial Model Inputs Page 2

Promotion:				
Year	1	2	3	constant
% conversions attributed to Assists	50%			Estimate, what % of conversions are based off non last interactions as measured by Google A
Conversions (last interaction):				As attributed by last interaction and measured by Google Analytics
SEO	0%	15%	15%	Search was the source of traffic for converting this % of Conversions
Local SEO	0%	15%	15%	Local Search was the source of traffic for converting this % of Conversions
Advertising	0%	15%	15%	Advertising was the source of traffic for converting this % of Conversions
CSE	0%	10%	10%	CSE was the source of traffic for converting this % of Conversions
Blogging	0%	5%	5%	Blog was the source of traffic for converting this % of Conversions
Facebook	0%	5%	5%	Facebook was the source of traffic for converting this % of Conversions
Twitter	0%	3%	3%	Twitter was the source of traffic for converting this % of Conversions
Mobile	0%	5%	5%	Mobile was the source of traffic for converting this % of Conversions
LBS	0%	1%	1%	LBS was the source of traffic for converting this % of Conversions
Mobile & Social Commerce	0%	1%	1%	eCommerce on mobile or FB was the source of traffic for converting this % of Conversions
LPO	0%	10%	10%	LPO was the reason for converting this % of Conversions
Email	0%	15%	15%	Email was the source of traffic for converting this % of Conversions
% of all possible Conversions:	0%	100%	100%	MUST be 100% or lower, of all the possible conversions what % will be counted
Assisted Conversions (previous interactions):				As attributed by previous interactions and measured by Google Analytics as Assists/Micro Co
SEO	0%	5%	5%	Search was the source of traffic for converting this % of Assisted Conversions
Local SEO	0%	5%	5%	Local Search was the source of traffic for converting this % of Assisted Conversions
Advertising	0%	5%	5%	Advertising was the source of traffic for converting this % of Assisted Conversions
CSE	0%	5%	5%	CSE was the source of traffic for converting this % of Assisted Conversions
Blogging	0%	15%	15%	Blog was the source of traffic for converting this % of Assisted Conversions
Facebook	0%	15%	15%	Facebook was the source of traffic for converting this % of Assisted Conversions
Twitter	0%	10%	10%	Twitter was the source of traffic for converting this % of Assisted Conversions
Mobile	0%	10%	10%	Mobile was the source of traffic for converting this % of Assisted Conversions
LBS	0%	5%	5%	LBS was the source of traffic for converting this % of Assisted Conversions
Mobile & Social Commerce	0%	10%	10%	eCommerce on mobile or FB was the source of traffic for converting this % of Assisted Conve
LPO	0%	10%	10%	LPO was the reason for converting this % of Assisted Conversions
Email	0%	5%	5%	Email was the source of traffic for converting this % of Assisted Conversions
% of all possible Assists:	0%	100%	100%	MUST be 100% or lower, of all the possible assisted conversions what % will be counted
Price Promotion:				
Price promotions activity	1	0	0	Dummy variable. 1 = active, 0 = inactive.
Price Elasticity	1			estimate (eg 1=same % increase in buyers as discount, or 1.5= 50% increase)
Price Promotion Discount (%)	20%			variable

Figure 4.11: Tony's Wine Store Years 1-3 Financial Model Calculations and Profit & Loss Statement

Revenue Calculations				
Year	1	2	3	Notes
Segment sizes:				
Enthusiasts	880	880	880	Wine Drinker Market Size * Segment % of drinker: Enthusiasts
Luxury Enthusiasts	293	293	293	Wine Drinker Market Size * Segment % of drinker: Lux. Enth.
Image Seekers	1,760	1,760	1,760	Wine Drinker Market Size * Segment % of drinker: Image Seekers
Luxury Image Seekers	196	196	196	Wine Drinker Market Size * Segment % of drinker: Lux. Image Seekers
Savvy Shoppers	1,467	1,467	1,467	Wine Drinker Market Size * Segment % of drinker: Savvy Shoppers
Traditionalists	1,565	1,565	1,565	Wine Drinker Market Size * Segment % of drinker: Traditionalists
Satisfied Sippers	1,369	1,369	1,369	Wine Drinker Market Size * Segment % of drinker: Satisfied Sippers
Overwhelmed	2,249	2,249	2,249	Wine Drinker Market Size * Segment % of drinker: Overwhelmed
Wine Drinker Market Size	**9,780**	**9,780**	**9,780**	Population * Adult % * Wine Drinker %
Customers:				
Enthusiasts	132	220	308	Segment Size * (Store Market Share of Segment * (1-% conversions attr
Luxury Enthusiasts	44	88	147	Segment Size * (Store Market Share of Segment * (1-% conversions attr
Image Seekers	264	440	616	Segment Size * (Store Market Share of Segment * (1-% conversions attr
Luxury Image Seekers	29	59	98	Segment Size * (Store Market Share of Segment * (1-% conversions attr
Savvy Shoppers	220	73	73	Segment Size * (Store Market Share of Segment * (1-% conversions attr
Traditionalists	235	235	235	Segment Size * (Store Market Share of Segment * (1-% conversions attr
Satisfied Sippers	205	68	68	Segment Size * (Store Market Share of Segment * (1-% conversions attr
Overwhelmed	337	112	112	Segment Size * (Store Market Share of Segment * (1-% conversions attr
Total Customers	**1,467**	**1,296**	**1,658**	Sum of Customers
Tony's Volume by Segment (bottles):				
Enthusiasts	13,731	22,885	32,039	Customers * Segment Quantity purchased pa
Luxury Enthusiasts	4,577	9,154	15,257	Customers * Segment Quantity purchased pa
Image Seekers	27,462	45,770	64,079	Customers * Segment Quantity purchased pa
Luxury Image Seekers	3,051	6,103	10,171	Customers * Segment Quantity purchased pa
Savvy Shoppers	11,443	3,814	3,814	Customers * Segment Quantity purchased pa
Traditionalists	12,205	12,205	12,205	Customers * Segment Quantity purchased pa
Satisfied Sippers	10,680	3,560	3,560	Customers * Segment Quantity purchased pa
Overwhelmed	17,545	5,848	5,848	Customers * Segment Quantity purchased pa
Total Volume (bottles)	**100,695**	**109,340**	**146,974**	Sum of bottle volume pa
Tony's Revenue by Segment ($):				
Enthusiasts	$205,967	$343,278	$480,589	Segment bottle Volume * Segment Price per bottle
Luxury Enthusiasts	$114,426	$228,852	$381,420	Segment bottle Volume * Segment Price per bottle
Image Seekers	$411,934	$686,556	$961,178	Segment bottle Volume * Segment Price per bottle
Luxury Image Seekers	$76,284	$152,568	$254,280	Segment bottle Volume * Segment Price per bottle
Savvy Shoppers	$114,426	$38,142	$38,142	Segment bottle Volume * Segment Price per bottle
Traditionalists	$122,054	$122,054	$122,054	Segment bottle Volume * Segment Price per bottle
Satisfied Sippers	$53,399	$17,800	$17,800	Segment bottle Volume * Segment Price per bottle
Overwhelmed	$87,727	$29,242	$29,242	Segment bottle Volume * Segment Price per bottle
Total Revenue	**$1,186,216**	**$1,618,492**	**$2,284,706**	Sum of revenue
Variable cost calculations:				
Year	1	2	3	Notes
COGS	$830,351	$1,132,945	$1,599,294	Revenue * (1 – Gross Margin)
Cost of Price Promotion Discount	$237,243	$0	$0	Revenue * Discount % * on/off
Variable costs	**$1,067,595**	**$1,132,945**	**$1,599,294**	Sum of variable costs above
Sales Contribution	**$118,622**	**$485,548**	**$685,412**	Total Revenue – Variable Costs
Fixed cost calculations:				
Year	1	2	3	Notes
Lease	$30,000	$30,000	$30,000	Store Lease per period ($)
Salaries	$115,000	$115,000	$115,000	Manager's salary + (staff salary * staff #)
Administration	$20,000	$20,000	$20,000	Administration
Internet Marketing Cost	$0	$65,000	$65,000	If % of all possible conversions=0% then 0, else internet marketing cost
Fixed costs	**$165,000**	**$230,000**	**$230,000**	Sum of fixed costs above
Profit & Cashflow				
Year	1	2	3	Notes
Profit (Loss) or Net Cash flow	**($46,378)**	**$255,548**	**$455,412**	Sales Contribution - Fixed costs

Notes:
Note this is for illustrative purposes only. Before starting a business you should get professional accounting and legal advice.
Sales tax, company tax, depreciation and interest is ignored for the sake of simplicity.
"Wine Marketing and Sales". Wagner, Olsen, Thach 2007

from low value customers to high value customers. For example a Satisfied Sipper is worth only \$260 pa in revenue (\$5 * 52 bottles pa) versus a Luxury Enthusiast who is worth \$2600 (\$25 * 104 bottles pa).

We'll look at how the internet marketing strategies affect customer numbers in the Measurement chapter.

Lastly let's keep internet marketing in perspective.

4.6 The Wine Retailer's Internet Dream

The internet is great but let's have reasonable expectations.

'So I'm going to be a multi-millionaire—with my own gleaming white super yacht— surrounded by gorgeous bikini clad women— right!?' Well, you might. . . but probably not due to a wine internet site. True, Gary Vaynerchuk (WineLibrary.tv) seems to have been able to build a business (for himself and his father) that's now worth millions. And perhaps that points towards a way where you could become internationally successful using video and social media.

More reasonable aims would be:

- take an extra day off a week
- increase your profits via an extra virtual salesperson
- protect your sales from your internet savvy local competitor
- extra profit which may help you put your children through university or buy a new car each year

I think those are sensible though they still require some serious work over a few years.

Remember back in 2001, when the high profile wine internet retailers in the US went bust post the internet stockmarket boom? The market wasn't ready. Since then some companies have started to make it work (see the chapter on wine online competitors) but very few companies have achieved the Amazon success that was hoped for.

The more reasonable aim is to see it as having just another very good 'salesperson', who knocks 'door to door'. Or, a superb 'call center customer service' team. Or a brilliant 'mail order' catalog.

In other words an excellent tool to boost your sales with your existing market. If you found that a direct mail campaign boosted business, a newspaper ad drove foot traffic, or suddenly word of mouth sales increased then you'd be excited about the extra profit but you wouldn't expect to be the next multi-millionaire. That's just an internet dream. . . .

4.7 Summary

Despite a very competitive online wine market the local wine store has some natural advantages. I've outlined some points of difference but believe that there is a particular advantage in leveraging your local status or focusing on a particular niche. A business plan helps you put into action this insight, though some market research may be required first.

4.8 Resources

- Retailer Company Discussion, Update, and Posts Page: `www.WineMarketingPros.com/cmychap/`
- *Wine Shop Financials* Spreadsheet, see Resources section on the above website page
- Tony's Wine Store Profit and Loss Statement Years 1-3, is from the *Wine Shop Financials* Spreadsheet

5 Company—the Winery

In the last chapter we looked at wine retailer company marketing plan in the context of the chapters on Customers and Competitors. In this chapter we do the same thing for wineries. The major difference is we take a professional brand management process approach. In this chapter I go through the complete brand management process including an illustrative marketing plan.

5.1 What is a Brand

A brand is a set of images and experiences in a person's mind. A product is a wine, winery, or wine store. The product you have direct control over; whereas, a brand you only have some influence over—because it's in the customer's mind.

It's an important distinction because wineries make a series of very rational decisions in producing or choosing their wine and perhaps feel that customers are similarly rational. However customers are emotional beings who make split second decisions based on how they perceive your brand.

Four key truths[34] about why people buy wine help to explain why brands are so important:

1. Wine drinkers never understand a premium wine as well as the winery company that sells it. Their relationship is not through months of hard and loving graft but rather fleeting and superficial.

2. Wine drinkers perceive premium wine brands in their own terms. Given they have imperfect knowledge of the wine they have to select something relevant to them perhaps by label design rather than taste.

3. Wine drinkers' perception will focus on benefits that are often intangible—this can seem irrational to wine growers. This is because consumers focus on what a wine can do for them rather than what it actually is. The benefits to them are intangible but are still real in their minds.

4. Wine drinkers' perceptions are not at the conscious level. When we ask people why they purchased a wine we may get a rational answer but not the whole story. Feelings about wine are not always easily articulated because they are complex and emotional.

This book is focused on premium wine, which requires good brand management to ensure higher prices, margins, and/or volume. Many wineries struggle to make a reasonable margin because they can't push through higher prices, sell though low margin distribution channels (e.g. supermarkets), and/or can't sell enough cases because they don't have sufficient demand.

5.1.1 Brand Management Process

The Brand Management process has 8 steps. Once you have completed all of the steps you will know:

- Your target market, competitors, and company goals
- Your points of differentiation from your competitors
- What your brand means to your customers
- Your marketing strategies
- An action plan with dates, responsibilities, and budget

The steps are:

Step 1: Understand your customers
Step 2: Analyze your competitors
Step 3: Look at your company goals, personalities, and stories
Step 4: Choose your niche
Step 5: Create or define your brand
Step 6: Review the marketing mix or 5 Ps
Step 7: Create your marketing plan
Step 8: Review

5.2 Step 1: Understand your Customers

A great wine product is a start, but, alas, for most wineries it is not enough. Great wines need to appeal to different customer groups in other non-sensory ways, including some not well-known. These customer groups are usually defined by demographics (age, gender, income, city, etc.) and psychological insights, though alcoholic beverage marketers also look at the particular occasion people drink wine as this seems to drive consumer purchase decision more than any other factor.

What the brand management process is doing is attempting to change how customers view your brand in their minds. Rather than only relying on one part of a customer's decision making process, the rational taste/smell of the wine, it also appeals to the other parts of their decision-making—the emotional and sociological.

One well-known way of looking at people is through a tool called Maslow's Hierarchy of Needs[35]. This suggests that a person must satisfy the most important and basic physiological needs before moving onto the higher levels of need. As each level is satisfied the next level is likely to become the focus of attention. The steps are outlined in Figure 5.1.

Figure 5.1: Maslow's Hierarchy of Needs

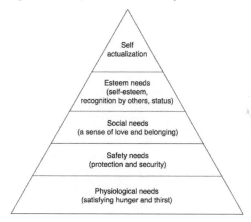

The experts, the market research psychologists, will give you a much more detailed and better explanation of human needs. For our purposes this is a useful way of giving a background to the psychology of customer decision making. In other sections we will look at how brands interrelate with customers on rational, social, and emotive levels.

A brand needs to appeal to a particular customer in a way that's important to them This is the realm of 'niche' or 'target' marketing. In short you have different groups of people (segmentation is the jargon) with a similar psychological make up.

These different groups of people want different things from wine. On top of this people want different things from wine depending on the situation they're in.

Some want that moment of savouring a great wine by themselves at home, others want to make an impression at an important dinner party, some want to show that they don't follow the conventions of the world in a trendy cafe, others just want to have unpretentious fun with close friends at a BBQ.

Rather than get lost in the detail of human psychology, market researchers simplify analysis by grouping similar wine drinkers and occasions, known as 'segments'. This way sophisticated, but terribly complex, analysis of human beings becomes a simple and usable model to make marketing decisions about niches.

Segmentation is a huge area of marketing, alcohol beverage companies have spent millions on researching it and academics have done numerous studies on it. I've covered two particular studies from Johnson & Bruwer and Constellation Wines in the Customer Chapter.

Having commissioned, analyzed, and utilized this sort of research, I've come up with my own version of what I believe to be a practical, usable, and pragmatic market model outlined in Figure 5.2. Note this uses insights from the two studies above but does not pretend to aggregate other research data to come up with 'meta analysis' of a number of studies in an academically correct manner. It's just an amalgamation of my reading, experience, and thoughts, and it helps me better illustrate the brand management process than the other studies.

A market model makes describing customers and brands simpler. It allows senior managers to talk strategically about customers and brands in ways that everyone can understand. It's at the center of brand management.

Each 'slice' of this model represents a particular wine drinker in a particular occasion. The ones of the most interest to premium wine brands are Creative Individualist, Inspiring Businessmen, and Knowledgeable Professors.

The rest of the segments are either too poor or unwilling to pay

Figure 5.2: Wine Market Model

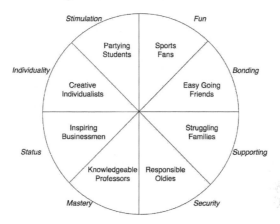

for great wine. They are Partying Students, Sports Fans, Easy-Going Friends, Struggling Families, and Responsible Oldies.

Marketers have extended and altered the use of Maslow's Hierarchy of Needs triangle to summarize a description of customer groups and occasions. It looks like Figure 5.3.

In a simple-to-understand way it describes the demographic, rational, sociological, and emotive make up of a particular segment.

Note that although I use Pinot Noir as the example premium wine, the key point is that your wine is premium, not mainstream. If it's mainstream then only some of this book is applicable to your situation. There are some very good books and blogs that provide very good information on mainstream wine marketing (differences include distribution choices, regular discounting, and traditional advertising). Point made, lets describe the three segments.

Inspiring Businessman

Imagine a businessman in a Hugo Boss suit, cufflinks, perfectly knotted tie, and groomed to perfection. He is sitting at a sophisticated restaurant in Chicago. He may be a merchant banker drinking with his peers. He's ambitious, he's smart and well... he's very egotistical. He wants to look successful and feel confident. Whether he is or not

Figure 5.3: Consumer Description

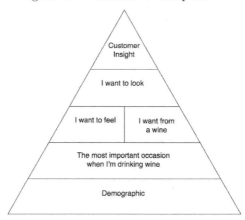

is irrelevant to us, our job is to give him what he wants to make him feel or look this way. If we do, he'll buy more of our wine and pay higher prices for it. Remember he's on US$250,000 pa—money is not the issue with this man, if your wine is too cheap it will not reflect well on him. See Figure 5.13 for the Inspiring Businessman Consumer Triangle.

Knowledgeable Professor

Imagine a 55-year-old hardened lawyer. He doesn't really care what people think of his clothes or his car, though he does appreciate authentic, high quality, crafted products. He's quite introverted (or doesn't like small talk) though he still likes sharing a good bottle of wine with friends at a fine dining establishment in Manhattan, New York. It's important to him that he comes across as being knowledgeable and discerning but not flashy or egotistical. He won't admit it, but he wants to impress others with his sophistication, yet he still wants to feel relaxed and confident.

By understanding what drives him we can change what we do to help him with his needs and wants. Of all the customer groups this sort of person is marketed to the most by premium wine companies by default. This is because most companies emphasize the product

Figure 5.4: Inspiring Businessman Consumer Triangle

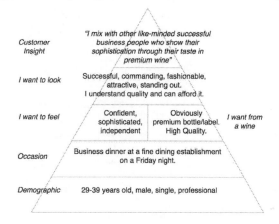

which is what he absolutely wants to know all about. See Figure 5.5 for the Knowledgeable Professor Consumer Triangle.

Creative Individualist

Imagine an artist, an architect or a designer. He or she dresses a little different, is adventurous and individualistic. They always seem to be a year ahead of everyone else. They may go through a couple of bottles of wine at a very trendy cafe in San Francisco on a Thursday afternoon. Then go to a play, poetry reading, art show, or music event that evening. They are very environmentally conscious and keen to be different from everyone else.

A fashionable wine from a faraway region that allows them to stand apart will get this group reaching for your bottle (and their wallet). See Figure 5.6 for the Creative Individualist Consumer Triangle.

Note that on average the segments above tend to be male so I've described male personas for that reason rather than being purposely irritatingly sexist. Most of the other segments would have female personas.

Hopefully the descriptions of these different types of wine drinkers illustrates why brand marketers focus on just one. Let's take the bottle and label to illustrate why it's important to focus on one niche

Figure 5.5: Knowledgeable Professor Consumer Triangle

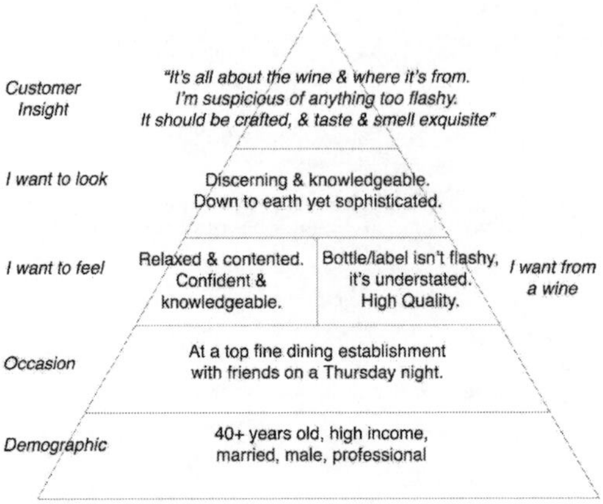

Customer Insight — *"It's all about the wine & where it's from. I'm suspicious of anything too flashy. It should be crafted, & taste & smell exquisite"*

I want to look — Discerning & knowledgeable. Down to earth yet sophisticated.

I want to feel — Relaxed & contented. Confident & knowledgeable.

Bottle/label isn't flashy, it's understated. High Quality. — I want from a wine

Occasion — At a top fine dining establishment with friends on a Thursday night.

Demographic — 40+ years old, high income, married, male, professional

Figure 5.6: Creative Individualist Consumer Triangle

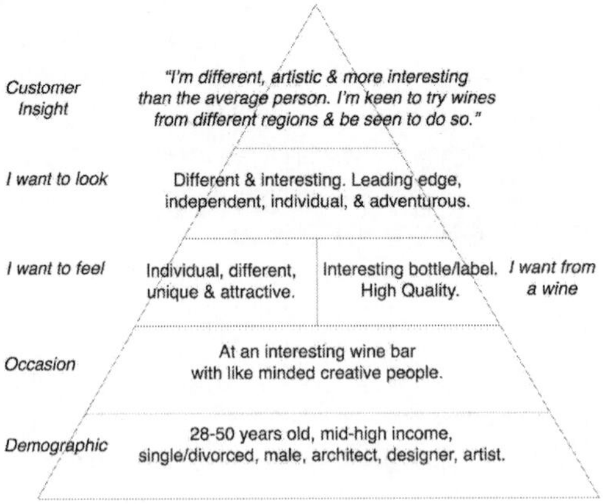

Customer Insight — *"I'm different, artistic & more interesting than the average person. I'm keen to try wines from different regions & be seen to do so."*

I want to look — Different & interesting. Leading edge, independent, individual, & adventurous.

I want to feel — Individual, different, unique & attractive.

Interesting bottle/label. High Quality. — I want from a wine

Occasion — At an interesting wine bar with like minded creative people.

Demographic — 28-50 years old, mid-high income, single/divorced, male, architect, designer, artist.

rather than many.

Which bottle/label combination suits which consumer group the best?

(1) Simple label and bottle, detailed tasting note on the back.

(2) Flashy gold label, heavy solid premium bottle.

(3) Superbly designed label with a different bottle shape.

Pretty obvious?

(1) Knowledgeable Professor.

(2) Inspiring Businessperson.

(3) Creative Individualist.

But it also applies to your price point, cellar door, website, advertising, retailers, trade strategy, events, and your whole marketing mix.

Different customers will want different things from your wine brand. If you try to market to them all you're going to have to make such compromises to their differing opinions you'll come across as confused or bland—a decision in effect by 'consumer committee'.

5.3 Step 2: Wine Industry Competitors

The majority of wine industry competitors are probably doing what everyone else does—they are trying to copy success.

They've looked at what others are doing and may have also chosen a less sophisticated form of analyzing niches e.g. women, Napa Valley, cool climate Pinot Noir. Indeed many may not be doing any brand management at all.

Before we look any further at competitors let's set the scene. Remember customers will have an image of your brand the moment they are first exposed to it. It may be at a friend's house over dinner, on a wine list at a fine dining establishment, or at cheap and nasty supermarket.

This initial impression will be based on the product's bottle/label (and hopefully the wine), its price, the place it's sold, the people who are drinking it, and any promotion via advertising, direct marketing, the web etc (the '5Ps' are covered later). Based on this set of images and experiences they will position your brand in their minds as a wine for a sort of person which might be themselves. Or if it makes no strong impression, just a bland brand appealing to no one particularly that will hopefully taste and smell great.

In Figure 5.7 is the market model but this time with some illustrative brands put in.

Figure 5.7: Market Model with Brands

Remember each 'slice' represents a consumer group in a particular occasion. Occasions are on the outside, consumers are in the inside.

Brand A represented by the dot in Creative Individualists segment strongly appeals to this group of people. It may be purchased by other groups, but it is most associated with this segment. Brand D, on the other hand, has no particularly strong association with any customer group and is floating in the center.

We would say Brand A is strongly positioned in the Creative Individualists segment. Brand B is also positioned in this segment but not as strongly as Brand A.

In a multinational alcohol beverage company's market research surveys, the positioning of each brand is worked out through some serious math formula (called multi-variate analysis). This formula calculates how closely the surveyed consumers associate Brand A with key words that are important to that consumer group and positions the brand in the market model accordingly. What you do here is a rough proxy for this expensive research.

Brand positioning is a key concept in brand management and marketing. Go through the series of prompts below, each of which says something about your brand. For example, a colorful label might appeal to one segment; whereas, a simple label will appeal to another. A low price will not appeal to some (in a certain occasion) but will be seen by others as a welcome bargain. These prompts are:

- Label
- Bottle
- Opening
- Price
- Medals/Ratings
- Point of sale
- Website
- Advertising
- Trade Promotions
- PR, media clippings
- Wine store promotions
- Fine Dining ('A class') Restaurant listings
- Premium Bar ('A class') listings
- Specialist fine wine stores
- Other retail
- Wine and Food Festivals
- Cellar Door experience
- Market research
- Marketing Plans
- Business Plans, Annual reports
- Customer emails, letters

From this analysis, map your wine brand on the Wine Market Model—is it strongly Knowledgeable Professor for example, or is it not really appealing to any one of these customer groups and occasions?

My experience is that wine brands do not give a consistent message and try to appeal to too many groups, thereby getting lost in a sea of brands. The outcome of this is what the market model below simply illustrates. Your brand may be sending strong product signals but is being overwhelmed by stronger brands that have a more consistent message and comprehensive brand management program.

Even worse, your brand may be sending very few signals at all and be lost in a sea of brands desperately trying to compete on smell and taste characteristics as per Figure 5.8. Is your brand the grey one in the middle of the wine market model?

A group of wine industry competitors in a particular price bracket

Figure 5.8: Lost in a Sea of Brands

are known as the customer's consideration set. In most industries a brand manager attempts to build awareness of a brand, then ensures that it is attractive enough to be considered one of a number brands customers will consider buying (consideration set), and finally attempting to become the most preferred brand. The process is known as Awareness >Consideration >Preference.

In the wine industry, customers tend to have a price bracket in mind for purchasing wine. They will have a number of varietals and regions they will consider but do not have a strong preference that is seen in other industries. So the aim is to be included in the consideration set. If a customer buys wine every week then a realistic aim is to be chosen perhaps every fourth week rather than expecting to be purchased every week.

Make an educated guess of who your competitors are. Put yourself in (for example) your (e.g. Californian) customer's shoes. They may consider an Oregon Pinot Noir, a Burgundy, and, perhaps, a New Zealand Pinot Noir.

Arguably you should include other varietals, but let's keep this simple. They should be in a similar price bracket in your major market(s). For Pinot Noir brand owners I suggest this price is retail $30-60+ per bottle (remember this book is for premium wines not mainstream ones).

They should be the market leaders in this segment—the ones customers would recognize and like the most on a wine list or wine store shelf. They are the consumer's consideration set.

Then use the same prompts above to decide what group of consumers your competitors brand most appeals to.

This is a proxy for customer research. Customers have imperfect knowledge and fleetingly focus on benefits relevant to them before making a decision. The time and effort you've spent looking at all of your wine industry competitors' brands' cues is probably a heck of a lot longer than customers ever will spend in making their decisions.

From this analysis map your wine industry competitors on the Wine Market Model. No need to use my Wine Market Model 'mashup' if you don't want to, check out Constellation Wines Project Genome research instead.

5.4 Step 3: Telling your Wine Business, Vineyard or Winery Story

What wine story will appeal to your target consumers? It is time to look internally for your winery story, an interesting story you can tell your customers.

You know what occasions and customer groups are out there using a market model. You've analyzed where your brand and your competitors' position is in the market, and know whether any brands appeal to one group of customers/occasions more than another.

What stories can you tell that will appeal to one of these segments? Who are you most comfortable with marketing too? Is your team happy with those who want to look and feel knowledgeable about wine, those who want to appear as creative alternative individuals, or those who want to appear successful and confident? When you create stories which group will you feel most at ease with? If you don't have an intuitive grasp and a sense of empathy for them your marketing activity may lack insight and effectiveness.

But why not appeal to more than one? Let's take a quick ground check. Your wine has to appeal in one of these situations, or people will skip to one of their other dozen options that appeal to them more strongly. If you try to appeal to all of these situations you'll end up bland and not appeal terribly well to any. Don't worry, other customer groups will still buy your wine but you will boost your margins and volume by focusing on just one because your brand appeals to them more strongly on different levels—product and emotive.

Also consider your business plan. It may suggest one segment over another especially if a high price is needed to cover a high cost base.

So what are your stories and company objectives? Soft qualitative analysis includes:

- About establishing vineyards/winery
- Owner's background and personality
- Wine maker's background and personality
- Sales and marketing team's background and personality
- Other company personalities? E.g. cellar door, viticulture team
- Who's extroverted and happy to travel
- Medals, ratings, reviews
- Do you believe you can be a 5 star or 90+ point wine in the next year or two
- Wine writers, bloggers, and other journalists' comments
- Distributor/trade comments
- Financial objectives in terms of volume and price/margin
- High cost structure including Cost Volume Profit analysis

Hard analysis will cover:

- Your belief in producing, say, a top 5 wine for your varietal and region
- High cost structure
- Empathy with customer group and occasion

Corporate alcohol beverage marketing teams cover each segment with its own brand and a professional brand manager. This collection of brands is known as a 'brand portfolio'. The brand manager can use various agencies (market research, ad, design, web, and direct marketing agencies) and hopefully some natural empathy. It's unlikely you will be able to afford to buy all that expertise, so you need to feel comfortable and empathetic with your chosen segment.

Soft analysis will cover the brand personality. Imagine that your company (or brand) was a person. He or she walks into a party full of other people who represent your competitors and customers. Would your company be the person who was loud, shy, quiet, extroverted, introverted, sophisticated, sexy, homely, etc.?

Indeed most companies have a person who is the company 'celeb'—

the one wine writers interview and the one who travels overseas to assist with distributor training, wine tastings, and festivals. Chances are he or she is the wine maker or major shareholder—and decision maker. He or she may be the face of the company and will be at the forefront of implementing the marketing plan.

What stories can we tell about this person? In the party above who would they be?

5.5 Step 4: Choose your Wine Niche

Time to make your niche choice. If you've looked at customers and competitors and also considered which segment you'd be most comfortable with, then it's time to choose which one is best. Ideally there is a segment that

- has no strong competitors
- you're already positioned in
- you have empathy for

Most likely you've got some hard choices to make. Weigh up company, competitors, and customers and decide what your ideal position in the market is. If you think there is a gap in the market and you're happy with marketing to that group of customers—take it. That's classic brand strategy at work, is called 'repositioning' and is illustrated in Figure 5.9.

5.6 Step 5: Creating, Describing, and Defining your Premium Wine Brand

Let's review where we've got to in the process. A great wine brand communicates to wine drinkers in ways that are important to them. Wine drinkers make brand decisions based on superficial criteria as well as the smell and taste of premium wine. Wine marketers appeal to this superficial criteria through brand management. Specifically they define a brand and keep referring to it throughout the wine marketing process.

Remember the four key truths about why people buy wine helps to explain why brands are so important:

1. Wine drinkers never understand a premium wine as well as the company that sells it. Their relationship is not through months of

Figure 5.9: Repositioning a Brand

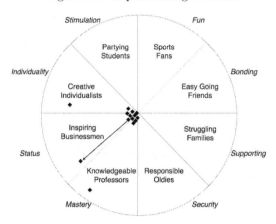

hard and loving graft but rather fleeting and superficial.

2. Wine drinkers perceive premium wine brands in their own terms. Given they have imperfect knowledge of the wine they have to select something relevant to them—perhaps by label design rather than taste.

3. Wine drinkers' perceptions will focus on benefits that are often intangible—this can seem irrational to wine growers. This is because consumers focus on what a wine can do for them rather than what it actually is. The benefits to them are intangible but are still real in their minds.

4. Wine drinkers' perceptions are not at the conscious level. When we ask people why they purchased a wine we may get a rational answer but not the whole story. Feelings about wine are not always easily articulated because they are complex and emotional.

We've also looked at Maslow's Hierarchy of Needs and the way marketers have evolved that into descriptions of customers in another web page.

That basic idea has evolved into a way to also look at brands and how customers relate to them. Figure 5.10 illustrates this relationship. Customers want certain things from the product itself—taste and smell characteristics. They also want the brand to make them feel and be seen in certain ways that are important to them—intangible, irrational benefits but very human.

Figure 5.10: Customers Relate to Brands on Different Levels

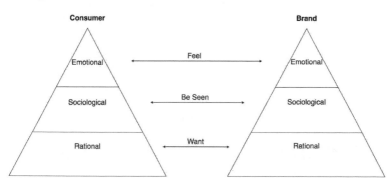

We are in effect defining what your brand looks like in a customer's mind. When we define your ideal brand much of it will simply reflect or 'mirror' your target customer. Figure 5.11 illustrates this.

Your definition will also include product elements and describe how it's different from competitors. Figure 5.15 illustrates this.

5.6.1 Defining your Wine Brand Example

The following brand definition process is not one I've made up. It's one that is used in different forms for the world's most well-known brands, a famous Chief Marketing Officer[36], and that I've picked up working in various international marketing teams. I simplify a lot of the process below, but it requires some hard, in-depth thinking on your part.

Once you've done this though you've got a tool that helps unlock sales from consumers all round the world. Why? Because you're communicating to them in ways that are important to them. Your consumer wants to feel and be seen in certain important ways. You want your brand to help make them feel and be seen in these ways.

Figure 5.11: Reflect your Customer

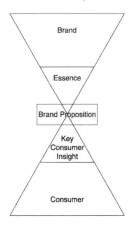

Figure 5.12: Brand Definition

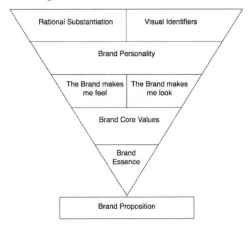

These form what your brand stands for and are called Brand Core Values.

So let's look at an example. Let's say you chose Inspiring Businessman as your niche. There are other Brand Core Value words that could also be used to describe variants of this niche (listed in this section below). But for the purposes of simplicity let's stick with the words in the Inspiring Businessman consumer description in Figure 5.13.

Figure 5.13: Inspiring Businessman Consumer Triangle

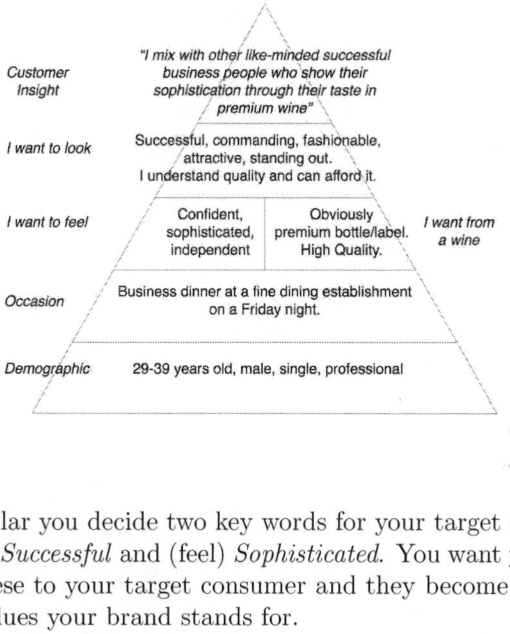

In particular you decide two key words for your target market are (be seen as) *Successful* and (feel) *Sophisticated*. You want your brand to signal these to your target consumer and they become two of the four core values your brand stands for.

In the premium wine category customers demand *High Quality*. This is pretty consistent whatever of the three segments you choose as they all prefer premium wine. We call this the 'rational' core value.

The last one differentiates your brand from your competitors'. This is an important step so

- Go back to the Wine Industry Competitor section's market model and look to see where you positioned your competitors
- Review the stories you have to tell from your Company Wine Business section

- In the Choose your Niche section you decided on where to position your brand including the target customer group.

Look at the relevant list of possible core value words by your chosen customer group in the Core Value Words lists below (these words also describe the segments themselves and resonate with them).

What word could you 'own' that separates you from other wine brands and resonates with consumers? This requires some hard analysis and thinking, but brand management isn't all long lunches and designing graphics.

In our case we are targeting Inspiring Businessmen, so let's say you decided *Contemporary* was a key point of difference. This might be because your company owner has great taste in the latest that the design world can offer—furniture, architecture, cars, watches, mobile phones, artwork, and clothes.

You also have access to a leading edge graphic designer and so can see how you could stand out from the crowd and appeal to this group of customers through this brand core value.

So, for example, competitor 1 has a bright Kangaroo label, competitor 2 a bland black and white label and simple bottle, and competitor 3 a flashy but 90s looking label.

You would have a very stylish bottle with cutting edge graphics that remind people of an Armani suit, a Ferrari car, or a Tag Heur watch. This would also flow through into point of sale, websites, cellar door, how you present yourself at wine shows etc—more of the marketing execution later. The point is not the actual ideas on bringing 'Contemporary' to life but illustrating why this differentiating core value is so important.

Inspiring Businessman Core Value Words

- Ambitious
- Assertive
- Attractive
- Boutique
- Brand Leader
- Brash
- Capable
- Commanding
- Competent
- Confident
- Contemporary
- Cool
- Crafted
- Determined
- Different
- Discerning
- Dominance
- Expensive
- Expert
- High Quality
- Holding Court
- Important
- Impressing
- Impressive
- In Charge
- Independent
- Individual
- Intelligent
- Interesting
- International
- Knowledgeable
- Leadership
- Natural
- Naturally Stylish
- Organized
- Personalized
- Popular
- Potency
- Potent

- Powerful
- Premium
- Premium Quality
- Professional
- Responsive
- Self Assured
- Smart
- Sophisticated
- Status
- Stimulating
- Strong
- Presence
- Stylish
- Subtle
- Successful
- The Best
- Uncompromising
- Understated
- Wealth
- Witty
- World Class
- Worldly

Knowledgeable Professor Core Value Words

- Advanced
- Boutique
- Capable
- Clever
- Comfortable
- Confident
- Conservative
- Considered
- Content
- Control
- Crafted
- Craftsman
- Different
- Discerning
- Discernment
- Down To Earth

- Effective
- Efficient
- Environment
- Focused
- Formal
- Genuine
- High Quality
- In Control
- Independent
- Individual
- Interesting
- International
- Knowledgeable
- Made-by-Craftsman
- Mastery
- Mature
- On Top Of Things
- One Step Ahead
- Organized
- Professional
- Refined
- Refreshing
- Relaxed
- Savvy
- Simple No Nonsense
- Smart
- Smart Value
- Sophisticated
- Structured
- Technical
- Understated

Creative Individualists Core Value Words

- Adventures
- Adventurous
- Alternative
- Ambitious
- Attractive
- Authentic
- Bold

- Boutique
- Challenging
- Charming
- Confident
- Contemporary
- Cutting Edge
- Daring
- Different
- Distinctive
- Doing Things Differently
- Doing Things My Way
- Dynamic
- Energetic
- Energy
- Exciting
- Exploration
- Fashionable
- Free Thinking
- Freedom
- Fun Loving
- High Quality
- Impressive
- Independent
- Individualist
- Individualistic
- Innovative
- Intelligent
- Interesting
- Knowledgeable
- Latest
- Leading Edge
- Live Life On The Edge
- Modern
- Party Lovers
- Proactive
- Quality
- Risk Taker
- Spontaneous
- Stimulating
- Stimulation

- Street Smart
- Stylish
- Superior Quality
- Trendy
- Try New Things
- Unique
- Witty
- World Class
- Youthful

5.6.2 Brand Essence

Coming up with the values got you thinking about your consumer and competitor. If you were to come up with a phrase that described the basic need that the brand is addressing, its 'Essence', what would it be?

The classic examples are from other industries are Volvo with 'Safety', and Marlboro with 'Strength and Independence'.

The Brand Essence is a short, easy-to-remember descriptor of the brand. In this illustrative case it might be *Contemporary Premium Quality.*

Regardless of the idea the point is that this is your brand short hand or a description of your brand's DNA.

5.6.3 Brand Proposition

Which brings me to the most well-known part of a brand—its proposition, unique selling proposition (USP), or promise. The brand proposition is how your brand benefits the consumer. Let's go back to the Customer Insight at the top of the description of Inspiring Businessperson. It reads, *I mix with other like-minded business people who show their sophistication through their taste in premium wine.*

Your brand's proposition to these customer may be, *Brand X brings out your contemporary style and sophistication.*

Figure 5.14 illustrates this connection between brand and target consumer.

Figure 5.14: Brand Proposition

5.6.4 Personality and Product

Bring your brand to life by describing the brand as if it was a person, known as the brand personality. Look for words that also describe your customer group (see core value words) as well as clothes, cars, popular brands for these customers etc. This will help bring more depth to explaining and understanding your brand.

Last but not least add in the product elements—your ideal tasting notes, substantiation of quality, such as top awards, visual identifiers such as logo, label and bottle, and region/nationality. See the example wine brand definition in Figure 5.15.

Once you put them into the Brand Triangle, you have defined your brand and can ensure you communicate to those seemingly superficial but actually very important criteria target market uses to choose a wine brand.

5.7 Step 6: The Wine Marketing Mix—The 5Ps

Customers' image of a brand is prompted by some key drivers, descriptions of which have been molded into words that start with 'P'. They could be considered a good check of your brand activity and

Figure 5.15: Example Winery Brand Definition

drive your marketing activities to reposition your brand as illustrated in Figure 5.16. . They are known as the 'marketing mix'. You can also look at using these to describe how you will deliver your brand to your customers in a shorthand brand plan. These drivers are: Product, Price, Place, People, and Perception.

Product

If you haven't got the product right all your branding effort will be in vain. However we're not just talking about the intensity of flavor, complexity, balance, texture, and length of flavor. We're talking about the bottle, the label, the closure, and the cases. Different customers groups will prefer different levels of quality and premium cues.

Price

The simplest indicator of quality to a consumer—if not always the most accurate! Given your cost base you need to be priced in the premium category, the choice is just how premium. In an occasion where a customer wants to impress others, a middling priced bottle on the wine list may not cut it.

Figure 5.16: The 5Ps Helping to Reposition a Brand

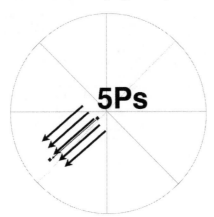

Place

'The right people at the right place drinking the right product', 'On Premise builds brands', and 'Brands are built in the Tasting Room' are key phrases you'll hear from professional alcohol beverage industry brand managers. For premium brands it's absolutely key to their brand development.

For mainstream popular brands other drivers are arguably more important including high profile advertising and the general visibility around a region, including billboards and signage. But that's more for a large mainstream brand to be worried about than a premium wine brand. Indeed some advertising can signal to consumers that you're not an exclusive and special brand but just another mainstream brand for the masses.

If it's listed in the best restaurants that's a superb cue for most groups of customers. If it's discounted at the local supermarket on an aisle end then it's time to panic—not only is your premium price point being destroyed, but you're seen as just another popular brand.

On Premise (restaurants, cafes, bars) or the Tasting Room (including a winery restaurant) are the venues for key occasions and experiences for your target market. For example, if your customers are at a fine dining establishment with some friends they may be enjoying exquisite food with some great wine.

This sort of occasion could well be one where the consumer is showing how discerning they are. Or perhaps at a flashy expensive place they want to impress others with their knowledge and wealth. Regardless a bottle of your premium wine on the table will be associated with an experience important to your customers and will hopefully prompt them to purchase your wine brand again.

Distributors are key in assisting you with this. They should have a good understanding of precincts (clusters of bars and restaurants) and whether they are, for example, more flashy or more foody. When you go through your target market ask them to identify what establishments have what sort of people. If they fit your target market then add them to your distributor listing objectives.

People

A key part of professional brand management is deciding on your niche or your particular group of customers. Once you've done this you want other potential customers in your niche seeing people like them (or people they aspire to be) drinking your premium wine. If it's more an older sophisticated drinker then think about what sort of place that is versus a young single merchant banker. Any images of people you use also need to reflect this sort of person.

Promotion

Small wine businesses generally can't afford traditional advertising. However direct marketing, internet marketing (this book), events, donations, PR, and cellar door sales are affordable and effective. There are some great examples of wine, food, and music events where people can have a great time and associate that with your brand. It's then up to you to use internet marketing, your website, point of sale stands, trade hosting, and cellar door promotion to let your target market know.

Events especially wine, food, and music, events are other good places where you can also be associated with experiences that are important to your customers. Remember with events to leverage them—that is for every dollar you spend on the event itself, spend another dollar on promoting your attendance/sponsorship of the event to your customers. Many brands do not leverage events and only gets a small part of the value of this expenditure as a result.

You can't afford advertising but you can afford internet marketing with online sales. Again it has to be relevant to your market. If it's people who want to appear knowledgeable to others—then lots of detail will be appropriate. If people are looking for your wine for other reasons then don't bother with detail and give them, for example, wine events they can attend.

Direct sales will boost your average margins so they will form a key part of your marketing plan no matter what your size. The challenge here is relevant, interesting information over the four seasons that will lead to lots of sales on the release of your wine as well as supporting wine retailer marketing efforts.

This book is all about Wine Internet Marketing and will take you through tactics that cover search engines, internet advertising, social media, and eCommerce in the following chapters.

5.8 Step 7: The Wine Marketing Plan

All your insights from analyzing your customers, competitors, and your company need to be put into an action plan.

However there's little point writing a Wine Marketing Plan (also called a Brand Plan) unless you've:

- decided how your brand is appealing to a carefully chosen target market
- looked at how you're different from your competitors
- looked at how you will achieve your company goals

By following the brand management process you should understand what your current situation (or brand position) is and what your ideal brand position should be. Your analysis of the Product, Price, People, Place, and Promotion will suggest ways in which you can move to your ideal position through various marketing activities.

As you start to move in this direction, you'll be able to increase your price, margins, and/or volume. When it comes down to it, this is the measurable benefit of great brand management. An additional benefit is the increased capital value or goodwill that you will get should your company choose to sell all or part of the business.

The brand plan will therefore follow a structure like this:

Company Financials 3-year volume, price, and margin target.

Customer, Company, and Competitor Section A summary of your customer niche, your company objectives, and competitor review from your workings in the relevant sections above.

Brand Definition and Positioning Your Brand Definition and where you're positioned in the Market Model.

Major Issue 1 Strategies to resolve it. With a responsible person, due date, and budget against each detailed task

- Product tasks
- Place tasks
- Price tasks
- Promotion tasks
- People tasks
- ... and then repeat for each major issue.

Note I don't bother with interesting but secondary sections, such as Market Trends. I've written these in the past and never really used them. If a market trend is relevant, perhaps bottling design, then build that into your 5Ps analysis—if it can't be included in a relevant section then it's probably peripheral to brand success.

Another quick and easy way of writing a brand plan is to use the headings Product, Price, People, Place, and Perception to analyze where you're going wrong and how you'll address this. It would look like this:

Price Strategy to resolve it. With a Responsible person, due date, and budget against each detailed task.

... and then repeat for Product, People, Place, and Perception.

I illustrate a brand plan below using the later 5P approach for the target segment Inspiring Businessman.

In practice, a brand often has a couple of key issues it needs to resolve. They may revolve around lack of awareness or consideration for your brand, low prices versus high costs, expensive inventory, or poor international sales. A better approach may be to address a few key issues that your marketing or business faces.

The Marketing Calendar

A Marketing Calendar is simply a very effective time management discipline for a marketing team or person.

It's a calendar of when activities or tasks are to be launched into the market and need to be agreed in detail with the CEO, owner, board (or husband or wife).

A company should be in a cycle of starting to prepare six months before an activity is to be launched and start to implement three months before it is visible in the market place.

The calendar provides a discipline for the sales and marketing team to get tasks done. Want to make things happen—this is the way! Some frequently encountered issues are budget, bland implementation, and sales vs marketing. I also use this for social media planning but call it a 'content calendar'.

Budget

No doubt you have many issues you'd like to resolve. The problem is there are always too many things you want to do and not enough budget. Either you'll invest more in your brand, or you'll concentrate on a few actions a year. With a 3-year action plan you achieve many of them—but not all, I'm afraid you're doomed to always wanting to spend more on branding, marketing, and sales than you can afford.

I suggest you cost out the plan and then balance your need for a profit vs the need to achieve long-term revenue and greater margin. If you are a well funded winegrower then you may choose to spend more on marketing for three years and perhaps even accept a net loss every year. If you're not so well funded then you'll need to prioritize your plan and do it more slowly over a few years.

Implementation

So you've gone through the brand process and written a great brand plan. Of course you already have a premium wine and a passionate sales and marketing team. All you have to do is implement it, right? Almost. The problem you're now facing is not strategic (you've done all that work)—it's now creative. If you write the perfect brand plan but execute the plan with blandness you're still not going to stand out from the hundreds of other brands in the market place.

This is a dilemma of being unable to afford an ad agency and therefore access their creative talent, but being unsure of the quality of local contracted designers. Frankly you'll need to take a risk on smaller designers but be prepared to move if you feel the creative is not performing.

Sales versus Marketing

A good marketing plan will provide the sales team leads, enthusiastic trade buyers, more effective sales calls, and more direct sales. By and large sales works hand in hand with marketing except the sales manager can turn your inventory into hard cash by negotiating a volume deal. By offering this discount it will mean a very happy trade account and, if the discount is passed on, very happy consumers.

On the other hand, a marketing manager is trying to change consumers' minds, thereby, boosting prices and encouraging future volume. If they see sales offering discounts repetitively then they will watch the discounted price become the actual price over time.

Discounting is a very treacherous area and I discourage its use outside of standard discounts for volume purchasing. I acknowledge it is endemic in the wine industry but no small business in the wine industry can afford to go down that track—leave it to the corporates and find other ways to compete (which is really what this book is about).

5.8.1 Illustrative Marketing Plan

In this section I bring it all together into a marketing action plan for targeting the segment Inspiring Businessman. I cover some differences in the marketing plan with another segment, Knowledgeable Professor, at the end of this section.

The quandary I face with writing this is if I become too specific it becomes irrelevant to a wider audience but if I'm too general then it isn't informative.

I haven't even tried to put in a budget but have instead covered some thoughts in notes below as its too dependent on company funds, size, and age. This Brand Plan is for the Inspiring Businessman segment and excludes company objectives and major issues.

The marketing calendar that I mention below is simply a calendar of when activities or tasks are launched in the market place. A company should be in a cycle of starting to prepare six months before an activity is due and starting to implement three months before it is visible in the market place. The calendar provides a discipline for the sales and marketing team to get tasks done. Otherwise they'll be spending all their time firefighting rather than engaging in productive marketing.

5.8.2 Brand Strategy

Record what customer group you are targeting, how your brand is perceived in the market now, and how you wish it be perceived in the future. In other words your customer, the current perception of your brand, and your desired brand position as described by your brand definition.

How you get from the current position to your desired position is explained through your marketing plan...

The 5Ps below would most probably be in table format with the headings being What, Who, Budget, When By.

5.8.3 Product

- Review label and logos to ensure they have visual cues of wealth and success. Action Point: Brief agency on new design if necessary
- Review bottle type—heavy, good punt
- Review opening—happy with screw top or does this market demand cork
- Review case—consider wood cases, single bottle boxes, or interesting design (case could be on display)
- Substantiation—what awards, reviews, ratings can you use in your marketing. Is there a famous international wine award you've won?

5.8.4 Place

On Premise: Restaurants

- Review account objectives with sales team and distributors.
- Make key objective being listed in at least one quarter of the best fine dining establishments in (for example) Los Angeles, San Francisco, San Diego, New York, Washington, D.C., Denver, Chicago, Austin, Houston, Dallas, San Antonio, Fort Worth, Miami, Boston, Los Vegas, Pheonix, Philadelphia, Baltimore, Seattle...
- Other major cities if you can afford to personally visit them.
- Look to the precincts that people go to 'be seen' as well as precincts around banking, legal, and accounting businesses.

- Is there a wine retailer you can work with who can help? Action Point: Put into Distributor brief

On Premise: Own Tasting Room and Restaurant

- Review exterior and interior design for brand fit
- Review service for brand fit e.g. professional or low-key and friendly
- Review menu for brand fit

On Premise: Bars

- Review account objectives with sales team and distributors.
- Make key objective being listed and prominently displayed behind the bar in at least half of the best Premium bars especially wine bars.
- Cities as above.
- Look to the precincts that people go to be seen as well as precincts around banking, legal, and accounting businesses. Action Point: Put into Distributor brief

On Premise Trade Program: Restaurants

- Supports the above and assists distributors with being listed in fine dining restaurants
- Host a trip for key restaurateurs and bar owners in your region to visit your winery and perhaps tied into an event. May only be able to afford 1-2 per year. Action Point: Write a marketing activity brief and implement as part of a marketing calendar.
- Wine maker and/or your key personality visits to the premises above as well as distributor training and media interviews.
- Should be supported with one pager of tasting notes and key product info. Action Point: Write a marketing activity brief and implement as part of a marketing calendar

Off Premise: Wine Retailers

- Review account objectives with sales team and distributors.
- The key objective is your wine being sold in fine wine stores in wealthy areas and precincts.
- Percentage of stores and actual number of cities dependent on your volume. Action Point: Put into Distributor brief
- Offer premium point of sale for these small stores and circulate every couple of months.
- Must be high quality and probably custom built. Action Point: Brief into local joiner.

- Action Point: Write an marketing activity brief and implement as part of a marketing calendar.
- Aim to be positioned on the shelf as near to the varietal category leaders of your price point as possible.
- Make this a clear objective with distributors. Action Point: Put into Distributor brief

Off Premise: Supermarkets and Liquor Store Chains

- Stop all promotional discounting to supermarkets and liquor stores.
- Offer large volume discounts only and look to reduce this over a period of time as a way to reduce your exposure to this channel (replaced by direct, fine wine stores, and on premise sales). Action Point: Price review

Off Premise: Distributor Review

- Can your distributor deliver the following tasks?
- Will your objectives of promoting a premium brand fit their objectives. If they want a cheap wine they can push to liquor chain stores—then find another distributor. Action Point: Discuss Distributor brief with distributors

Direct. In order to boost your net price/margin you need to sell more direct through cellar door, your website and internet marketing. See Promotion below.

5.8.5 Price

- Review top same-country, same-price-range varietal category leaders in your key target cities—can you match their prices or get close to them? Aim is to be in top 10% in the next few years. Action Point: Price review

5.8.6 Promotion

Internet Marketing Which is really what this book is about. Read the following chapters and decide what type of how internet marketing will help position your brand and drive sales. Note most of internet marketing will involve producing some sort of content and this content should be driven by your brand proposition and target market.

Direct Marketing This is all about lists, offers and creative. You need to focus on lists as it's by far the most important. Create your own wine club list through website sign up, sign up at the cellar door, and sign up at events.

Next most important is the offer you make:

- If you have the perception of limited stock then offer allocation
- Otherwise promote key news and events that are important to the target market. This will be more about restaurants and events rather than harvest information. Awards and reviews are good too
- Could offer a discount on case lots or for ordering every month or so over a period of time (volume discount) but your aim is to boost margins by encouraging direct sales and maintain a premium price point—try and avoid

Lastly is the creative. Email marketing is the most cost effective though postcards can be affordable. Sign up to an email marketing service, such as MailChimp, and send it out every month or so.

You really need good customer service people and/or sales person and/or marketing person to run a good internet and direct marketing operation. They'll need to do all of the above but also interact with customers by phone, social media, and email. And sort out the inevitable problems with delivery.

Action Points:

- Write a marketing activity brief and implement as part of a marketing calendar
- Brief in agency to upgrade website to offer wine sales and email sign ups
- Ensure you have a form to capture email sign ups at cellar door and events
- Ensure you have available staff or contracted resources

Tasting Room

Review or open a tasting room operation. Does your tasting room operation reflect your high quality brand value and appeal to your target segment? If you've attached a restaurant are you happy your chef can cook similar high quality food and does the restaurant have the ambiance that your target market will enjoy?

PR

What stores do you have that will help a journalist write interesting articles? About the wine and something else—review your company stories.

Action Points:

- Write a media kit, ensure you have professional photos
- Write a media strategy

5.8.7 People

People are also covered in your good work in On Premise Place above. However, events can also show the right people at the right place drinking the right product. Assuming your customer has a great experience at the event they will also associate it with your wine.

Events

Wine festivals that will be attended by your target audience—probably in their home cities or even home suburbs. Offer list sign up. Remember to spend resources on marketing your association with the event rather than just attending the event. Action Point: Write an event strategy and implement as part of a marketing calendar.

Charity and Donations

Look for a charity or business event that wealthy, successful people are supporting i.e. your target market. Perhaps a charity ball or banking awards dinner to contribute wine. Of course, also contribute to community requests etc but that is more community obligation than marketing strategy. Action Point: Include in event strategy and implement as part of a marketing calendar.

5.8.8 Difference for Knowledgeable Professor and Creative Individualist

Product: Different bottles, openings, cases, and product information—simpler for the professor, more cutting edge for the individualist.

Place: Focus on different precincts—more top quality food type establishments for the professor, more trendy/artistic precincts for the individualist.

Price: Carefully consider the value for money equation for the professors as they actually understand quality wine, may not be able to increase prices as much compared to the other customer groups.

Promotion: Very product focused for the professor, lots of information about vineyard and wine making progress, significant interaction in social media. Very event focused for the individualist.

People: Wine tourism and wine events for the professor, donations to business/opera type events. Music and artistic events for the individualist as well as donations to artistic events.

5.9 Step 8: Review your Wine Marketing Plan

Sure, review your Wine Marketing Plan but stay the course! Consistency is more important than consistently conducting Wine Marketing Reviews.

It's common knowledge with market research companies (that monitor consumer's brand awareness etc) and media planners (those people who recommend ad placements) that consistently advertising the same brand message works best. Each campaign builds on the previous ones.

So keep to your overall plan, but keep refining it at the edges (especially with internet marketing testing). I'm guessing it will take at least three years for you to implement all your changes from your first marketing plan. So your review should be of successful implementation of the Marketing Plan not the plan itself (in the short term).

What you're doing is changing consumers' minds, and this takes time as your target market is slowly exposed to all your marketing activities. Sales activities, like a price discount promotion, may lead to immediate, measurable volume increases, but marketing is implementing a series of well thought through activities. Some of these (web sales) can lead to immediate profit improvement, others (fine dining listings) can take a while to positively affect your sales.

Large wine companies track supermarket data and use regular surveys to measure sales and consumer awareness respectively. As a premium wine brand you won't really be selling in supermarkets and can't afford the market research surveys. You will get direct feedback on internet and direct marketing but that's about it.

However, three years after implementing your marketing plan, it would be an excellent idea to see whether you've managed to hold your price increases, boost your margins through direct sales, and generated higher demand through a more attractive brand.

If your profits are still not increasing and you're happy that discounting or product quality hasn't held you back then it maybe time to completely review your marketing plan. After three to five years markets do substantially change so it's worthwhile doing a complete review.

In which case go through the complete process again...

5.10 Summary

Wineries should follow a brand management process for their marketing plan. This involves understanding customers, competitors, and your strengths/personality. Then positioning your brand by creating an ideal Brand Definition and using 5Ps and the marketing plan to move the brand from the current position to an ideal position over a period of years.

5.11 Resources

- Wine Brand Management Discussion, Update, and Posts Page: www.WineMarketingPros.com/winerycmpchap/

6 Internet Marketing Measurement

6.1 What is Internet Marketing Measurement

Internet Marketing Measurement is making sure that your marketing strategies are actually achieving a business objective through measurement. These measurements also allow us to change the strategy if it's doing poorly or invest more time and money in it if it's doing very well.

These measurements are called different things by different people and include phrases such as Key Performance Indicators (KPI), Benchmarks, Metrics, Goals, Desirable Outcomes, Objectives, Targets, Segments, or Measurements of Success. I choose to use the terms *KPI* and *KPI target*.

Internet marketing has access to a huge amount of data that can be measured, and there is a whole profession of Web Analysts who are experts at sifting through this data. The problem is not one of finding the data, but turning that data into information.

In this chapter, we will look at web analytics software, social media monitoring, some serious problems with internet data, analysis, and reporting and then show how Tony's Wine Store resolves them.

6.2 Google Analytics

The most common way to collect website data is to install Google Analytics on your website. To install it requires just a few lines of code in each webpage—there is usually a simple way to do this depending on your website software. Google Analytics is offered for free by Google, and it tracks everything that a visitor does on a website. It allows a wine store owner to see the what, how, when, where, and who of all his visitors (in aggregate, not individually identified for privacy reasons). It is remarkably easy to use and allows you to measure such things as traffic sources, web page, and keyword popularity, eCommerce conversion rates, average length of visit, new vs. repeat visitors, and much more.

However, it is not as comprehensive and all encompassing as an internet marketer would like, here's why.

6.3 The Problem of Multiple-Attribution

We'll use a short story to illustrate the problem of multi-attribution. Let's go back to Larry, the Luxury Enthusiast,

> Larry, let's say, first heard about Tony's new competitor, the specialist wine store across town, from his wife who happened to be driving past it. A week later, he saw one of his friends mentioning on Facebook that he'd found a hard-to-find bottle of Pomerol at the new wine store. The next day he was reading through a wine blog when he saw a banner ad promoting the store. Two weeks later he saw a tweet from one of his colleagues saying they were buying a bottle of Russian River Pinot Noir from the wine store for Friday night drinks. When he spoke to the colleague on Friday night the colleague was effusive about how knowledgeable the staff at the wine store were.
>
> But it was on the other side of town, whereas, the big bland liquor discounter and Tony's Wine Store were just down the road.
>
> The following Monday he was browsing the internet for a gift to buy for one of his customers. He was reading a local wine blog and noticed that it had recommended a great vintage Burgundy with a link to purchase this at the new wine store. He clicked on the link and started reading about the wine when the phone rang, so he closed the internet browser and answered the call. An hour later Larry had forgotten about the Burgundy and was once again browsing the internet by searching Google with the search phrase 'corporate wine gift'. He noticed a Google Ad from the new wine store selling a Burgundy Wine in a wooden box—perfect. He knows all about the wine store by now, had read and heard good things about it, and had kept seeing it pop up all over the place. So he clicked

on the ad, which went to the new wine store's eCommerce
website's Corporate Wine Gift web page, and within moments he had made his first purchase from the new wine
store. Which started his new relationship with a competing wine store, and the slow death of his relationship with
Tony's Wine Store.

Google Analytics would measure whether the click on the Google
Ad mentioned above resulted in a sale i.e. a 'conversion'. *The natural
inclination of the wine store owner is to then attribute the sale to the
Google Ad.* Yet this seems unfair as any one of the mentions of
the new wine store from wife, to Facebook, wine blog ad, Twitter,
colleague, wine blogger, or Google Search could have been the key
driver for the sale. Indeed most probably all the mentions combined
to lead to such a level of trust that Larry was happy to purchase a gift
from the new wine store. Yet the Google Ad conversion is directly
measurable by Google Analytics (and is the last measurable click) so
it gets the credit.

This problem is known as *multiple attribution*, as in you're unsure
where to attribute the success of a sale. It is seen in advertising
of all types (including TV, newspaper, radio, and magazine) but is
particularly galling for internet marketing given the amount of data
that is available.

In August 2011, Google Analytics was upgraded[37] and is now able
to report many of the traffic sources that led up to the sale as an
Assisted Conversion. The report is called 'Multi Channel Funnels',
and Google Search and the wine blog ad in the story above would
be shown as responsible for an Assisted Conversion. However, what
it won't show is any influence that doesn't have a direct interaction
with the website. In the example above, these influences include
the conversation with his wife, the Facebook mention (unless he had
clicked on a link on the Facebook post to the website), the banner
ad impression (unless he clicked on the ad), and the tweet (unless he
clicked on a link to the website in the tweet).

With this attribution problem in mind internet marketers do two
things. Firstly they accept that they can never achieve analytics
nirvana—analytics tools will only ever be an approximation. Secondly, we also use other measurement software, usually for social
media, that can measure things that Google Analytics cannot see,
such as store related mentions that take place on third party web-

sites.

This social media measurement software includes Facebook Insights (Facebook's own Google Analytics type software), PeerIndex, and Klout for Twitter (Twitter is close to releasing its own Twitter Analytics software), simple email alerts such as SocialMention and Google Alerts a specialist wine social media monitoring and management service called VinTank Social Connect. Because these tools cannot usually tie sales conversions with sources, we need to make a judgement as to what to measure. We'll cover each of those in relevant chapters.

However with that explanation of multi-attribution problems we are in a position to explain how internet marketing can be accounted for in the store's future Profit and Loss Statement.

6.4 Tonys' Wine Store Internet Marketing Measurements

The Customer numbers, Volume, Revenue calculations in Figure 6.1 are copied from the Profit and Loss Statement, as per Figure 4.11.

The Internet Marketing report calculates the increase in customers per segment from internet marketing, see Figure 6.2.

The increased customer numbers are then spread across the Conversions and Assisted Conversions as per the Input Variable *% conversions attributed to Assists*, see Figure 6.3. We are managing the attribution problem by splitting internet marketing conversions into two sections:

1. Conversions based on the traffic source of the last interaction before purchase—which is easily measured by Google Analytics.
2. Assisted Conversions, based on the previous ('non-last') interactions before purchase. This is sometimes measured by Google Analytics.

Given we don't know which traffic source can really be attributed to the decision to purchase, we are covering both types in the model. It is necessarily subjective and imperfect. If you believe it is more the last interaction before purchase then you can lower the Input Variable *% conversions attributed to Assists*. If you think it is more previous interactions before purchase then you can increase this. I believe it is about two-thirds in favor of Assisted Conversions so have

Figure 6.1: Internet Marketing Report—Revenue

Revenue Calculations			
Year	**1**	**2**	**3**
Segment sizes:			
Enthusiasts	880	880	880
Luxury Enthusiasts	293	293	293
Image Seekers	1760	1760	1760
Luxury Image Seekers	196	196	196
Savvy Shoppers	1467	1467	1467
Traditionalists	1565	1565	1565
Satisfied Sippers	1369	1369	1369
Overwhelmed	2249	2249	2249
Wine Drinker Market Size	**9780**	**9780**	**9780**
Customers:			
Enthusiasts	132	220	308
Luxury Enthusiasts	44	88	147
Image Seekers	264	352	352
Luxury Image Seekers	29	59	98
Savvy Shoppers	220	73	73
Traditionalists	235	235	235
Satisfied Sippers	205	68	68
Overwhelmed	337	112	112
Total Customers	**1467**	**1208**	**1394**
Tony's Volume by Segment (bottles):			
Enthusiasts	13731	22885	32039
Luxury Enthusiasts	4577	9154	15257
Image Seekers	27462	36616	36616
Luxury Image Seekers	3051	6103	10171
Savvy Shoppers	11443	3814	3814
Traditionalists	12205	12205	12205
Satisfied Sippers	10680	3560	3560
Overwhelmed	17545	5848	5848
Total Volume (bottles)	**100695**	**100186**	**119512**
Tony's Revenue by Segment ($):			
Enthusiasts	$205,967	$343,278	$480,589
Luxury Enthusiasts	$114,426	$228,852	$381,420
Image Seekers	$411,934	$549,245	$549,245
Luxury Image Seekers	$76,284	$152,568	$254,280
Savvy Shoppers	$114,426	$38,142	$38,142
Traditionalists	$122,054	$122,054	$122,054
Satisfied Sippers	$53,399	$17,800	$17,800
Overwhelmed	$87,727	$29,242	$29,242
Total Revenue	**$1,186,216**	**$1,481,181**	**$1,872,772**

Figure 6.2: Internet Marketing Report—Customer Number Differences by Segment

Customer # Difference by Segment			
Segments	Original Y1	Difference Y2	Difference Y3
Enthusiasts	132	88	88
Luxury Enthusiasts	44	44	59
Image Seekers	264	88	0
Luxury Image Seekers	29	29	39
Savvy Shoppers	220	-147	0
Traditionalists	235	0	0
Satisfied Sippers	205	-137	0
Overwhelmed	337	-225	0

Figure 6.3: Internet Marketing Report—Strategy Attribution

Internet Marketing Strategies:			
Year	1	2	3
% conversions attributed to Assists	65%		
Conversions (last interaction):			
SEO	0%	15%	15%
Local SEO	0%	15%	15%
Advertising	0%	15%	15%
CSE	0%	10%	10%
Blogging	0%	5%	5%
Facebook	0%	5%	5%
Twitter	0%	3%	3%
Mobile	0%	5%	5%
LBS	0%	1%	1%
Mobile & Social Commerce	0%	1%	1%
LPO	0%	10%	10%
Email	0%	15%	15%
% of all possible Conversions:	0%	100%	100%
Assisted Conversions (previous interactions):			
SEO	0%	5%	5%
Local SEO	0%	5%	5%
Advertising	0%	5%	5%
CSE	0%	5%	5%
Blogging	0%	15%	15%
Facebook	0%	15%	15%
Twitter	0%	10%	10%
Mobile	0%	10%	10%
LBS	0%	5%	5%
Mobile & Social Commerce	0%	10%	10%
LPO	0%	10%	10%
Email	0%	5%	5%
% of all possible Assists:	0%	100%	100%

set this at 65%.

The model then lists all the internet marketing strategies under Conversions and again under Assisted Conversions. Beside each marketing strategy is a % number and total 100%. In essence, you are saying how influential each marketing strategy was within Conversions or Assisted Conversions.

So in our example there are 293 Luxury Enthusiasts in the local market. In Year 1, Tony's Wine Store has a 15% Market Share of Luxury Enthusiasts (44 customers), then 30% (88 customers) in Year 2, as per Figure 6.1. This additional Market Share equates to 44 more Luxury Enthusiasts as seen in Figure 6.2.

In Figure 6.3, *% conversions attributed to Assists* is 65%, so (44*65%) 29 of the new customers conversions can be attributed to interactions with traffic sources other than the last one before online purchase. Of the 29, only 15% (2) came from SEO (probably Google Search), see Figure 6.4.

Figure 6.4: Internet Marketing Report—Conversions Luxury Enthusiast

Conversions: *Luxury Enthusiasts*	New Customers Y2	New Customers Y3
SEO	2	3
Local SEO	2	3
Advertising	2	3
CSE	2	2
Blogging	1	1
Facebook	1	1
Twitter	0	1
Mobile	1	1
LBS	0	0
Mobile & Social Commerce	0	0
LPO	2	2
Email	2	3

Assisted Conversions: *Luxury Enthusiasts*	New Customers Y2	New Customers Y3
SEO	1	2
Local SEO	1	2
Advertising	1	2
CSE	1	2
Blogging	4	6
Facebook	4	6
Twitter	3	4
Mobile	3	4
LBS	1	2
Mobile & Social Commerce	3	4
LPO	3	4
Email	1	2

One of our Measurements of the success of SEO will be that we have two Luxury Enthusiasts acquired through SEO (Google Analytics calls this traffic source 'Non Paid Search') as measured by the eCommerce Conversion report. Specifically we want two new customers in Year 2 to every month purchase $65 of wine made up of at least two bottles being worth $25+ each. This measurement comes from the Financial Model. Luxury Enthusiasts purchase 104 bottles pa, Tony's Wine Store's target market share of this segment's annual purchases is 30% in Year 2, the segment's average bottle price is $25. The equation is: 104 bottles * 30% share * $25 12 months = $65.

Note Tony will also need to do the following to achieve his *Business Objective 2. Boost Margins and Volume by changing to a Higher Value Customer Mix*:

Five Enthusiasts: 104 bottles * 25% share * $15 price * 12 months = $33 per month

Two Image Seekers: 104 * 25% * $15 * 12 months = $26 pm

Two Luxury Image Seekers: 104 * 25% * $15 12 months = $65 pm

He will set up a custom report in Google Analytics that automatically calculates this each month. If he fails to meet these targets then he will need to put more effort into SEO.

These measures are examples of the ones you will see in the Measurement section of each of the following chapters.

6.5 Social Media Measurement

As mentioned above social media is unlikely to feature as a source of traffic for a Google Analytics Conversion and probably never as an Assisted Conversion. We will need to come up with separate measurements for these important sources of sales. We will assume there is an Assisted Conversion when a certain social media KPI is reached. This KPI will be based on interactions over time. For example, in Facebook we may measure the number of Facebook user wall posts per month vs. last month on our business Facebook Page.

The Web Analytics expert Avinash Kaushik[38] calls something similar a *Micro Conversion*, that is an important event on your website as measured by Google Analytics that is not strictly an eCommerce sale conversion. For example, sales leads from the Contact Us form, or email newsletter sign-ups. I've taken that idea and applied it to social media measurement and called it an Assisted Conversion.

Wineries are lucky enough to have a wine specific tool for measuring social media mentions of their wine brand. It is called Social Connect.

6.5.1 Wine Specialist Social Media Monitoring Tool

Social Connect is software from a Californian wine tech firm company called Vintank. It is somewhat similar to Google in that it has a robot that crawls over 15,000 wine specific platforms, 170,000 social sites and blogs, and over 90,000 forums including Twitter, Facebook, and even CellarTracker. The robot looks for mentions of wine brands and records every mention. It has measured over 300 million wine conversations and has profiles from more than 10 million social wine consumers.

Wineries can sign up to Social Connect (`vintank.com`), verify they are the winery owner and get reports on social media mentions by type of media, day of week/month, time of day, top social media customers, recent mentions, and much more. Most importantly they can then track their social media success by comparing the number of mentions last month vs this month. They can also add a custom campaign to track mentions of a competitor or appellation.

It is a free service for this level of functionality but you can pay for additional features that gives you more data and user accounts as well as allowing you to manage your social media accounts from within Social Connect. At the time of writing they were also about to launch a new service that offered integration with your own CRM systems as well as the ability to measure influence.

6.5.2 Wine Directory

Vintank also assists the wine industry by providing a wine internet database called the Wine Directory.[39] The aim of this free service is to help wineries ensure that businesses use accurate wine information. In particular this is very useful to wine retailers who have struggled to find accurate wine information for their websites and end up spending significant resources to do the simplest eCommerce wine product descriptions.

But lets leave it to Vintank to explain the issue,

> Is your brand being displayed properly in every digital outlet? Clean data is the #1 problem inhibiting the

success of wine online. We found this problem to be endemic & added it to our engine, so you can enter it once and it is distributed to over 300 outlets. But the rub is that most of these sites dont have access to clean wine data. Just 'google' your brand and see how many different ways your wine is being presented in the market. And the companies behind these sites are spending 30% to 50% of their resources generating or scraping data from various sources to try to cobble together information about wine products. And who benefits? Not the consumer, the winery, or the digital platform. We found this problem to be the greatest inhibitor for the entire industry and also a challenge we were facing in matching wines with conversations. Ideally, your wines should be presented with consistency and accuracy across these various outlets. Displaying clean data helps you sell more wine, and it helps consumers find your products quickly and easily. Reality, unfortunately, never quite matches our needs or expectations, and in truth, consistent data distribution is a tremendous problem for the wine industry. All too often, your wines are displayed with incorrect pricing, wrong (or missing) images, and content that is incomplete or inaccurate. We chose to champion this solution not as a company, but as a community of companies (now over 300 strong) by leveraging all the data connections we had to help wineries and tech companies solve this inhibitor to success.

It is not only fixing the inaccurate data issue but also providing a wealth of information wine retailers can use to help sell wine. Wineries upload accurate winery and wine product information including photos, videos, QR codes, location, and even tasting room details that wine retailers (mobile app developers, wine writers/bloggers, wine social networks) can use to more accurately portray your wine.

6.6 Resources

- Internet Measurement Discussion, Update, and Posts Page: www.WineMarketingPros.com/anachap/

- Web Analytics including Google Analytics: Avinash Kaushik `Kaushik.net`
- Vintank Wine Directory and Social Connect: `vintank.com`

Part II

Traffic

The chapters in this part of the book cover most of the ways to increase traffic to your online shop. Indeed how to increase traffic is usually the first question retailers ask when approaching me for advice. However, I think its importance is overestimated. It should be seen as just one part of the process, and it is arguably more important to convert traffic to sales than to build traffic.

Note that I've left social media and location-based services out of this Part. Not because they don't drive traffic, they do, but rather they better fit the Engagement part of the selling wine online process. Indeed social media is increasingly influencing the search engine result page rankings and being used by comparison shopping engines, location based services, and is inherently part of Facebook advertising. So where it makes sense I'll include social media strategies in this Part, but I'll purposely try to leave most of social media to Part III.

7 Search Engine Optimization (SEO)

7.1 What is SEO

Search engines help users find information on the internet. The users enter a search query or 'keyword phrase' and then get presented with a list of results. Search engines create this list by finding most of the web pages on the internet ('crawl' and 'index') and then ranking them for usefulness for particular search queries. These ranked results are then presented in the search engine results page in mere fractions of a second. Its impressive technology with the biggest search engine being Google and the only other one of significance being Bing (which runs Yahoo and Facebook search).

Note that because Google dominates the search engine market, I'll focus almost exclusively on His Majesty's pronouncements and his 'courtiers' analysis of what these really mean.

The search engine results page, see Figure 7.1, has three general parts:

- the left sidebar with search filtering options
- the middle listings (sometimes with Ads at the top in a yellow box or as 'Sponsored' shopping results)
- the right sidebar with advertising listings, also known as Ads, and 'PPC' or 'pay per click'

This chapter is all about the middle results listing also known as 'organic' results. Ways in which you can increase your traffic from the middle section are known as 'search engine optimization' or 'SEO'. However, the way Google makes money is from the advertising listings on the right sidebar. The better Google's search engine results, the more people use Google, the more advertising Google sells, and the higher its profits. Note, confusingly, there are sometimes advertising listings at top of the middle section like the one shaded in yellow in Figure 7.1 and just below the yellow ad is a set of Sponsored shop-

Figure 7.1: Screenshot of Google Search Engine Results Page for 'Napa Valley Merlot'

Web

Images

Maps

Shopping

More

Any time
Past hour
Past 24 hours
Past week
Past month
Past year

All results
Verbatim

Ad

Buy Napa Valley Merlot - The #1 Rated Online Wine Store
www.wine.com/Napa-Valley-Wines
wine.com is rated ★★★★★ (1,582 reviews)
Scheduled Delivery for All Orders.

Sponsored

Shop for **napa valley merlot** on Google

Hall Napa Valley	Duckhorn Merlot	Irony Napa Valley	Provenance Vineyards N...	Stags' Leap Winery
$31.99	$44.97	$13.99	$32.99	$23.97
Wine.com	WineChatea...	Wine.com	Wine.com	Ultimate Win...

Wine reviews and ratings - highly rated **Napa Valley** proprietary red ...
www.amusebouchewine.com/press.html - Cached - Similar
Amuse Bouche wine - a cult **Napa Valley Merlot**. In the ... Highly rated **Napa Valley Merlot** review by Robert Parker Wine Advocate, Jim Laube Wine Spectator , ...

The Chronicle Wine Selections **Napa Valley Merlot** - SFGate
www.sfgate.com/.../The-Chronicle-Wine-Selections-Napa-Valley-Merlot-3183972.php - Cached
Nov 21, 2008 ... Rating: TWO STARS 2005 Cosentino Reserve **Napa Valley Merlot** ($42) Oak spice and toast wrap around savory Chinese herb, graphite and ...

Napa Valley Merlot: Napa Merlot, California Merlot , Merlot Wine
www.hallwines.com/hall-napa-valley-merlot - Cached - Similar
Hall's **Napa Valley Merlot** is crafted from intense aromatics of cedar oak accented by roasted coffee beans with hints of violets and roses. This California Merlot is ...

Napa Valley Merlot: Compare Prices, Reviews & Buy Online ...
shopping.yahoo.com/red-wine/napa-valley.../merlot-wine-varietals/ - Cached
Yahoo! Shopping is the best place to comparison shop for **Napa Valley Merlot**. Compare prices on **Napa Valley Merlot**. Find **Napa Valley Merlot** deals and save.

2010 **Napa Valley Merlot** - Napa Cellars -
www.napacellars.com/Wines/Merlot/ - Cached
The Oak Knoll district of **Napa Valley** is an ideal location for cultivating **Merlot** grapes. Warm days and cool morning fog, rich and well-drained soils all contribute ...

Ads

Merlot Wines
www.winechateau.com/merlot
Buy Great Merlot Wines Here!
On Sale Now Plus 30% Discounts

Buy 90+ Rated Merlot
www.wineaccess.com/
Compare Prices on a wide selection
Great Prices, Service and Selection

Duckhorn Wine Company
www.duckhornwineshop.com/
Voted One of the Top 3 U.S. Wine
Brands. Find Your Varietal Today!

Slingshot Wines
www.slingshotwines.com/
Napa Valley Cabernet Sauvignon
Only $23/bottle or $276 for a case

Napa Valley Visitor Guide
www.napavalley.com/
The best visitors guide to plan
a visit to **Napa Valley**.

Napa Valley Limo Tour
www.napavalleylimos.com/
Expert Wine Touring Guides
Specializing in **Napa** Wineries

Napa Valley Merlot
www.midwestsupplies.com/Homebrew
Your Complete Homebrew Supplier.
Fast Shipping. Order W/ Confidence!

Cakebread Cellars Merlot
www.jbuckley.com/
Over 6000 Fine Wines In Stock.
Wine Concierge Service. Buy Now!

ping results that are just another type of ad called a Google Adwords Product Extension. Ads will be covered in the Internet Advertising chapter.

Companies want to rank higher in the search engine results because they'll get more traffic. Position 1 on the results page doesn't get 10% more traffic than position 2 but rather almost double the traffic[40] (depending on the keyword phrase). Likewise position 2 vs 3, 3 vs 4 etc—think of a logarithmic scale.

Note that ranking is only a means to an end—traffic. So strictly speaking, we measure our SEO results by traffic it generates not the ranking. What's more the ranking you see on your search engine results page will be different from what other people see because Google personalizes results based on a user's browsing history.

Search engine users want the most relevant results for their search query. They want to type in a keyword phrase and see the solution to their search problem straight away. So if someone searches for a popular Napa Valley wine brand name they may want to (a) buy it (b) get information about it, or (c) navigate straight to it. It's difficult to work out what a user wants from a simple phrase. So the search engines provide a list of possible answers hoping that one of them will solve the searcher's problem.

When I searched Google for the merlot product in Figure 7.1, Amuse Bouche winery headed the list, then a newspaper article, then Hall Wines, a Yahoo wine shopping result, a Napa wine store, a wiki website, two more wineries, a price finder website, and lastly a gift company. A nice set of possible answers to an unclear query—and the reason why most people use Google. Google knows users want a list of different answers—not a list of the same answers from different websites (see the 'duplicate content' section later in this chapter).

Google's break-through in search engine accuracy was based around the idea of the number of links or 'votes' that a specific web page got from other websites. Votes were not equal, however. Important websites' votes were regarded as having more authority and given more weighting than other websites. By using this now famous technique, Google took over the search world in the early 2000s.

However, it is not just external links that determine a web page's ranking, there are hundreds of factors. These factors make up a complex mathematical formula called 'The Algorithm'.

7.2 The 'Algorithm'

The relevance and external links to a web page dominate the algorithm. However, in the last couple of years links from other web sites have reduced in importance. [41]

Let's look at the factors in the algorithm. SEOmoz, a leading search engine researcher and commentator, undertook various surveys and studies in 2011 and found that the following factors make up the algorithm, with each factor's weighting in brackets. [41]

Note a 'Page' means one specific page on a website e.g. 'www.example.com/the-specific-page.html'. A domain means the website as a whole e.g. 'example.com'.

7.2.1 Search Engine Factors

Page Level Links was the most important factor in the early days of the algorithm.

1. Page Level Links (22% weight in the algorithm). Key elements are:

- The number of external links to a specific page. The more diverse sources and the higher their authority and trust the better.
- Anchor Text of External Links contains keywords (anchor text, or hyperlink text, is usually blue and underlined). Preferably varied anchor text using targeted keywords from authoritative and trusted websites. Google nowadays also considers the surrounding text around the link.

Page level links are steadily reducing in importance and are half as important as they were in 2009.

2. Domain Level Links (21%). Key elements are:

- How far away your website is linked from a trusted seed set of websites. Trusted seed sets are respected government, university, and large corporate website that Google believes is careful about what webpages are linked to. It has been found that the fewer links your website is from these trusted websites the less likely it will be a spam website.
- The number of external domains that link to your website. The more diverse sources and the higher their authority and trust the better. Having a large quantity of domains is less important

than diversity of domain names.

3. Page Level Keyword Usage (14%). Key elements are:

- Use of keywords earlier in the title tag, headlines, and internal anchor text
- Longer web pages tend to rank better

4. Domain Level Keyword Usage (11%). Key elements are:

- Use of keywords in the website name, the closer the match the better

5. Page Level Social Metrics (7%). Key elements are:

- Facebook shares can be seen by Google, the quantity of shares is important, though Google struggles to see the authority of the sharer
- Tweets are also seen by Google, and their authority can be seen, both authority and quantity are important
- Google+ can be directly influence results both in terms of shares and authority of the sharer

Social signals are likely to increase in weight in future years. Despite not being able to see most Facebook data, Google can use Chrome, Android mobiles, and logged in Gmail users to see social data on external pages, such as shares, likes, and comments. Google+ and '+1' has also become important in 2012 and is increasingly being used to personalize search results[42]

6. Other factors. Key elements are:

- Domain level brand metrics, such as how often it was searched for, the number of mentions on news, and social media websites, social media accounts, Wikipedia citation (7%)
- Other Page factors, such as content uniqueness, load speed, internal links (7%)
- Page Level traffic, such as the percent of users who click on a search result, and the users who click but immediately return to Google (6%)
- Other Domain Level factors, such as content uniqueness across whole website, load speed, internal links, and percent of users who click on a search result, the users who click but immediately return to Google (5%)

7.2.2 Search Engine Strategy in a Nutshell

There are scores of factors which have been summarized above. Put simply though you need to get lots of links from (preferably) high authority web pages where the anchor text of that link includes your keywords. Increasingly, you need a large number of social media shares, especially Facebook, and if you're a local business then you have another chapter to go on this—the Local SEO chapter.

Note that the only significant control you have is what you do on your own website or 'On-Page'—everything else is controlled by third parties. So getting to the top of Google rankings, with the resulting huge boost in traffic, comes down to getting other quality sites to link to, or share links about, your website. In my humble opinion, and in the opinion of other people with far more expertise like SEOmoz and even Google, this is mostly about creating unique and compelling content, while making sure you have done the technical on-page basics well enough.

A web developer will often say they have made sure your website is 'search engine optimized'. By which they most often mean the keywords are in the right places, and there is nothing technically stopping the website being crawled by Google. What they don't mean is that they have helped you get external links to your website, encouraged social sharing, and worked with you to build compelling content. SEO is more of an ongoing process than a web page development. Here's the process I recommend.

7.3 SEO Process

The process has eight stages.

1. Objectives. Like all internet marketing campaigns SEO should start with a particular Business Objective in mind. We'll cover our example wine store at the end of this chapter but other goals may be to be build brand awareness for a new winery, send leads to retailers, and of course sell wine online.

2. Search Personas. We covered wine consumer research extensively in the Customer Chapter so we're off to a good start. Who is your target market, and what are they interested in? There is likely to be a difference between the segments. The Enthusiast will be much more interested in technical data, regional information, interesting varietals, vintage charts, etc. The Image Seeker is going to

be more interested in who is drinking this wine, what places stock it, and how it's rated.

3. Keywords. Here we list all the keyword phrases that our personas are likely to use when searching. Some will be more important for traffic reasons, and others will be more important for sales reasons. Some can be discarded as unimportant or perhaps too competitive. Each page on your website will have a primary keyword phrase it is targeting.

4. Competitors and Rankings. For each important keyword phrase how do we stack up versus our competitors? For a wine store, this is the few other wine suppliers in a block, suburb, or town. However a winery will have to look at competitors in a sub region by varietal by price point or some such categorization. A winery may even need to add location onto this as Californian wines will be a source of competition in San Francisco but French wines may be a bigger competitor in London.

5. On Page SEO. This is where you make sure your keyword is prominently displayed on your website in all the right places like headlines and anchor text. You may also want to make sure that you have a strong call to action of some sort (like a Buy button) to drive an action that will deliver your business objectives. Nowadays, Google also measures how easy to use and professional-looking your website is.

6. Technical Analysis. Here you make sure that you do not have technical issues with your website that stops the Google robot crawling and indexing your web pages or sends it confusing signals (e.g. broken links, robot.txt file, too many navigation levels, duplicate content).

7. Link Building. SEO success is traditionally from getting high value links from high authority relevant websites. There are all sorts of ways you can do this not the least being creating great content.

8. Analyze Results. Most companies use Google Analytics to measure how well their SEO tactics are going and whether they are meeting business objectives. Google Analytics will show you how much organic search engine traffic you are getting for each keyword and whether it is leading to conversions.

We've covered objectives in the Company chapter and Personas in the Customer chapter let's start with keywords.

7.4 Keywords

Both SEO and PPC rely on search keywords (keywords are the words you type into the Google search box on google.com). There is a continuum of keywords from browsing words like *wine* through to category phrases like *merlot* through to purchasing phrases like *buy Andrea's Vineyard Napa Valley 2005* with lots of different combinations of these along the continuum e.g. *Californian merlot* or *Andrea's Vineyard wine.*

About 10-20% of searched for keywords in the wine industry will form the 'fat head' of a long tail graph. That is about 10-20% will make up 60% to 90% of all searches. Then about 10-20% of keywords a chunky middle will make up a further, say, 20% of searches. With the last 60-80% making up the remainder of keywords. [43]

My own research shows that fat head keyword phrases will be dominated by country/region plus varietal, and varietal phrases. For example, a fat head keyword would be something like 'wine', 'French wine', or 'merlot'. Chunky middle keyword phrases will be dominated by smaller regions plus varietals and less popular varietals plus regions phrases. A chunky middle keyword would be perhaps 'willamette valley wine'. A long tail keyword may be 'buy Andrea's Vineyard Napa Valley Merlot 2005'.

Let's look at that purchasing phrase a bit more closely, specifically the words:

buy + Andrea's Vineyard + Napa Valley + Merlot + 2005

buy + brand + (sub)region + varietal + vintage (in various combinations)

To see this on your own website, ask your webmaster to send you the keyword phrases from your server logs, and/or run a Google Analytics report for keywords.

The closer to the 'long tail' phrase the more likely they are to purchase. They may have started with 'Californian wine', found too many results, changed the search keyword phrase to 'Californian merlot', and found some interesting results. From browsing those results they see Napa Valley being mentioned time and again so they search on 'napa merlot'. They click on various results and see that a number of good results that may include wine retailers, wineries, and appellation websites including your website. Finally they decide to buy our example winery's wine, Andrea's Vineyard Napa Valley Merlot 2005, so they search for 'buy Andrea's Vineyard Napa Valley Merlot 2005'.

In SEO we want your website to appear as far up and down that search continuum as reasonably possible—reasonable expectations would be in the long tail and hopefully the chunky middle. Unless you are a well-known retail or winery brand in which case you stand a chance to feature in the big head of search results (also note that location helps too but that is the next chapter, Local SEO).

7.4.1 Short Head Keywords

These will make good 'category' pages in a wine retailer's website. These tend to be the varietal. For a wine retailer, I'd suggest at least the following varietals (based on US keyword data):

- merlot
- pinot noir
- cabernet sauvignon
- syrah, syrah
- zinfandel
- sauvignon blanc
- chardonnay
- moscato
- sparkling
- and other varietals depending on your sales mix, such as pinot grigio, malbec, riesling, muscat, barolo, gewurztraminer, tempranillo, white zinfandel, viognier, bordeaux wine, burgundy wine, sangiovese, carmenere, grenache, barbera, chenin blanc, pinot gris, albarino, cabernet franc, petite sirah

The regions should also probably be included (based on US keyword traffic):

- french wine
- spanish wine
- italian wine
- german wine
- australian wine
- californian wine
- as well as some other regions depending on your sales mix

e.g. new zealand wine, bordeaux wine, burgundy wine, virginia wine, argentina wine, chilean wine, portuguese wine, croatian wine, oregon wine

Exactly what regions will depend on where your store is. If it is in Oregon or Central Coast then you may want to list the Oregon or Central Coast sub regions for example.

These Short Head keywords may well form the product (left hand) navigation menu of a normal wine retailer's web site. Each page would have a keyword rich description of the varietal or region with the top wines from each sub category page listed. Note it will be difficult to rank well for these keywords.

In the case of a winery, you may want to write a blog post or web page about each fat head keyword, though you will probably want to start with the chunky middle first. You may choose to make these fat head keyword pages on your navigation, though I think chunky middle keywords are better ones to target first.

7.4.2 Chunky Middle Keywords

In the case of a wine retailer, the sub category pages would then be the sub region and varietal combinations, for example Napa Merlot or Santa Maria Pinot Noir. These chunky middle keywords make good sub category pages for SEO purposes. They have enough traffic and are close enough to purchase phrases to be worth continually investing time and money in, rather than just at the web page set-up stage. Work hard on creating as great sub category page content though it shouldn't be too long as you want your products to appear high up the page not invisible 'below the fold'.

This is also the most likely keyword phrase for a winery to focus on first for the same reasons though probably in a blog post format rather on an eCommerce subcategory page. As mentioned above, you could also link to it in your main navigation menu. Note they are also good internet advertising keywords for both wineries and wine retailers.

7.4.3 Long Tail Keywords

Long tail keywords are all the variations of 'buy + brand + subregion + region + country + varietal + vintage'. These keywords are very important as the searcher is much closer to having purchase intent vs higher traffic, though more research-focused, fat head, and chunky middle keywords. Your product purchase pages will focus on these. I believe the best practice is to have pages focused on the product regardless of vintages if possible. Where vintage is important, as in cult wines, I accept that you may need to have vintage pages for each product. In the case of a winery, these product pages should also be focused on wine product information with links to separate vintage sales pages. By separating out vintage from product the page will never go out of date and can build up links over a number of years not just on the vintage release year.

7.4.4 Wine Retail Store Categories

Imagine your 'brick and mortar' wine retail store had no categories— you had the varietals and regions all mixed up, not sorted into shelves, with no signs indicating categories. Ridiculous right? This is what search engines face every day. If they come across a website with all sorts of products haphazardly spread across the website they struggle to work out what the website is all about.

If a Google user searches for *merlot*, Google will know that the top online wine retailers have a part of their website about *merlot*. That's because they clearly 'theme' parts of their website. These themes are based on important keywords, including *merlot*. Google is happy to list these websites in their search results page over other less clearly optimized websites. When building a wine retail eCommerce site, we want to decide what keywords are most important and create 'themes' or 'silos'[44] for these.

Search engines want to assess your site for subject matter expertise. It's pretty easy to show them you sell wine. It's much harder to show them that you are a subject matter expert on Napa Merlot. It's even harder to show them you have more information about Andrea's Vineyard Napa Merlot than your competitors. And it's harder still to tell them that you are a subject matter expert for:

- wine buyers
- who live near your store
- who want to buy Andrea's Vineyard Napa Merlot 2007

There may be hundreds of wine websites that sell a particular wine brand. Most of them may have respectable eCommerce websites with a Merlot category. Many of them are in your town. How do you show your website has a better search result than any of your competitors? Clearly show Google that you are a subject matter expert for wine categories. In this case the category, or what I call a 'theme', would be merlot. With a sub theme of Napa merlot and the product Andreas Vineyard Napa Merlot. You clearly flag to Google your subject matter expertise by keeping your products in strict themes. You write unique content about each theme and sub theme, and carefully delineate themes through internal links.

Now when Google looks at your site it sees that:

- the major theme is *wine store* and there are clearly some other (sub) themes
- one of them is *merlot* and there is some interesting unique content about your merlot range that Google's users may find very useful
- there is clearly another sub theme in the merlot theme about *Napa merlot* with some more interesting content
- you can buy Napa merlot products

Note that you can reuse this content in your advertising campaigns, as I'll cover in other chapters. You can also use this content to spread your word in the social media world, which I cover at length in later chapters as well.

What are the most important themes or keyword phrase search terms? I have spent more hours over the last few years working on this than I'd care to admit. The answer is the actual product names e.g. Andrea's Vineyard Napa Merlot. This is because these are keyword search phrases that people often buy on. However, I'll argue below to use varietals if you have many products.

If you're a wine retailer then you probably have hundreds of products so you need to sort them into categories for your human customers and search engine robots. For wine website themes, this is how I do it:

- Your major theme is pretty obvious: wine (and probably spirits, but I'll ignore spirits)
- The sub themes are the popular varietals, see the Short Head Keyword section above
- Your sub-sub themes are the varietal regions e.g. Napa Merlot. If you have thousands of products you may need to have a subset of regions e.g. Los Carneros Merlot
- Your product page (or 'buy' page) is the wine itself e.g Andrea's Vineyard Napa Merlot, this may remain the same as vintages

come and go, or you may need another layer of product page by vintage

Any wines you want given special attention would be linked from higher theme levels. So if you wanted to promote Andrea's Vineyard Napa Merlot then you would link it to the merlot sub theme page or even the home page. The wines you choose to feature this way are likely to be the ones that provide you with the best sales contribution i.e. good sales volumes at great margins.

You then build a 'Pyramid' to support these themes. Think of the top of the pyramid being supported by the themes below, which in turn are supported by the themes below that. The thinking goes like this:

- The home page is the theme of our website: *wine*
- We will focus our initial SEO effort on *merlot* and create a sub theme page with unique and compelling content about our store's merlot range. The keyword *merlot* has much more volume than *Andrea's Vineyard Napa* or *Napa wine*. These *category* pages are very important for SEO and also for internet advertising
- We create a sub-sub theme page with unique and compelling content about our store's Napa merlot range. Or perhaps this is a Californian merlot page if you can fit all the products on one page. These *sub-category* pages are also important for SEO and also for internet advertising
- If you have a large store then you may want to create a sub-sub-category page but the aim is to limit the number of clicks to 3-4 from the home page. Any more than that and we may lose the human's interest as well as the Google robot
- We then ensure that the Napa merlot products we most want to promote (high margin and good sales volume) are listed on the Napa merlot category page

The diagram in Figure 7.2 shows this using an organizational chart.

You could sensibly argue that if you're a wine expert on particular regions then it may make sense to sub theme by region not varietal. Alternatively you may specialize in particular wineries or brands in which case you could even sub theme by winery or brand. In the end it may depend on your particular circumstances.

Note 'siloing' or theming was first published by a well-known SEO

Figure 7.2: Wine Silo Categories

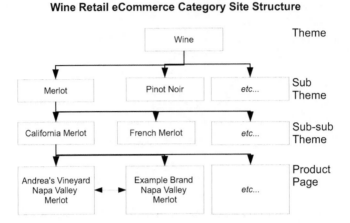

expert Bruce Clay.[44] Given that only the search engines know exactly how their algorithms work, SEO experts are simply using their experience and testing to estimate what works best. This siloing strategy is not accepted by all SEO practitioners.

Also note that wineries that only have 5-10 products can put product listings on the home page of the website (with no categories). It makes it easy for Google (and humans) to find your most important 'buy' pages directly from your home page. No need to bother careful sub-theming if you have only have a few products.

We haven't covered all sorts of other keyword phrases you could target such as 'top Napa Merlot wines' or 'Paso Robles Pinot 2011 ratings and reviews'. There is a wealth of keywords you can find by searching Google Analytics, web log search phrases, top competitor websites, and Google Adwords Keyword tool.

We also haven't covered the keyword phrase wine store plus location e.g. *wine store chicago* because we'll cover optimizing for local search in the Local SEO chapter. What will be important is having a Google+ Local account and ensuring you clearly identify your wine store with a city on your webpages.

7.5 Competitors and Rankings

Having decided on the keyword phrases we want to rank for, we now need to measure how we stack up versus a competitor set. To decide on competitors, we look at this online as well as those physically nearby.

When you are searching remember to append the search parameter *&pws=0* to the end of the search result url to ensure you turn off any personalized results. Otherwise, you will be getting results skewed towards your own search history.

Wine Store. For a wine store firstly list the other key local competitors in a block, suburb, or town depending on whether you are in New York or a small town. Then for your most important keywords, search Google and record the rankings of your store, local wine store competitors, and big online competitors (e.g. wine.com, Amazon) in a spreadsheet, along with the exact web page address as displayed in Google search.

Winery. Listing competitors for a winery is more difficult. A winery will need to look at competitors in a sub region by varietal by price point or some such categorization as described in the Competitor section of the Company—Winery chapter. Then for your most important keywords, search Google and record the rankings of your winery and competitors in a spreadsheet.

A regular task of your SEO efforts will be to gauge how successful your ranking efforts are each week or month vs your competitors. This is a good proxy for how much traffic you can expect to get and hopefully sales. There are good search engine tools you can use, such as SEOmoz, that help you do this automatically.

Now we need to analyze why your competitors are doing so well. There may be issues with your website that you can fix, called Crawl Diagnostics and On-Page SEO, or your competitors may have external website links that you don't, called Link Analysis.

7.6 Basic On-Page SEO

Now we have a list of every keyword phrase we want to rank well for that includes the relevant web page, meta description, keywords in the right places, and call to action of some kind. In particular, have your wine keyword phrases in the:

- Title tag
- Anchor text
- Headline and Body copy
- Meta description tag
- URL

No point in trying to out-game Google, just write naturally, but make sure you have the targeted keywords in the places above.

Title Tags

A title tag is the strip at the very top of your browser, see Figure 7.3. The title tag tells search engines what the topic of the particular page

Figure 7.3: The Title tag is at the top of this screen grab 'Selling Wine Online' using one of my websites as an example

is about. It is generally regarded as being the most important factor for On-Page SEO. Your eCommerce software will provide an obvious place to edit the title on the admin page where you edit the content itself.

Unwittingly, many businesses don't do this. Instead, they use a default title (e.g. *Tony's Wine Store*) on all pages and lose crucial search engine influence. You should ensure your keywords, perhaps *Andrea's Vineyard Merlot Napa Valley* or *Merlot Wine*, are the title tag, thereby, sending a strong signal to search engines about this page. You also gain favor from your search engine results page human readers.

This same title tag is used as the first blue line in search engine results (the first line below). So if a consumer was searching for *Merlot Napa Valley*, then the result will look like Figure 7.4. Notice how the keywords the consumer searched for are in bold in Figure 7.4. Direct response copywriting also says that the headline is the most important influence on consumer response rates. The consumer is trying

Figure 7.4: The 'Title' tag is the first line in the Google search results
Andrea's Vineyard Merlot Napa Valley
www.tonyswinestore.com/andreas-vineyard-**merlot**-**napa**-**valley**.html
This **Napa Valley Merlot** is made in an intense fruit forward style and reveals black berry fruit aromas of plum, cherry, blueberry with a complex. . .

to purchase this wine as easily as possible. He's on a 'scent trail' and the search has given him 10 results. The wine he is searching for is in one of the listings, in blue at the top, and in bold. He's on to something and will click it to find out more.

Now assuming that Tony's Wine Store used a default title tag, then it will look like Figure 7.6. It is too general and not directly linking

Figure 7.5: Default title tag as the first line
Tony's Wine Store
www.tonyswinestore.com/avnb1232?mnp+cfsd.asp
Tony's Wine Store offers a great range of wines at great prices with personal service. Find out what specials we have on today and buy it online

the inquirer's search to the listing result. Make your titles unique to the content of the page—for the robots and the humans.

Anchor Text (internal)

A website link, or hyperlink, is made up of two layers. The top visible layer that a reader can see (usually blue and underlined) e.g. Merlot Wine. Beneath that is the linked web page address (URL) that they often can't see e.g `http://www.tonyswinestore.com/merlotwine`. The text that they can see is called an 'anchor link' and is a very important SEO factor especially when linked from external websites to your website—though we are referring to links within your website here.

When you are linking, make sure you use an important keyword phrase as the anchor text. Never have, for example, click here or read more... , but rather Merlot or French Wine .

Keep this in mind for navigation menus as well. An 'Adobe Flash' or image based navigation menu that hasn't been set-up to be read by Google will limit the power of this SEO factor.

Headline and Body copy

The 'headline' or 'heading' (but not the title which is confusing some-thing else in the internet world) is usually the first bolded large font phrase on your webpage. Headlines are bigger and bolder than the rest of the page so they are seen by humans as an important relevance indicator (just like direct marketing headlines). When you write your content, your editor will usually allow you to highlight a phrase as Heading 1, Heading 2, Heading 3, etc. Or it may automatically make the product name or blog post title a Heading.

Google uses basic html code called an <h> or heading tag to find headings. It sees an <h1> as a more important indicator of keyword phrase relevance than a <h2> or <h3> tag. So you want to ensure that your targeted keyword phrase is included, preferably in the first few words of the headline (if that reads well).

The 'body copy' is the text below the headline. You also want to make sure you have your targeted keyword phrase in the body copy, preferably in the first 100 words (the theory is these words are given greater weight by Google). No point in trying to out-game Google, just write naturally, but make sure you have the keywords in place in this section. There used to be a fair amount of focus on 'keyword density'—the % of keyword phrases vs total words on the page. As long as you write naturally, you can just ignore this, but do not purposely 'stuff' your page with your keyword phrase or forget to include it.

The Meta Description Tag

Like the title tag, the meta description tag tells searchers what the page is about. Whereas, the title tag is restricted to just a sentence, the meta name description tag can be a short paragraph. You see the Title tag at the top of the web page; however, you don't see a meta description tag displayed on your web page though it exists as I'll show you shortly. You don't want it too short or too long, nor do you want to duplicate it across pages. So let's go back to our search engine result example in Figure 7.6. The description appears in lines 3 and 4.

Google will look at your page and aim to find a snippet of text that best describes what the page is all about. It may decide that

Figure 7.6: The meta description tag

Andrea's Vineyard Merlot Napa Valley
www.tonyswinestore.com/andreas-vineyard-**merlot**-**napa**-**valley**.html
This **Napa Valley Merlot** is made in an intense fruit forward style and reveals
black berry fruit aromas of plum, cherry, blueberry with a complex . . .

this meta description is best. Or it may choose another snippet if it thinks that offers a better description. Your aim is to recommend the description that you think is representative and will get people to click on your link. If Google agrees then your carefully written statement will be displayed. Note that the consumers' query words will be bolded in this snippet as well as on the other lines.

The meta description is shown on the 'head' part of your web page (I promise to keep the technical stuff to an absolute minimum). Essentially a web page is html code that is made pretty for readers. Under this pretty presentation, the web page is ordered and structured as follows:

- I'm an html page
- Here's some stuff you need to know about how to present me to humans, search engine robots, and other software—the 'head'
- Here's my the text (and photos) for humans and search engines to read—the 'body'

Still reading? Because I'm about to ask you to look at the code of a webpage. Open up a browser go to www.WineMarketingPros.com. Go to your browser menu and View >Page Source[1]. A new page will open and at the top of the page, usually around lines 4 to 11 will be the html tag (a tag is html code that is enclosed in <>brackets):

```
meta name = "description" content ="A community..."
```

Where it says *content ="A community of wine businesses providing online marketing support and advice. Led by the author or Wine Marketing Online, Bruce McGechan"* is what the Google robot reads and may display in its search engine results page (unless it feels there is a better phrase to use).

---

[1]Internet Explorer: View >Source. Firefox: View >Page Source. Safari: View >View Source. Chrome: View >Developer >View Source.

On a wine eCommerce website administration product page, it usually has fields for the Meta Title, Meta Keywords, and Meta Description. Meta keywords are no longer considered by Google, so ignore this field. In the case of the Magento eCommerce system, it's on the product set up page. The normal (but not necessarily the best) practice is to fill this out with a short tasting note.

The ability to view the Page Source code means you can see all the invisible elements that are obliquely referred to in this section.

URLs

The URL (Uniform Resource Locator) is what you type into a web browser e.g. `http://www.winemarketingpros.com` and is also known as a web page address. Remember the name of the game is for Google and humans to rate you highly for certain search term queries or keywords (listed in this previous post). See Figure 7.7 for how the search phrase *Napa Valley Merlot* appears. The URL is on line 2.

Figure 7.7: A good search engine results page listing.

Andrea's Vineyard Merlot Napa Valley
www.tonyswinestore.com/andreas-vineyard-**merlot**-**napa**-**valley**.html
This **Napa Valley Merlot** is made in an intense fruit forward style and reveals black berry fruit aromas of plum, cherry, blueberry with a complex ...

Let's compare it to our poor example in Figure 7.8.

Figure 7.8: A poor search engine results page listing.

Tony's Wine Store
www.tonyswinestore.com/avnb1232?mnp+cfsd.asp
Tony's Wine Store offers a great range of wines at great prices with personal service. Find out what specials we have on today and buy it online.

We have two audiences—Google and those good ol' humans. Both of them are going to be confused or skeptical about:
avnb1232?mnp+cfsd.asp

But it gets even worse. Say a wine blogger recommends on their blog that a wine be purchased through your website. They may not bother providing anchor text, they'll do the easy thing and just copy

and paste whatever URL they see. If their readers see,
www.tonyswinestore.com/andreas-vineyard-merlot-napa-valley.html
then they'll be a lot more reassured that the URL is taking them to
a relevant page than,
www.tonyswinestore.com/avnb1232?mnp+cfsd.asp.
Make your URLs suggest what the page content is—for the robots
and the humans.

Most eCommerce software does a good job providing fields for entering custom title tags and meta descriptions. It's not always the
case with URLs. An easy way to check is to find a prospective ven-
dor's wine eCommerce website, click on a product page, and check
out whether the URL is complete gobbledygook or has the relevant
keywords in them.

A good web page also has a strong call to action probably to buy a
wine. This is such an important area it has its own name, Conversion,
and its own chapter called Conversion Rate Optimization.

7.7 Technical Analysis

You may be doing everything well but there is a technical issue with
your website. Infamously, WordPress websites use to be installed
with a Privacy option selected that blocks Google from crawling the
website.

Here are the key critical issues:

- Broken links resulting in Error Page codes starting with 4 e.g.
  404 Error code
- A server error resulting in Error Page codes starting with 5
- Duplicate Page Content is where there is content on one page
  that is similar to content on other pages on your website. This
  may result in search engines not knowing which page to include
  in their index and reduce the ranking of all the affected pages.
- Search engine crawlers blocked by robots.txt in where you un-
  intentionally block Google from crawling your website resulting
  in your pages not appearing in search results.

All of these can be fixed by your web developer or a savvy technical
SEO person. Other issues include long meta descriptions, title tags,
temporary web page redirects, and overly dynamic URLs. Likewise,
these can also be fixed.

There are also other technical elements to a website that a good

SEO person will provide advice on these include having a good xml sitemap and ensuring you don't have too many pages in your results. Doing both of these will ensure Google crawls all of your website.

7.8 Link Building

We know our keywords, we've identified our competitors, ranked us vs them, we've made sure that keywords are in the right places, and there aren't any technical issues. The next step is to boost our rankings by earning links.

This is also the area of 'blackhat' and voodoo SEO. That is websites such as those that manipulate results by listing in cheap low quality (directory) websites, send you those annoying emails asking you to link to their websites (sometimes offering to pay), ask for simple reciprocal link pages, make spam blog comments, and create 'link farms'. Google hates these sites as they ruin their search engine results and make for poor user search experience. These tactics may work for awhile but then Google finds a way to block them from showing up in search engine results page through updating its algorithms. These Google updates, which have vague names like Farmer, May Day, Penguin, and Panda, become big news in the internet marketing world. This book does not cover blackhat techniques as any advantage is both fleeting and insecure.

7.8.1 Competitors Links

Ranking by pages by analyzing the quality and quantity of high authority relevant external links is at the heart of Google's search engine accuracy and success. Many more things have happened to the Google Algorithm since those heady days at the turn of the century, but good links remains highly important to doing well.

Ranking is by its nature relative. You only need to be doing a bit better than your competitors to be ranked higher in Google's search engine results page. So naturally the first place we head is to a tool that helps compare our website to other competitors, it's called `OpenSiteExplorer.com` by SEOmoz.

This tool is a close-enough approximation to Google's algorithm and is based on some hefty software coding by SEOmoz that replicates Google's search engine processes. It has some metrics across the top, along with six tabs that show more detailed information.

Take each competitor's web page address as recorded in the spreadsheet you created and paste it into the box at the top of the page. OpenSiteExplorer will then find all the inbound links for that web page (the free version limits this to the top few). Now you know where their most powerful links are coming from, and you can target these websites yourself.

When you approach a website directly, it's called 'outreach'. The best way to do this is to carefully research who owns the website and then help them out first, perhaps write a blog post and link to them, tweet their blog posts, post about their service on your Facebook page, or refer people to them. Then at some stage send them a friendly email asking the person if they would mind linking to your particular web page. You want to make this linking as hassle-free as possible. Perhaps you offer to write a guest blog post they could use[45].

Some of these links may come from (non local) directories and other sources that do not require the effort above. Absolutely target these, but beware that Google has started to ignore such easily-built links.

On the positive side, Google is becoming so sophisticated (and so determined not to lose the blackhat battle) that they are prepared to accept citations rather than links. This is where your brand is mentioned on the web near an important keyword phrase with no hyperlink back to your website. They also attach trust to websites that have indicators of physical addresses, followed social media accounts, clear contact information, and register with government organizations.

The other way is to create great content and attract inbound links without asking. Let's look at this some more.

7.8.2 Creating Great Content

What you shouldn't do is use wineries' wine descriptions at the top of the page. Let's be honest, we sometimes don't bother writing new wine descriptions for our website. We're tired, we've got a lot to do, and sometimes we're just not up to sitting down in front of the computer writing about wine for a future sale. Especially when there are more immediate tasks that need to be done.

Copying wine descriptions isn't really an issue with wineries given that they are usually very happy with wine retailers using their wine description (note there could be copyright issues though). The issue is with Google. Google is smart; it is very user-focused and knows that searchers do not want the same content for every link in a Google search results page. So Google detects duplication of page content.

Here is how one of Google's top search engineers, Matt Cutts, answered this question, 'What are your opinions on optimizing an eCommerce website where the main pages/products may not necessarily be rich in content?', on the Google YouTube channel, [46]

That's a tough question, alright. Essentially you are saying here's a place where you can buy products and there's not a lot of content or may be the content is duplicated from a bunch of places. So my short answer is put on your user-hat.

If you type in a product and you get a ton of places to buy things and there's no real information on that page, and there's no real value add, and all you get is places to buy then you get pretty annoyed. In fact whenever we ask your users, 'whats the top issue for you these days?' it's less about web spam like cloaking or hidden text or other stuff like that and more about search quality issue, 'Oh I don't like how many commercial results I see' or 'I get too many products or too many comparison shopping sites' or things like that.

So that's the sentiment that we've heard a lot, and what you should be asking yourself is, 'do I want to take that step, do I want to make an eCommerce site if I dont have a lot of original content or value add? Or if I have a lot of duplicate content or if it's in a filler feed and if there's really not that much that I'm adding to it.'

And so I'd ask you, 'if you really want to jump into that and start optimizing that?', or do you want to look into something more original, something more compelling, some other hook that you could get a lot of visitors for?

And so my advice is, if possible think about how you can move towards that high value add, unique sort of site not just a site that somebody might view it as cookie cutter, or they get annoyed about if they land and find a page just looks like 500 other pages that they have just seen on the web. So those are the sort of things to think about.

Top ranking websites have unique content. That means using winery descriptions as secondary information below your unique content. Google knows if a wine description is a duplication of the winery's description. It only wants to include the 'best page' and probably regards the 'best page' as the winery's product page. Therefore, the winery will get the ranking for its own page. The rest of the pages using the same content will be either discarded or given a poor ranking in organic search results.

Combine it with your own original content, so you could have:

- your unique wine description
- wine experts reviews
- the winery description
- and hopefully customers reviews

Or at the very least reword the winery's description. That might be enough for Google to regard it as unique and not a duplicate. Though no one really knows because Google only reveals a few of the elements of its algorithm.

So what should we do with wine descriptions? If you have lots of new releases and you want to get them onto the website soonest then here are the options,

- Use the winery description; just accept that you will be ranked poorly in the Google organic results
- reword the description enough (just what that means needs testing and experimentation but will most probably mean completely rewriting the first 100 words)
- write your own descriptions and combine them with wine writers' and wineries' reviews to ensure a unique and useful page (hopefully with customer reviews as well)

I recommend the last one.

Writing Content

If you draw people to your site through great content then Google will start to notice and rank your site higher. Because you are ranked higher you will get more visits. More visitors will comment and share (on blogs, forums, email, chat, various social media sites) which Google will also notice, and rank your site higher as a result...a virtuous circle. Having done this for a while, you get lots of traffic.

This is hard work, I agree, but given it's probably the most important thing you can do here are some tips.

Take apart any information provided by the winemaker, such as:

- winemaker's tasting notes
- other winemaker's notes (% de-stemmed, days skin contact, oak, % new oak, fining, filtration, indigenous/cultured yeast fermentation, etc.)
- winegrower's notes (yield, vine age, clones, soil, canopy system, etc.)
- images of the label—either the bottle or the label itself

Add your review and rating with this information in mind. This should give you unique content that may reference key winery facts (also check out vintank.com's Wine Directory for a central, accurate wine information database from participating wineries).

If it's for an important keyword then:

- have a chat with the winemaker or wine grower
- have a chat with a local sommelier
- use terroir as a thought provoker: soil type, weather, topography, people
- if you're a foodie then use food pairings as a thought provoker

Ideally you'll also have:

- user reviews
- user ratings—5-star or 100-point systems
- expert reviews and ratings
- badge systems with accompanying text—the wine is representative of a particular style (e.g. wine blogger Joe Roberts badge rating system)
- recommendations—if you like this popular wine X then you might like this related but unknown wine Y

Indeed you may want to become an expert for a sub region varietal, write and report about this topic.

Tasting events are going to become a big deal for content creation—at your store or elsewhere. This provides ways to discuss your thoughts with others helping to coalesce your thoughts on important keyword web pages.

Other topics for a keyword phrase might include:

- the best wine ever tasted
- the most expensive wine you've ever drunk

- blind tasting of wines
- local chef's (and trade customer's) thoughts on what wine goes with what dish (joint promo in effect)
- gift ideas, by occasion—birthdays, weddings, Valentine's, etc.
- maps of particular regions and why a vineyard does well there
- personal wine travel experiences to this region and that vineyard

Other ways may include:

- video—with written transcript and important keywords in description
- podcast—with written transcript and important keywords in description
- blog posts—entries that capture your thoughts as wines come in or topics arise

Also, don't forget to ask your customers in person, via email, or with a social media post what interesting information they want to know about your keyword and use that to drive ideas as well.

Write conversationally but well. I try to make my posts easy to read by using headings, bullet points, and short paragraphs (unlike this book which tends to be more formally formatted).

I never have a long paragraph in my blog posts. If a paragraph becomes longer than I would prefer, then I bold key phrases for the 'scanners'. People don't read web pages so much as scan them, so your key points need to stand out to ensure attention. Also, split out your topic into sub blocks with sub headings—good for readability as well as Google robots.

7.9 Case Study: How a Cheese Store did better than a Wine Store with Google

In June 2010, I was investigating wine SEO for wine internet shoppers who lived in CA 90210. I kept seeing K&L Wines pop up. I was impressed by their results and with their physical wine stores, so I decided to delve into why they were doing so well. The results were not what I expected.

K&L Wines had disappeared from organic results. My original intention of working out what K&L Wines was doing correctly had been replaced by what it was doing incorrectly in organic search.

Don't get me wrong, K&L Wines usually does a great job with local search ('local business results') and adwords (right hand side). They were just struggling with organic search for searches with 90210 location related phrases in them (organic search is the normal listings in the center of a Google search results page). The reason why was because they had some strong competition.

Meet the Cheese Store that is beating the Wine Store!

The Cheese Store of Beverly Hills was ranked in the top two places in local search and organic search—check out their site: `www.cheesestorebh.com`. It is a good functional website with no obvious reason to be doing so well. Let's dig into them a little more.

This cheese store has 686 external links from 250 unique websites (as at June 2010)! Sure they also sell wine but not prominently on their website. I visited the store in 2012 and saw that perhaps one quarter was wine and the rest was cheese.

It is the external links that are driving the store up the Google rankings. The links are from well-trusted sites like `www.privatechefsinc.com/chefs.htm` and `www.thefoodpaper.com`. They also seem to be well covered by journalists as I see loads of reviews (mainly about cheese) in the external link listings. They do well with suppliers linking to their store from supplier websites—a good thing to ask your rep the next time they see you!

So what had K&L Wines done wrong (when it had already done so much right)?

- It only had one external link (as of Jun-10; it has many more now)
- It was not clearly separating its stores

In comparison, Beverly Hills Wine Merchant has 15 external links, and Vendome Wine & Spirits has 25. Both of these stores have Beverly Hills in their web address— a great local business SEO practice. If K&L wants to do better they need to create a Beverly Hills 90210 website presence.

Here's what they should look at doing. Firstly, let's be clear—the internet marketing team behind `kandlwines.com` are very professional. They just had a gap in their armor—'organic SEO'. Secondly, SEO metrics suggest that this local wine internet market was not overly competitive especially for wine related pages. So K&L Wines is/was still in the game.

My Local Wine Store SEO recommendations for K&L

Note some long URLs have been truncated.

1. Location. Their overall website was excellent, but they were not being associated with their locations—in particular the Beverly Hills location. This is because they have three stores; whereas, the others seem to be sole stores. The three K&L store addresses appeared on the same single K&L 'Locations' web page. Their Beverly Hills competitors all have a physical store address on most of their web pages. So what K&L Wines could do is create webpages that are dedicated to various stores. Here are some options:

- They might even go as far as using new websites with new domain names for (two of the) stores e.g. `HollywoodKandLWines.com` (note using Magento eCommerce a company can have many websites but with just one backend system for administering orders)
- Or different stores in different subdomains e.g. `beverlyhills.kandlwines.com`
- Or different stores in different subfolders e.g. `kandlwines.com/beverlyhills/`
- Or they may get away with very good web pages optimized for local searches e.g. `kandlwines.com/wine-store-hollywood.html` with a Google Map insert and address text

They also needed to be more consistent with their results in Google Maps by updating their Google+ Local account. Sometimes they were listed as K&L and sometimes as K&L Wine Merchants. On their website location page they say K&L Hollywood. Each listing of each store needs to be exactly the same everywhere from phone number to character spaces in the retail address.

2. External Links. They then need trusted websites from LA to link to their LA pages. Check out these high value links for some of their competitors :

- KCRW Radio Guest Interview about Cheese Store of Beverly Hills Comme Ca's Fromager `www.kcrw.com/etc/programs/gf/gf080315mood_foods_american_`
- KCRW Radio Directory Listing for a Fringe Benefits card Wine Valet at Two Rodeo Drive: `www.kcrw.com/benefits/list?c=35`
- Local Directory Listing for the cheese guys: `www.at-la.com/biz/@la-market.htm`

- A number of wine retailers listed in supplier La Fenetre's website, e.g. `www.timelesspalateswine.com/home/index.php`

And lastly, an external site that has all sorts of issues but some good links, it's from Beverly Hills Conference and Visitors Bureau:

- Tasting with the cheese guys, e.g.`beverlyhillsbehere.com/cvbgeneral.asp?id=411`
- Then a listing of the cheese guys, e.g.`beverlyhillsbehere.com/cvbmembers_print.asp`

There are hundreds of other links but I choose these as they were rated highly in my SEO software (SEOmoz Pro).

3. Anchor Text of these links. The anchor text (usually blue and underlined) from the LA websites to K&L should promote Beverly Hills K & L Wines—not just K & L Wines. This anchor text is important for Google in deciding what keyword phrases to attach to the recipient website. There's lots more they could do, such as having better URLs and better meta name descriptions, but external links are worth hard work, so I'd concentrate on that.

Here's what I would recommend to K&L based on their local situation:

- Approach food and wine journalists with story ideas. Ideally a wine journalists's blog would write about K&L Wines Beverly Hills store with a link to their Beverly Hills optimized page. The Cheese Store has done brilliantly by using mostly cheeses to get lots of reviews and links!
- Wine bloggers are good sources of links (note DrVino has a good page about Best Wine Stores in LA that K&L Wines is listed on—but to the general website of course not the LA one)
- Do a search for Beverly Hills Business Directories and if they look reputable then list in these e.g. Beverly Hills Chamber of Commerce
- Ask their customers to write them reviews on Google Maps and yelp.com (put the stickers they offer in your shop window)

7.10 Measurement

7.10.1 Recap

You may remember Tony's Wine Store Business Plan in the Company chapter. He has two issues.

Issue 1: Competitor is discounting which Tony has tried to match, the resulting losses are destroying his business profitability. So his first Business Objective is to *Boost Margins by stopping discounting while maintaining or growing the customer base.*

The marketing strategies are to do with *Price* rather than Internet Marketing *Promotion.* In summary, the strategies are to renew the wine range, reduce and then stop discounting, and rely on other non-price promotions. Given this book is not about Pricing it will not cover this objective and related marketing strategies. Instead, we will focus from here on Issue 2.

Issue 2: Low Value Customer and Product Mix. Tony's Wine Store's average order value has decreased which is due to (1) discounting as per the previous issue, and (2) attracting more customers who purchase lower-priced wine. What's more, these customers are purchasing fewer bottles. There are fewer customers who purchase higher-priced wine and purchase many bottles of high-priced wine. It seems many premium customers are now going across town to a new wine specialist store or shopping on the internet. The Business Objective is to *Boost Margins and Volume by changing to a Higher Value Customer Mix.*

The marketing strategies cover Service, Product, Place, and Promotion. Given this book is only about Internet Marketing we will only cover this from here on. The format in this section will be:

Business Objective: Boost Margins and Volume by changing to a Higher Value Customer Mix (same objective each time)

Marketing Strategy>Promotion>Internet marketing: (Marketing Strategy e.g. SEO)

KPI: (Measurement of Success)

KPI Target: (Numerical Target)

7.10.2 SEO Measurement

Tony has decided to work with an agency to launch a new eCommerce website that is very SEO friendly with all the elements mentioned in this chapter. Indeed, he has started the website project with SEO in mind and has researched his keywords, created unique interesting content about wine varietals and wines that Luxury Enthusiasts love.

Some local wine bloggers have been very impressed and have already linked to these ultra premium wine product pages. Some of his

Luxury Enthusiast customers have already added their own reviews to some wine product pages.

This is a great start, but we need to tie the Measurements back to the Business Objectives. In other words, let's make sure we are using SEO to achieve our Higher Value Customer Mix objective.

Business Objective: Boost Margins and Volume by changing to a Higher Value Customer Mix.

Marketing Strategy >Promotion >Internet marketing: Increase 'organic' Search Engine Traffic that leads to conversions.

KPI: Conversion Average Order Value (AOV); Conversion Average Bottle Value (ABV). As measured in Google Analytics filtering for 'Non Paid' Search, excluding traffic from his city Notown (which will be included in Local SEO measurements instead).

KPI Targets: For Year 2, see Table 7.1.

Segment	Conv.#	Ass. Conv.#	AOV	ABV
Luxury Enthusiasts:	2	1	$65	$25
Enthusiasts:	5	2	$33	$15
Image Seekers:	2	2	$26	$15
Luxury Image Seekers:	2	1	$65	$15

Table 7.1: KPI Targets: SEO (Year 2)

Conv.#, Conversion numbers, is the number of customers who will purchase every month directly as a result of the SEO marketing strategy as measured by Traffic Source 'Non Paid' search (as measured in Google Analytics).

Ass. Conv.#, Assisted Conversion numbers, is the number of customers who will purchase every month, where SEO is the primary influence on their purchase decision. Before purchase their last interaction was not with a search engine but rather another traffic source (as measured in Google Analytics).

AOV, Average Order Value per month, is the customer's average order revenue amount each month. AOV is a proxy or indicator to help us determine which segment they belong to.

ABV, Average Bottle Value per month, is the customer's average bottle price for each order in that month. ABV is a proxy or indicator to help us determine which segment they belong to.

KPI Target Sources: Segment numbers come from the *Wine Shop Financials Spreadsheet, Internet Marketing* tab, in the section, starting at about row 96, titled *Segment Conversions Report.* Conversion Average Order Value equations are:

- Luxury Enthusiasts: purchase 104 bottles pa * 30% market share * $25 average bottle price 12 months = Average Order Value of $65 per month
- Enthusiasts: 104 bottles * 25% share * $15 price * 12 months = $33 pm
- Image Seekers: 104 * 25% * $15 * 12 months = $26 pm
- Luxury Image Seekers: 104 * 25% * $15 * 12 months = $65 pm
- The various bottle figures come from the Profit-Loss tab, Financial Model Inputs section.

SEO will directly add 11 more customers and through assisted conversions six more customers. If you do the math you'll see these customers are worth $8700 in revenue per annum.

However, as per Tony's marketing strategy he is focused on his primary segment—getting 44 more Luxury Enthusiasts in Year 2. He is following this Primary Segment KPI the closest. He expects SEO to deliver three Luxury Enthusiasts. This is a good start, but he has 41 more to go before he reaches his target. Time to move to another internet marketing strategy in the next chapter.

7.11 Summary

SEO is made up of five major parts, four of which were covered in this chapter: 1) having good overall website legitimacy, 2) having your webpages linked to by relevant and trusted external websites, 3) having important keyword phrases included in external website anchor text, 4) having these keyword phrases in particular parts of your webpage, 5) having interesting unique content and 6) having clear website themes around wine varietals and regions.

7.12 Resources

- How well did you understand? Visit my website to discuss or ask questions about Wine SEO: `www.WineMarketingPros.`

com/seochap/
- *Wine Shop Financials* Spreadsheet, see Resources section on the above website page
- Segment numbers come from the *Wine Shop Financials Spreadsheet, Internet Marketing* tab, in the section, starting at about row 96, titled *Segment Conversions Report*
- SEOmoz seomoz.org
- OpenSiteExplorer www.opensiteexplorer.org
- Google Keyword Tool adwords.google.com/select/KeywordToolExternal

8 Local Search Engine Optimization (SEO)

One in three searches are about finding information about locations and places according to Google[47], and this increases to 50% for mobile searches.[27] For example, Maria Baugh from a shop called Butter Lane Cupcakes in New York City was quoted in a Google study[7] as saying,

> There's simply no way to succeed, really, if we're going to rely on foot traffic and just our one little storefront. We ask people how they find out about Butter Lane Cupcakes, and a lot of people find out about us on Yelp, a lot of people find out about us through Google AdWords, tons of food bloggers, tons of people going online. Its like built-in marketing and a built-in consumer base.

In this chapter, we look at how a small local business can take advantage of their local status in Google search. It is a crucial chapter for local wine shops, so I'll focus mainly on them. However, it is just as important for any winery that has a tasting room.

8.1 What is Local SEO

Local SEO is optimizing your website to increase search engine traffic for local search queries. For example, if you search for 'Chicago Wine Stores' on google.com you may see a search engine results page like the one in Figure 8.1.

Figure 8.1 shows 'organic' and 'local' results. The local listings are the ones with the address details beside a teardrop or pin icon. The organic results have no pins. When we have both results the search engine industry jargon is known as a 'blended' results page. If there are only organic then it is known as a 'pure' results page. So we have two organic listings at the top, followed by seven Google local

Figure 8.1: Searching for Chicago Wine Stores on Google—Blended
result

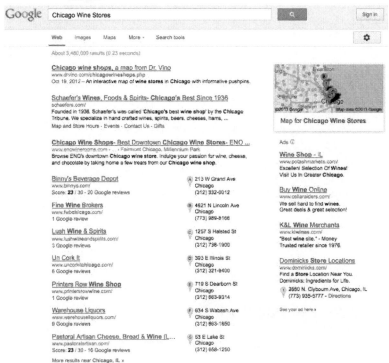

listings of which you can only see three. To the right is a map with local Adwords results below it.

These local listings are known as Google+ Local pages because Google has integrated Local listings into their Google+ service. They use to be called Places and before that Maps. Only a year or so ago the map would be in the center column with 3-7 business listings down the side. Before that it was just organic results with no local listings. Local listings have become important, and it's expected that this prominence will increase. If you are business which hopes to attract customers to a physical location, i.e. a store or tasting room, this chapter is for you.

Let's see how to increase traffic from local SEO.

8.1.1 Local SEO in Detail

Local SEO at its simplest is to just claim your Google+ Local[48] account and fill out the fields as comprehensively as possible. Of course, there is much more to do if you want to be one of the top listings for your city.

Name, Address, and Phone: NAP

When you fill out the fields there are three you need to pay particular attention to: Name, Address, and Phone number. The Local SEO jargon is to call this 'NAP'. Google crawls the web looking for as much data as it can about your local business. This data comes in all sorts of different formats and can lead to low levels of confidence as to whether the data is about your business or another. The best way to clearly signal that the data, perhaps a great review, is about your wine store or wine tasting room is to have an exact standard way of describing your NAP, down to every comma. This:
Tony's Wine Store
100 Example Avenue, New York, NY 10017
(212) 600-0000
Is different than this:
Tonys Wine Store
100 Example Ave, New York 10017
(212) 600-0000
In the second one Tony has no apostrophe, Avenue is spelled Ave, there is no state, and there is no comma after New York.

Note that is the physical address not a PO Box or postal address that Google is looking for. To work out the USPS standard address look it up in their website zip code finder.

Many times you have complete control over how you list your NAP, e.g. directories, and can ensure you list it the exact same way each time. Often times you also have influence, e.g. on a supplier's website, in which case you should assertively ask that your NAP is used. Other times you don't have much influence at all, e.g. a magazine review, and you just have to hope that your business name is in close proximity to an address and phone number that is very similar to your standard NAP.

Local SEO Factors

A survey is done every year on Local Search Criteria by one Local SEO expert called David Mihm. In mid 2012, he asked 41 prominent Local SEO experts to rate the importance of about 100 factors as to how they influence local search engine results rankings in Google. Note this survey is only about the search engine results for a query with *local* intent not a general search query (see the previous chapter for information about general search queries). Local intent is a presumption made by the search engines based on device (mobile or desktop) and word modifiers like city or zip code.

Here are the top 10 from a wine industry perspective (if you're interested check out David's Local Search Ranking Factors Report).[49]

1. Physical Address in City of Search

Put simply, you need to have a physical address in the city that users are searching in. There is some sort of invisible border for each city and you need to be inside it. If you're at the border or in the suburbs then you are at a disadvantage.

2. Proper Category Associations

Google+ Local has a section for categorizing your business. The relevant pre-set categories in Google+ Local are probably 'Wine Store', 'Liquor Store' and 'Beer Store'.

3. Proximity of Address to Centroid

How close are you to the center, or 'centroid', of the search area. To work this out do a search for your zip, suburb, or city and look for the blue pin in a Google map.

4. Domain Authority of Website

This is the general SEO concept of the signals about the website as whole that search engines use to determine authority and trust. See the previous SEO chapter.

5. Quantity of Structured Citations (IYPs, Data Aggregators)

In the internet world 'citations' means links or NAP listings from other websites. IYP stands for Internet Yellow Pages. The more of these local directory links the better. Yelp.com is likely to be the most important.

6. City, State in Places Landing Page Title

Ensure that when you enter your business title in Google, it is something like 'Example Wine Store Chicago IL' not 'Example Wine Store' without the city (and state). By the way, if your store is called something like 'Vinowonders' that does not have the important keywords 'wine', 'store/shop' (liquor/beer/spirits) in it then consider a Company/Organization title like 'Vinowonders, Wine Store — Chicago IL'.

7. Quantity of Native Google Places Reviews

How many Google+ Local reviews, not other review sites, do you have? You want at least 10, note the sentiment of the rating doesn't matter for this factor.

8. Quality/Authority of Structured Citations

Do you have accurate Local listings on relevant and authoritative websites e.g. Yelp.

9. Local Area Code on Place Page

Does your phone number local area code match the area you claim to be from on your Google+ Local page.

10. HTML NAP Matching Place Page NAP

Is the physical address on your website exactly match your Google+ Local page address? An easy one to check and correct.

In 2012, the number Google+ Local customer reviews and the proximity to the center of the area searched leaped in importance.

This survey has been done for the years 2008, 2009, 2010, 2011 and 2012. Each year the factors change as Google takes note of other important ways to and means of making their local search results as accurate and informative as possible. For instance, in 2008 Google+ Local (or Places) did not exist so other Local Business Listing sources were the number 1 factor. In 2009, it was making sure your business address was inside the invisible boundaries that Google set for each town. In 2010, it was clearly claiming and filling out your Google Places listing. In 2011, Google was sometimes showing a pure list of Local results and sometimes showing a blended list of normal lists and Places listings and this continued in 2012. In 2013, we will start to see the effect of Google+ Local, which wasn't covered in this survey.

8.2 Local SEO compared to General SEO

Remember that general SEO is more about sending trusted signals to search engines about:

- Trust/Authority of the Host Domain (i.e. 'www.example.com')
- Link Popularity of the Specific Page (i.e. 'www.example.com/the-specific-page.html')
- Anchor Text of External Links (anchor text is the hyperlink text, usually the blue and underlined)
- On-Page Keyword Usage (e.g. keywords in the title tag—usually seen at the top of your web browser)
- Social media signals from Facebook and Twitter

Local SEO is more about sending trusted signals to search engines that your website:

- is geographically relevant to a local search query and close to the center
- is in the proper business category in Google+ Local
- has a good volume of local listings, ratings, and reviews, especially in Google+ Local.

This also illustrates a key difference between SEO for wineries and SEO for local wine retailers. Wineries should focus on normal SEO practices; whereas, local wine retailers should focus more on local SEO practices. An exception would be if a winery is pushing cellar-door sales as part of a wine tourism marketing strategy then they need to be doing well in local SEO for local searchers.

8.3 How to Set Up Google+ Local

Of all the Local listing services Google+ Local is the now the most important. Here's some tips on setting this up.

Make sure you have a Google account (getting a gmail account is the easiest way to do this) then submit your site at the Google+ Local. Note this used to be called Local Google and then Google Local Business Center.[50]

Just follow the instructions. Google will ask you to fill out the basic information about your business. This includes:

- Company/Organization: This is the official/registered name of your business
- Address (required): The address should look exactly the way you'd write it on a paper mailing envelope
- Phone Number (required): Be sure to include your area code with your phone number.
- Website: This can be a maximum of 255 characters
- Categories: Enter several categories to describe your business to make it easier for others to find when they search Maps. Google will automatically suggest categories as you type and I'd choose *Wine Store*, *Liquor Store*, and *Beer Store*
- Hours of operation: Select your hours of operation using the dropdown menus
- Payment options: Select the checkboxes next to the payment methods that your business accepts
- Photos: Use the photo uploader to add a photo from your computer or specify a URL to add a photo from the web

- Video: To add a video, upload it to YouTube and enter its URL
- Additional details: Use this section to add your own information fields to your listing. For example, parking availability or whether your business allows pets

Google will verify this either by phone or postcard. I suggest you be beside your business telephone and choose verification by phone as I've found mail takes a while. You'll get an automatic phone call where you enter a code (so this is the quickest way also).

Note usually there will already be a preloaded listing of your business so you need to 'claim' this listing before doing the steps above.

When people search for a wine retailer with a zip code, suburb, or city, your listing will gain prominence and ranking depending on how relevant it is to the search query. In Google Maps you'll get a little red bubble with your listing on the side—this prominence really assists driving online and in-store traffic. All the work that the Google search engine does comes down to filtering out the 90% of the pages on the web that are spam. If it has verified you are a real business then you'll stand in good stead for high rankings. Usually Google would have to rely on yellow pages and other third parties to assess whether you are local to a person's search query or not, and it seems queasy over accepting the accuracy of these. So verifying the Google+ Local account is best. Other great features:

- Statistics—you can see how many people have visited and what zip code they were requesting this information from, great information to have for a local Adwords campaign
- Photos and Video—you can upload a small number of photos and videos which can make it a mini local website in effect
- Reviews—Google also automatically trawls the web for reviews on your business and people can review directly. Don't worry they're usually good, and if they're bad you may be able to lobby Google to remove them
- Adwords integration—gives you a 'local' advantage on the advertising listings on the right hand side of the search results page. This is because it shows your local address immediately under your ad. It's called Ad Extensions and will be covered in the Internet Advertising chapter.

8.4 Other Local Services

There are a number of local search and review services that offer searchers the chance to find, review, and rate local businesses. The most important review engines in the US, in order of how important they are for a wine retailers Local SEO efforts are:

1. Yelp.com
2. Yellowpages.com
3. Facebook.com
4. Superpages.com
5. Local.Yahoo.com

Note that this is my estimate for wine retailers based off a study done for other types of retailers in 70 local search categories across 53 large US cities, 20 medium-sized cities, and 20 smaller cities by David Mihm and Darren Shaw.[51]

Yelp

Yelp is consistently shown as a top Local listing. Let's look at Yelp in a little more detail.

In Yelp's words,

> 'Yelp is the fun and easy way to find, review, and talk about what's great—and not so great, in your area.'

It's easy for a business to set up: you 'unlock' your account (verification by phone) and add/edit your hours and contact details.

The benefits of Yelp (and local review sites):

- Word of Mouth—the internet way. You get your customers reviewing and recommending your store to their friends. Given friends are a trusted source this is valuable
- Search engine juice—get links to the search engines for a particular area
- Reduce those annoying calls about opening hours and location
- Provides your location on a map (highlighted for sponsors)
- You can interact, privately and publicly, with your reviewers which can be more informative in its own right
- Can add photos
- Have some reports that can give you some great marketing information about your customers

It started in San Francisco but now offers this service throughout the world. It also has social networking features (adding friends, groups, etc.) to share reviews with their network of friends. The idea is that people generally trust their friends' recommendations. Google was so impressed with Yelp it apparently[52] almost purchased the company. Certainly it dominates the local ratings and reviews space with

- Google taking more of a business listings and search approach
- Foursquare taking a social and mobile phone check-in approach
- Groupon taking a social discount approach

I'll cover these sorts of local services and 'location-based services' in a later chapters. Yelp makes its money by offering you, the lucky local retailer or wine tasting room, the chance to have a sponsored listing at the top of the search results. For example, search for wine store in San Francisco and you might see that K&L Wines has got the top organic listing. They also have 318 reviews, most of which are 5 star ratings at the time I write this, which is pretty impressive (well done folks at K&L!). The normal number of reviews seems to be about 10-100.

Claim your listing and give the advertising a test (you can get reports on page views etc).

8.5 Measurement

Tony knows how important Local SEO is for a local business and has followed the advice above. He has made sure his website pages clearly have his physical address and phone number. He has comprehensively completed his Google Places, Yelp, and City Search pages, and been encouraging his customers to review his store (especially those Luxury Enthusiasts). Let's have a look at his Local SEO measurements.

Business Objective: Boost Margins and Volume by changing to a Higher Value Customer Mix

Marketing Strategy >Promotion >Internet marketing: Increase 'organic' local Search Engine and local directory referral Traffic that leads to conversions

KPI: Conversion Average Order Value; Conversion Average Bottle Value. As measured in Google Analytics filtering for (1) 'Non Paid'

Search only including traffic from his city Notown; (2) Referrals from Yelp, CitySearch and the other local directories

KPI Targets: For Year 2. see Table 8.1

Segment	Conv.#	Ass. Conv.#	AOV	ABV
Luxury Enthusiasts:	2	1	$65	$25
Enthusiasts:	5	2	$33	$15
Image Seekers:	2	2	$26	$15
Luxury Image Seekers:	2	1	$65	$15

Table 8.1: KPI Targets: Local SEO (Year 2)

KPI Target Sources: Segment numbers come from the Internet Marketing spreadsheet *Segment Conversions Report.* Conversion Average Order Value equations are:

- Luxury Enthusiasts: purchase 104 bottles pa * 30% market share * $25 average bottle price 12 months = Average Order Value of $65 per month
- Enthusiasts : 104 bottles * 25% share * $15 price * 12 months = $33 pm
- Image Seekers: 104 * 25% * $15 * 12 months = $26 pm
- Luxury Image Seekers: 104 * 25% * $15 * 12 months = $65 pm
- The bottle figures come from the Financial Model Inputs section.

Local SEO will directly add 11 more customers and through assisted conversions six more customers (the same as general SEO). If you do the math you'll see these customers are worth $8700 in revenue per annum.

As per Tony's marketing strategy he is focused on his primary segment– getting 44 more Luxury Enthusiasts in Year 2. He is following this Primary Segment KPI the closest. He expects Local SEO to deliver three Luxury Enthusiasts. Along with general SEO, he has 38 more to go before he reaches his target. Time to move to another internet marketing strategy in the next chapter.

8.6 Summary

Local SEO is becoming more important for any search that Google deems local in nature. The best way to boost your ranking is through verifying your Google+ Local listing and by ensuring your NAP (name, address and phone number) are exactly the same on all websites, including your own.

8.7 Resources

- Local SEO Discussion, Update, and Posts Page: `www.WineMarketingPros.com/localseochap/`
- Google Places: Help customers find you on Google Maps `http://www.google.com/placesforbusiness`
- Local Search Ranking Factors David Mihm `http://www.davidmihm.com/local-search-ranking-factors.shtml`

9 Internet Advertising

9.1 What is Internet Advertising

Internet Advertising are ads on the internet. They may come in the form of the small text ads on the side of search engine results pages, image banner ads on blogs, posts on Facebook, tweets in Twitter, or featured videos on YouTube.

In 2012, the US internet advertising market was \$34 billion large[53] and had grown by about 15-20% per annum. Search ads make up about half, display/banner ads about 20%, and mobile ads 8%. The big mover was mobile, which has almost doubled versus the previous year.

The retail industry made up about 20% of internet ad revenues[53], financial services and auto 13% each, telecom 12%, computing and travel 8%, and Consumer Package Goods 5% with health, media, and entertainment making up the rest.

Two-thirds of Internet ads were purchased on a performance click basis with the other third on an impressions viewing basis.

The most popular internet advertising network is Google 'Adwords'. Ninety-six percent of Google's revenue comes from its advertising networks.[54] It dominates the Search advertising category but shares Display with Facebook (and to a much lesser extent Yahoo with Microsoft and AOL).

Although Search drives Google's consumer success, it is the ads on Google and its partner websites that drive Google's financial success. A few years ago Adwords was relatively inexpensive and provided excellent measurable 'return on investment' (ROI). Nowadays, the advertiser competition for prominent ad spots has made it much more difficult to achieve high returns on advertising expenditure. This chapter starts by showing how a wine retailer can use Adwords to drive traffic while keeping costs down. We then look at the other internet advertising methods of banners, mobile, and Facebook.

Confusingly, internet advertising is often referred to as 'PPC' or 'Pay Per Click', sometimes even as 'Paid Search' (Google Analytics), and at other times as 'Search Engine Marketing' (SEM—which may also include other internet marketing). Adwords is simply Google's trademarked brand of internet advertising. To confuse you even more, advertising is not always paid on a per click basis, but, rather, it can be paid on impressions or even on a time basis. In this book, I use the phrase internet advertising or, where appropriate, Adwords.

9.2 Google Adwords

If you have a website then I believe you should just jump in and give Adwords a try.

Sign Up. Signing up to Adwords is really easy - just follow the instructions at `adwords.google.com`:

- If you don't have a Google account then I suggest you get one. The easiest way is create a gmail account and use that as your sign in for all Google products including Adwords
- I've used both credit card and internet banking to manage payments. Perhaps reduce your risk and just use internet banking for this first time by prepaying $20. It can take a couple of days for the banking to go through (credit card will just require responding to some verification emails). You can, however, start making a campaign, though the campaign won't start until the payment is verified

Create your First Campaign. We'll just call the campaign *Varietal* (note we can change this later). Note that the Google Adwords website regularly changes so the following process may well have changed post publication of this book.

- Select *Search Network only* and *Standard*
- Select *Networks >Let me choose >* and leave *Google search* ticked but untick *include search partners* (each of Google's networks have their own characteristics, we want to target each one separately)
- Choose All Devices (you may choose to alter mobile bids later)
- Choose your city or even suburb. Do not choose *All countries and territories*! Wine retailers at this stage should stick to an area that is cost-effective to deliver to or for local customers to pick-up orders. Wineries should probably have separate campaigns for separate cities.

- For the moment enter $1 for the *Default bid* which you will change. For *Daily budget* enter $20, you are unlikely to use that in a week much less a day if you are targeting one city

We'll ignore the Extensions for the moment and *Save and Continue* to the Ad Group page.

On the *Create Ad Group* page

- Choose a varietal and region that you stock lots of or even specialize in. For our example, we'll use Napa Valley Merlot
- Make the *Ad Group Name*: Napa Valley Merlot
- *Headline* will be: Napa Valley Merlot
- *Description line 1*: Wide Range, Great prices!
- *Description line 2*: Your Merlot Expert
- *Display URL*: www.YourWebsite.com
- *Destination URL (http://)*: www.YourWebsite.com/NapaMerlotCategoryPag
- In *Keywords* put the following on separate lines: *Napa Valley Merlot, 'Napa Valley Merlot', [Napa Valley Merlot]*
- Ignore *Placements*
- In *Add Group Default Bids* make the bid between $0.50 and $1.50. The higher it is the quicker you'll see results. (Note that these are not special default bid prices just suggestions to get you started. You should review these daily as you gain Adwords experience and skill.)
- *Save ad group* to start your campaign

In fact, your campaign has probably not started, rather it is 'Pending'. Google will generally tag wine industry ads as 'Non-Family' content status thus in need of approval. The Adwords Alcohol policy reflects normal liquor laws, though it does not allow the sale of 'hard alcohol'. You'll see them go 'Enabled' after a day or two.

Also note that you cannot advertise direct sales of wine on the Google Display Network. The Display network is the third party websites that display Google ads and does not show Non-Family ads.[55]

Keywords

Next we'll do some more work on Keywords. In particular, the difference between broad match, phrase match, and exact match.

Exact match is easy to understand, if someone types in the exact keywords *Napa Valley Merlot* then you have told Google you would like to bid for that search, and if your bid and your keywords' Quality

Score are high enough, then you will be shown on the right hand side under 'Ads' (what use to be called 'Sponsored Links'). I'll go through Quality Score later, it's a little tricky to understand (but very important). Square brackets are often used to delineate exact match keywords.

Phrase match is when someone types in something like:

- napa valley andreas vineyard merlot
- napa valley merlot
- napa north valley cabernet merlot

Google will show your *Napa Valley Merlot* ads if the search query has all your keywords, in the correct order, with other words between your keywords. It will also show for the Exact match above. Quotation marks are often used to delineate phrase match keywords.

It will not show our ad if they have searched for:

- merlot napa valley (out of order)
- napa valley (no merlot)
- napa merlot (no valley)

Broad Match had been very controversial in Adwords circles, but has become much more acceptable as Google's technology improved. Here's what Google says,[56]

> ...your ad may show if a search term contains your keyword terms in any order, and possibly along with other terms. Your ads can also show for singular or plural forms, synonyms, stemmings (such as floor and flooring), related searches, and other relevant variations. Keywords are broad by default, that is without any punctuation.

So it will show for

- merlot napa valley
- napa valley
- napa merlot
- buy merlot from napa valley
- buy merlot wine from napa
- information about napa merlot wine
- and all the other examples above

Broad Match +

The controversy with broad match is over synonyms and other related searches. This could be good if someone was looking for

Napa Valley Cabernet Merlot. That's a pretty close match, as are *Nappa Valley Merlot,* or *Californian Merlot.* So far so good, however, sometimes Google may also theoretically extend it to searches such as *French Bordeaux* or even *Napa Valley Pinot Noir* which are not really that close. To avoid this problem you can add the plus sign modifier in front of important words. This will exclude synonyms but still show it for close variants of this phrase. For our example we might change our keyword phrase to '+Napa Valley Merlot' to ensure that only Napa wines are shown.

Regardless, regularly check what the search queries were for each click you got. You do this by going to the keywords section of your Adwords account and choose the tab *See search terms. . .* and choose *All.* You then select irrelevant keywords to tell Google to exclude these in the future (called 'negative keywords' which we look at more below). In effect you are providing boundaries to Google's search algorithms. My recommendation for a beginner Adwords wine user is to use all three types but every day check your Search Query Performance Report and exclude irrelevant keywords.

Here's the example ad we created above, though I've replaced the URL with the imaginary wine store—'Tony's Wine Store':

Napa Valley Merlot
www.TonysWineStore.com/Merlot
Wide Range, Great prices!
Your Merlot Expert

Ad Copy

Headline

- I would always recommend you have your keyword in the headline as above
- It's what people are searching for and their query words will be in bold
- Some people believe that headlines can have 50%+ influence as to whether the ad is clicked, not just for Adwords but also landing pages and sales letters as well
- Don't put your store name in there, it's not about you—rather it's about the consumer solving their wine search problem

Description

- My example above is pretty bland to be honest it needs the following:
- A call to action e.g. buy or order now
- Something that is relevant to our target market, though Your Merlot Expert isn't too bad e.g. line 1: Widest Range of Napa Valley, line 2: Merlot in Texas might be better
- Expressed in the feature—benefit approach e.g. line 1: Widest Range of Merlot, line 2: Favorites Easily Found

Different consumers want different things—indeed a good part of my career was working this out. For example, why does someone drive a Mercedes, or why does an aspiring businessman drink a Rousseau Chambertin Grand Cru at a restaurant when he doesn't know much about wine: Status. See the Customers chapter for more detail about wine consumer research.

Display URL

Usually `www.YourWebsiteHere.com` but sometimes relevant subdomains like

`www.YourWebsiteHere.com/Merlot` can work well.

Destination URL

It's one thing getting people to click on your ad, it's quite another to get that converted into sales. The best start to this process is having a relevant and congruent landing page. In our case, the URL would go to a Napa Valley Merlot page or at least a Merlot Page but not the home page! Your searcher is trying to buy a particular wine. Make it as easy as possible rather than forcing them to start their search again from the home page.

Landing pages, consumer research, testing different ad copy, testing landing page copy, or 'optimization' also are important and will be covered later in the Conversion Rate Optimization chapter.

Quality Score

Next let's look at how to steadily improve your wine adwords results (essentially more clicks at less cost). Google uses something called a 'Quality Score' to rank competing ads for the limited number of spots on each search engine results page. It aims to make the ads the most relevant possible for its users. Just like SEO results, the higher the ad on the right hand side 'sponsored listings', the more prominent the ad and more likely it will be clicked.

In order to assess ad ranks, Google applies a Quality Score discounter to your Cost Per Click bid: Ad Rank = CPC bid x Quality Score.

The key point is the higher your Quality Score the less your CPC bid needs to be, and the more times your ad will be shown on the search engine results page (i.e. 'impressions'). For a good example see Google's detailed quality score help page[57]. Here's what Google says:

> Quality Score is broadly determined by three main factors:
> 1. Click through Rate
>
>   - The historical click through rate (CTR) of the keyword and the matched ad on Google
>   - Your account history, which is measured by the CTR of all the ads and keywords in your account
>   - The historical CTR of the display URLs in the ad group
>
> 2. Relevance
>
>   - The relevance of the keyword to the ads in its ad group
>   - The relevance of the keyword and the matched ad to the search query
>   - Your account's performance in the geographical region where the ad will be shown
>   - Other relevance factors
>
> 3. Landing Page Quality
>
>   - The site should have relevant and original content
>   - Be transparent and explicit about the nature of your business: how your site interacts with a visitor's computer, and how you intend to use a visitor's personal information
>   - An easily navigable site with quick load times and a minimum of pop-ups or pop-unders

Click through rate (CTR) is probably the best proxy for changing your Quality Score. The better your CTR, the better your Quality Score—it's a simple rule of thumb (but like all rules of thumb it doesn't always apply). To steadily improve our wine Adwords results we'll use testing and measure results using CTR. Here's our ad:

Napa Valley Merlot
www.TonysWineStore.com/Merlot
Favorites In-Stock and Easily Found
Buy from the Widest Range of Merlot

Remember the Destination URL should go to the Napa Valley Merlot page not the home page. We'll create a second ad that tests which headline drives more clicks and sales conversions. That ad will have one simple addition to the headline, the word 'Boutique' as follows:

Boutique Napa Valley Merlot
www.TonysWineStore.com/Merlot
Favorites In-Stock and Easily Found
Buy from the Widest Range of Merlot

We do this by clicking on the campaign we created in our Google Adwords account. Then the *Ads* tab >*New Ad* >*Text Ad*.

Notice the following:

- We have not changed anything else. If we did then we would be unable to isolate the reason for any difference in the test results between two ads (an 'A/B split test').
- We changed the headline because that's the most powerful part of the ad copy.
- I may have chosen 'Boutique' because I might have noticed that my best customers were wine Enthusiasts who like to explore little known boutique wines (actually they exist see 'Experimenters' in the Customer chapter).
  I also take the following crucial step:
- I click on my campaign. Then *Settings* >*Advanced Settings* (at the bottom), expand *Ad delivery: Ad rotation, frequency capping* and edit *Ad rotation*.
- Change this to *Rotate: Show ads more evenly* and *Save* (ignore the yellow warning).

What we've just done is to get Google to show each ad evenly over time so we can choose which is the best ad—not Google. Depending on your traffic you can then check to see which ad works the best by comparing the click through rates (CTR). Once you have found the winner, you delete the loser and create a new ad to test something else.

The idea is to achieve large CTR increases over a year or so by getting small increases over a month. The amount of traffic before you decide which ad is a winner is contentious. A rule of thumb is at least 200 impressions for each ad, though this sacrifices certainty of the test versus speed of testing. I want to quickly improve each part of my sales process, including the ad copy, so I can get larger overall increases over a 12 month period, so I use this rule of thumb. However, large companies with lots of traffic may wait for 200 clicks or even 200 conversions (sales) before making a decision. They have the luxury of high amounts of traffic, which a small business does not.

Next we'll carefully add some more keywords to the Wine Adwords ad group. Back in 2008, Google advertisers used many different tools from companies other than Google to come up with a great keyword list. In 2009, Google redeveloped its keyword tool and now gives excellent keyword ideas for free. What's more, it's based on an accurate Google database of keyword searches; whereas, the other tools were not.

- Go to `https://adwords.google.com/select/KeywordToolExternal`
- Choose your market: *Results are tailored to* we'll use English, US
- Select *Descriptive words or phrases*
- Type: napa valley merlot
- Check *Use synonyms*
- and click on the button *Get keyword ideas*

This shows the following wine adwords data by column and sorted by relevance.

- The keywords (that Google's database of user search queries shows) are related to napa valley merlot
- The amount of advertiser competition for these keywords
- The local search volume for each keyword, in our case for English and US
- The global search volume for each keyword i.e. all countries and all languages
- A match type selector to see the difference between match types

Here's what I see in these wine adwords keyword ideas:

- That napa valley merlot has a lot of search and competition
- That napa valley vineyards merlot has more than 1000 searches per month and so is a strong second keyword phrase
- That, as normal, consumers have different ways of constructing their wine search query (e.g. sometimes with the year at the

start, or end, or middle, or not all)

I would suggest a beginner advertiser do the following:

- If you stock any of the brands listed then add them to your keyword list by going to *Adwords >Campaign >Keywords* tab >then click on the button *+ Add Keywords.*
- Also add napa valley vineyards merlot
- Add them for all match types: broad, phrase, and exact
- Look at your bestselling Napa Valley Merlots and add those as well

If you're a little more advanced then create three more ad groups and put all the broad match brands in a Napa Valley Merlot Broad Match Ad Group, all the phrase match in its own Phrase Match Ad Group and likewise for Exact match. This way you can track what group gives you more clicks and more sales. Then you adjust your bid prices and the time you spend on the particular ad group based off its importance (80/20 rule). Do not add merlot or the other regional merlots to this ad group as we want it tightly focused on this theme. In particular, we want to use the headline Napa Valley Merlot.

A CTR benchmark for a Google Search ad is 0.5% to 4%, which is very similar to the direct marketing industry results for mail. Note Display advertising will be much lower, about 0.01% to 0.05%. A CTR rate comparison only makes senses within an advertising network rather than across advertising networks. What does matter when comparing networks is the Cost per Conversion which we'll discuss in the Measurement section below.

There is much more you can do (see the section *What I haven't covered in this Chapter* below), but those are the key Adwords fundamentals.

Google Display Network

The Google Display Network is the third party websites that display Google ads. A wine business cannot directly advertise wine on the Google Display Network because the ads have probably been tagged as Non-Family. Non-Family ads include wine, beer, and spirits. Though occasionally ads do seem to slip through this process.

Google does allow alcohol accessories, such as wine storage, alcohol-related collectibles, packaging, and containers. Google also allows, 'wineries, wine tours, sommelier courses with no direct promotion of drinking, alcohol, or direct sale option.'[58]

9.2.1 Local Adwords

If you're a Wine Store in Chicago, you don't want to spend money on ads being shown to Miami residents. On the other hand if a Miami resident wants to buy a bottle of wine for a friend in Chicago, then you do want them to see your ad so they can buy in Chicago and save on freight costs. This is the realm of local Adwords. In this section I'll go through how you do this in Google Adwords by using geo-targeting, ad extensions, keywords, ad copy, and landing pages.

Google lets you target specific areas. They can be defined by country, region, city, or even a custom sales area. Google limits results to locations in several ways:

- if google.com is being used (not google.co.uk etc)
- if a search query contains a recognizable zip code, city, or region, e.g. *Chicago* Wine Store
- the IP address, or in Google's words 'when possible, we determine the user's general physical location based on their device location, which is usually based on their computer's Internet Protocol (IP) address'[59]
- Google Search personalization: if you've told Google where you live (gmail?) then they'll use this

If you are part of a national network, e.g. a franchise, then you'll want a national office to co-ordinate the respective sales areas. Otherwise you'll not only increase costs through internet bid competition, but you'll also violate Google guidelines (overlapping areas). The idea is to have strong national and local campaigns working simultaneously, but you need clear rules for each branch.

Ad agencies also need to have a clear strategy on how they'll do this for clients competing for the same keywords, especially for clients in the same town.

Ad Extensions

In the previous chapter I mentioned I'd cover how to integrate Google+ Local with Adwords. We do this using an Ad Extension. An Ad Extension is where a standard text ad has a little something extra added to it by Google.

The Google+ Local (also confusingly sometimes still called Google Places) integration is through the Location Extension, which is accessed in the Campaign Settings page. You have two choices: manual entry or Google Places. I'd choose Google Places. Having integrated the Adwords and Places accounts we can now use Places to show our physical address in ads.

Sitelinks are where you can add links below one of Google larger dimension ads, such as Store Locator or Order Online.

The Call extension enables your phone number to show at the bottom of an ad. Note this is a powerful option for mobile ads given customers' large thumbs and small mobile screens.

The Social extension shows '+1's. That is any Google+, the Google Social Network, users who '+1' your website content on Google+, on a third party website with a +1 button, or on the ad itself. This social media endorsement is proving to be an effective form of advertising. Note you will not be charged if people +1 your ad, only if they click through to your website.

Dynamic search ads are shown not on a keyword basis but on what Google sees when it crawls your website. You nominate an ad template and destination web pages, and Google does the rest.

Mobile App extension allows you to add a link to an ad that directs people to the Google or Apple app store. This is a great way to advertise your mobile app, something I will be encouraging in a latter chapter.

Town in Ad Copy

Geographical targeting doesn't always work. IP addresses are especially problematic. So I would also add new keyword phrases that attach all the towns and suburbs you service to your keywords, e.g. Chicago to Wine Store as in 'Wine Store Chicago' or 'Wine Store 60611'. Don't replace the generic ones, just add to your keyword list (advanced accounts should have local keyword phrase in their own Ad Group).

Ad Copy (the text you use in your ads). The usual practices apply with a local twist. The local twists are:

- Use your target town in your title (remember it will be bolded if it is part of the search query)
- Possibly put your town in the descriptions and Display URL as well—but that may be overdoing it

- Adding a phone number will also show you're local (and appear in computer ads as well as mobile ads)

Google will be making an algorithmic assessment as to how well your landing page ties into the search query phrase. Since it's a local query, the landing page should also have *Chicago Wine Store* in the title tag and headline (see On-Page SEO in the SEO chapter) as well as having the store's physical address and other contact details somewhere prominently.

9.2.2 Negative Keywords

If you search Google for *wine*, guess what may be the top search result? Nothing to do with the beverage wine but rather *Wine Development HQ*. Wine also stands for *windows emulator*, usually used on the operating system called Linux, which is very popular software. Indeed, the Linux wine is so popular it outranks the beverage wine.

Wine, broad match, has thousands of searches per day. The problem is that many of these searches are for the software so if you bid on this keyword you're wasting money and will probably end up with a poor click through rate and therefore quality score. A poor quality score means that Google will price you out of bidding for this keyword. So what you do is add negative keywords by adding a minus sign in front of the keyword e.g. *-software*. Here's some good negative keywords to add to your wine Adwords campaigns:

- -open source
- -software
- -windows
- -applications
- -operating systems

This should eliminate software queries, but not other irrelevant searches.

UB40 was a great band when I grew up and I loved 'Reddd reeeeddd wiiiiiiine'. It looks like many people still do because when you use the keyword 'red wine' many of the searches are for the song not the wine. So add negative keywords such as:

- -ub40
- -mp3
- -music
- -[red red wine]

The last one is an exact negative. That is if someone enters that exact word combination in Google search then it will exclude your ad from showing. If you added *red red wine* then that could actually catch *red wine* searchers.

Staying with the music vein, watch out for *Amy Winehouse*... negative keywords is an on-going task.

A last example is *new wine*. This looks promising with thousands of searches for it, possibly what some people call a new vintage or a new release, a bit odd but if that's what they're searching for... if you do a Google search then you'll probably find the top two listings are for a church group called *New Wine*. Followed by a Norwegian electronica band on myspace called *The New Wine*. Then *new wine records*. Then it was *new wine into old wineskins*. Then it was *wine glasses*. Actually there were no wine beverage listings at all on the first page of Google—one to add to your negative keyword list. Now given the religious overtones of wine, what about the phrase *blood into wine*?

Google Adwords is purposely easy to use and should provide a moderate return on advertising expenditure. However, to get the best return, you'll need to spend some time learning the system—or hire a pro if you spend $1000s per annum. Experts will know already about other topics, such as the display network, image ads, remarketing, google website optimizer and analytics, conversion tracking, delivery times, and position and much more.

Note you can also advertise through the Bing network. It has such a similar system (Yahoo uses it as well) though I will not being going through it here. However I will cover, mobile, and Facebook advertising below.

9.3 Mobile Advertising

Mobile advertising is worth talking about on its own because, like other mobile marketing, it has the advantage of being in the right place at the right time—your customers' pocket. No matter where they are, they can easily and naturally bring out their phone in ways you can't with a laptop or PC.

Here are the various mobile advertising types:

- SMS (and MMS)
- WAP

- Social network ads
- Mobile banner ad on web browsers
- Inside mobile app (often in games)

First, picture message (MMS) ads just haven't seemed to have taken hold—so let's just ignore this. SMS on the other hand is an established form of advertising. It usually involves:

- sending a text code to a shortcode number
- an opt-in to receiving an offer or information

This is used extensively in traditional advertising to get some form of direct response. For retailers, it's often used for competition entry and access to discounts. It can also be used to build a list to send text messages to, usually with offers or event announcements of some type. When used this way it is essentially just another form of direct response marketing, but unlike email marketing it is expensive with shortcodes, setup, and delivery. For a 140 character text message I'm just not convinced the budget, time, and effort is worthwhile.

There was a hope that a system as seen in the movie 'Minority Report' would be the Next Big Thing. Remember Tom Cruise walking down the street with local businesses sending him personalized marketing messages? Well that has been technically possible with cell tower triangulation and SMS. But frankly I think everyone involved balked at sending this sort of spam and it never took off.

Do you even remember those days back in the nineties? You got an expensive phone, opened the poor resolution tiny mobile screen, and waited ages for simple info to be downloaded (via technology called WAP)? Probably not. I worked in mobile new product development, at that time and it's downright embarrassing what we thought would work. It was a pretty hopeless experience and needed the usability of the smartphone, e.g. iPhone, plus the bandwidth of 3G and WiFi, to make it as good as it is today. Anyhow, the point is back then you could get simple text ads along the top of these screens.

Moving on to 2007, Apple at last got mobile phone technology right. Great screens, touch navigation, easy to use, and good speed, and at last non-SMS mobile advertising started to gain traction.

In 2012, Facebook and Twitter launched mobile ads. These ads have seen significant growth as their ad format natively fits mobile devices. These ads are being shown in the home page News Feed of Facebook or Twitter mobile apps leading to many more clicks than expected.

Mobile Ad Market

The US mobile ad market is \$3.8 billion large[60] with Google's share about half of this. The market is still relatively small but growing extremely fast and expected to take over radio in 2016. Facebook and Twitter have gone from zero to 9% and 4% respectively in 12 months. Pandora (a music streaming business) makes up 6% and Apple's iAd 3% with others making up another 5%. Currently all the action is with Google, Facebook, and Twitter, with Apple's iPad being a dark horse.

Mobile ads can be split into two types: Search and Display. Search is mainly Google's ads, and Display is mainly Facebook's Sponsored Stories and Twitter's Promoted Tweets, rich media and video on mobile sites, and embedded in-application/in-game advertising.

Most of the ad revenue is still in Google Search. A Google mobile search campaign is now been absorbed into a normal campaign set-up, now called an 'enhanced campaign'. You can choose to increase or decrease your bids for mobiles vs computers. Likewise you can increase or decrease your bid for where people are located and even time of day. A good option for bidding on Adwords would be to increased bids for mobiles within a few miles of your wine store or tasting room. A wine store may increase its bids during Friday afternoons.

If you advertise with Google you've covered more than half the mobile advertising market. But if you advertise on Facebook you have two-thirds covered.

9.4 Facebook Advertising

Facebook makes more than \$2 billion from its ads[61], only Google is a bigger player in this Display market.

Traditionally, Facebook advertising were ads on the right hand side of a Facebook page. They tend to be a Headline, Text, and an Image. They would have a 'Like' thumbs up icon and sometimes show friends who have liked your Facebook Page (which we'll discuss in more detail in the Facebook chapter).

Facebook now offers the following ad types:

- Ad
- Sponsored Story
- Promoted Post

- Offers
- Check-Ins
- Retargeting

To create an Ad, Sponsored Story, or Promoted Post you simply click on the Settings button and choose 'Create and Ad'.

A *Standard Ad* is what you see in the right-hand column. It can link to your website or to you Facebook Page. You can add a small image and 90 characters of text. This is a very important way to grow a Fan base.

When a user interacts with a Facebook Page, their friends may see stories about it in their news feeds depending on EdgeRank. A *Sponsored Story* is where you pay to get past the EdgeRank filter so the user's friends see this interaction with the brand in their News Feed. This interaction is most probably going to be a Like, and the users' friends will arguably see this Like as an endorsement of your brand. This is a unique form of advertising that only social media can offer.

A *Promoted Post* is where you pay for your post to get past the EdgeRank filter and be shown to most of your Fans. 'Most of' because not all Fans may use Facebook during your campaign or there may be too much competition for News Feed space for your ad to be shown to all your Fans. Once you have 400 Fans or more then a Promote button will appear under your post.

Offers are a way to promote a discount or coupon that can be redeemed online and/or in-store. You can choose to set a budget when you set up the Offer or choose to promote it later using the normal Ads Manager. It is a simple process but is only available to Pages with at least 400 Fans.

Check-In Deals are a way to encourage users to check-in to your wine store or tasting room. Check-In means that a user is clicking a button on their Facebook Post that gives the location of where they are to their Facebook friends. There are various types including discounts, gift with purchase, loyalty, group and even charity. Check-Ins are only available to Pages with 400 Fans and, at the time of writing, were only available in the US. Facebook labels this ad type 'Beta' which means it could change or be cancelled at any time.

Retargeting is where you show Facebook Ads to anyone who has previously visited your website. That's right your external www website not Facebook itself! This is done by putting some code on your website that downloads a cookie on to the user's website browser.

Then the browser goes to Facebook which sees the cookie and displays your Facebook Ad. You will need to go through a Facebook ad service partner (I use adroll.com) and put some simple code onto your website so it is a little more complicated than the other methods—but very effective. [62]

You are most probably going to use a standard ad, sponsored story, and/or promoted post first. Facebook advertising best practice is very similar to Google Adwords. You split test your ads, measure your results, and set a daily budget. However, in Adwords you target audiences based on keywords, in Facebook you target audiences based on their interests and demographics. It is this targeting that makes Facebook a different and effective advertising medium.

Facebook Targeting

Micro-targeting[63] is central to success with Facebook ads. This is where you begin with a large audience and then refine your campaigns into smaller targets or 'segments' based on the resulting data. The following are ways you can target:

Location. You should target your local customers by choosing your city or suburb (though if the numbers seem unusually low choose your State).

Demographics. A premium wine marketer is best to target people aged greater than 30 years with high incomes.

Connections. You can target those connected to your Page already (repeat customers), their friends (new customers), anyone not connected to your Page (new customers), or all three. Who you should target depends on your business objectives. If it's to develop new business then focus on the non-connected customers, if it's repeat business then it's connected customers. Friends of connections will see that the connection has 'Liked' your Page, which can be a powerful social endorsement and very effective way to attract new customers. I suggest you split these into separate campaigns.

Interests People can choose to share interests on their Facebook profile. Wine Interests include *wine, wine tasting, food & wine, wine bar, wine cellar, drinking wine, wine enthusiast, wine festival, I Need Glass Wine, great wine, I Love Wine, Its Wine Oclock Now, wine library tv, wine lovers, wine ladies, wine month club, No Wimpy Wines,* and many more. There should be similarity between your Adwords keywords and Interests.

Precise, Topic, and Broad Targeting. Similar to the Adwords Exact, Phrase, and Broad match you have three different ways to reach your audience: Precise Interests, Topics, and Broad Categories.

Precise interest targeting is for advertisers who carefully manage detailed lists of specific interests. It is arguably too detailed for most advertisers. The obvious keyword is to type *wine* into the Interests field and see what comes up. Also try varietals and region combinations.

Topic targeting is like a phrase match in Adwords. You put a # in front of the interest. This captures every interest with that interest word in it, so you don't need to target every interest like you would with Precise Targeting. The obvious interest is *#wine* and the varietals.

Broad targeting uses categories that Facebook creates based on interests and other profile content. It can't be used with Precise Interest and Topic targeting, but you can switch your campaign to Broad at any time.

Campaigns are Ad Groups. In the Adwords example at the start of this chapter, we started a campaign that was focused just on Google Search not any of the other networks. Think of your Facebook as the same thing, just another network where the Facebook 'Campaigns' are really just Google 'Ad Group' levels of similar interests. So if we have one Google Adwords Ad Group focused on *Napa Valley Merlot*, we might have one Facebook Campaign focused on *Napa Valley Merlot*.

Google Analytics Tagging. In order to track Facebook Advertising in your Google Analytics account place the following code at the end of the external website url:

```
?&utm_medium=social&utm_source=facebook&utm_campaign=NAME
```

where NAME is a shorthand name for the campaign. If you don't then you'll not be able to split the Facebook Page and Facebook Ad traffic in Google Analytics.

Ad Fatigue and Testing

With Adwords you may find a particular ad works with no challenging ad able to beat it—possibly resulting in the same ad (or tiny variations of it) being shown for years. In Facebook, your ad will probably be shown hundreds more times than a Google Ad, and users will become 'blind' to it—it will 'fatigue'. In order to avoid this, you change the image, headline, and copy regularly by turning similar campaigns on and off.

In Adwords, your key element to test is the headline, while in Facebook it is the image. Don't assume that this is a wine bottle or a beautiful woman drinking wine—test different images to find what works in your market.

Campaign Measurement

Many Facebook marketers aim for simple Engagement measures of success, for example 'Likes'. This may be a perfectly acceptable way of monitoring Ad quality as would clicks. However, the overall aim of internet advertising is not Engagement but Traffic and Sales Conversions. We will cover this in the Measurement section below, and Engagement measures in the Facebook chapter.

Note that Google Analytics cannot automatically distinguish between normal Facebook traffic and Facebook advertising traffic. Google Analytics is closely integrated with Adwords and automatically distinguishes any traffic from its advertising networks as advertising or what it speciously calls 'Paid Search', and any traffic from other Google sources as 'Non Paid'. In order to distinguish between the two, you should paste some characters after the website url of any Facebook advertising that directs to your website as per *Google Analytics Tagging* above.

9.5 What I Haven't Covered in this Chapter

Internet Advertising is a large topic to cover in one chapter; indeed, it deserves its own book, if not three or four books (see Resources below). If you'd like to build your own skills in this area then look into the following:

- Adwords: Search Partner Network, Conversion tracking, Search Partner Network, Display Network, Display Ads, Image Ads, Display Automatic and Manual Placement, Categories, Retargeting
- Bing and Yahoo advertising
- YouTube advertising
- Twitter promoted tweets, accounts

- LinkedIn Ads (business to business advertising for trade rather than consumer customers)
- Yelp and other local directories, and Location Based Services advertising
- Other Banner Advertising Networks

An important part of Adwords is the sister services that have been integrated into it—Google Analytics and Google Website Optimizer. Google Analytics is partially covered in each Measurement section of every chapter in this book. Google Website Optimizer is covered in the Landing Page Optimization chapter.

This book takes an 80/20 approach to internet marketing, that is to show you 20% of the internet marketing strategies that provide you with 80% of the commercial benefit—all from a wine retail angle. However, in the case of internet advertising, you may wish to read more about this from dedicated sources such as outlined in the Resources section below.

9.6 Measurement

Tony has really got the hang of internet advertising. Not only is he using Adwords, including the extensions, but he's asked his agency to help him with banner, mobile, and Facebook advertising. His advertising is carefully targeted at wine varietals that Luxury Enthusiasts like. Before we look at his Internet Advertising measurements, let's cover Customer Acquisition Cost.

9.6.1 Customer Acquisition Cost

There is no point in using internet advertising if the cost of acquiring a new customer is hundreds of dollars. It is, however, arguably acceptable to break even on the first sale from advertising, as it's assumed that the customer will make repeat sales directly and therefore be profitable.

This calculation is called Cost per Acquisition. This simply is the Advertising Cost divided by the number of customers per period (usually month). For example, if you have an Adwords campaign that has 100 clicks in a month at $1 per click then your cost is $100. Let's say of those 100 clicks only 5 converted into sales. The cost per each of those sales, the Cost per Acquisition, is $100/5=$20.

If your gross margin is 30% then each of those orders has to be worth $66.67 of revenue (or profit of $20) or else you have lost money on this Adwords campaign. Tony may know that his average order value is about $45. So he needs to bring the Cost of Acquisition down to $13.50 or increase order value to $66.67.

Note that you can work on various ways to bring down the Cost per Acquisition. You can reduce the cost per click or increase conversions, for example, and we'll look at a good process to do this in the Landing Page Optimization chapter.

9.6.2 Internet Advertising Measurements

Business Objective: Boost Margins and Volume by changing to a Higher Value Customer Mix.

Marketing Strategy >Promotion >Internet marketing: Increase 'Paid' Traffic from Search, Banner, mobile, Facebook that leads to conversions.

KPI: Conversion Average Order Value; Conversion Average Bottle Value; Cost per Acquisition. As measured in Google Analytics filtering for 'Paid' Search, and all other internet advertising tagged 'ppc' (see Facebook Campaign Measurement above). Cost per Acquisition is manually calculated.

KPI Targets: For Year 2. Cost per Acquisition = $13.50. For other KPIs see Table below.

Segment	Conv.#	Ass. Conv.#	AOV	ABV
Luxury Enthusiasts:	2	1	$65	$25
Enthusiasts:	5	2	$33	$15
Image Seekers:	2	2	$26	$15
Luxury Image Seekers:	2	1	$65	$15

Table 9.1: KPI Targets: Advertising (Year 2)

KPI Target Sources: Segment numbers come from the Internet Marketing spreadsheet *Segment Conversions Report*. For Conversion Average Order Value equations see SEO Measurement section.

Internet Advertising will add 17 more customers. Tony expects advertising to deliver three Luxury Enthusiasts. Along with general and local SEO, he has 35 more to go before he reaches his target. Time to move to another internet marketing strategy in the next chapter.

9.7 Summary

Internet advertising covers ads appear on search engines results pages, websites of all types, and social media. Google calls its network 'Adwords'. You can easily set up an account and publish an ad, though there are various best practices in order to make it effective and to control costs, including targeting different keywords with separate Ad Groups, testing especially headlines, and using negative keywords. Other networks include banner, mobile, and Facebook advertising all with their own idiosyncrasies.

9.8 Resources

- Internet Advertising Discussion, Update, and Posts Page: `www.WineMarketingPros.com/advchap/`
- *Adwords for Dummies* by Howie Jacobson
- Facebook Marketing `www.facebook.com/marketing`

10 Comparison Shopping Engines (CSE)

10.1 What is CSE

In the SEO and Internet Marketing chapters, I wrote about a 'keyword search continuum'. One side of the continuum is browsing and the other side buying. So a word like *wine* is just a 'browsing' word; whereas, a word like *Andrea's Vineyard Napa Valley Merlot 2009* is a 'buy' keyword. The same can be said about different types of sites.[64] A website that is about general wine news is less likely to result in purchasing than a website that lists specific products at specific prices purchasable at specific online wine stores. The latter exists and is called a 'Comparison Shopping Engine' (CSE) also known as a price comparison service, price engine, shopping sites, and various derivations of these.

Websites, such as pricegrabber, shopzilla, shipping.com, and nexttag, service the general retail industry and often attempt to provide wine information. Shopping.Yahoo.com and the Amazon Marketplace are two of the more prominent Comparison Shopping Engines that sell wine. However, the wine industry is lucky to have some very effective specialist CSEs called Snooth and Wine-Searcher. Google Product Search used to be a CSE, but they have relaunched this service as an Adwords 'Extension', in effect changing it from a CSE to another form of Adwords.

Although comparison shopping engines may have smaller amounts of traffic than social media sites, such as Facebook or the search engines, their traffic is worth more given the purchase propensity of visitors and their higher conversion rates.

10.2 General Set Up

This part of the internet ecosystem has it's own peculiarities and optimization techniques. Its usually an easy process to get started. You'll be asked to submit your products. The easiest way to do this is by downloading a sample excel or csv file and filling this in for your products. You then upload it and in about 24-72 hours you're being displayed in the CSE at no charge. However, it's a manual process that can better be done with an automated feed.

By setting up an automated feed, CSEs can poll your site and receive a file that has structured product information. The structure code is specified by the CSE and would have a series of fields that cover basic product information. For example, one line of code may look like this, <price>19.99</price>. Google, therefore, knows that this product has a price of $19.99. Often eCommerce software will do this automatically or by allowing easy set up.

I suggest you visit the mentioned websites while reading this chapter.

10.3 Snooth

Snooth.com is a very interesting shopping comparison site that specializes in wine. It was launched in June 2007 by Philip James who has become a well known wine tech entrepreneur. It has a large wine database and online community, with over 1 million wines and prices from 11,000 merchants and wineries worldwide. Snooth says the site currently handles over 5 million searches per month and has over 400,000 registered users. It's certainly got some big names behind it and has established a lot of credibility in the wine and tech world. It is big but also free, as in you can list your products for free. It's only when you choose to get greater exposure through 'featured' listings that you start to pay any fees.

The set-up is reasonably standard and has some excellent suggestions for fields (* means this field is compulsory), see Table 10.1. Don't worry if it looks daunting—there are many ways to do this quickly other than doing it one product at a time. Also don't worry if you don't fill in most of the fields (though if you do you will most likely give you preference in a CSE's results). Your eCommerce software probably has a way to do this. According to Snooth, as long as

Table 10.1: Snooth Fields

Snooth Wine ID*	Name*	Vintage
Winery	Region*	Type
Color	Release Status	UPC
Organic	Kosher	Non-Alcoholic
Biodynamic	All-Natural	Vegan
Certified Sustainable	Varietal	MSRP
MSRP Currency	Container Notes	Amount Produced
Closure Type	Sugar	Alcohol
pH	Acidity	Your Price*
Your Sale Price	Product URL	Bottle Size*
Winery Notes	Vineyard Notes	Vintage Notes
Tasting Notes	Serving Suggestions	Aging Details
Review 1	Review 2	Review 3

it can identify SKU, price, URL, and wine name then it should work.

When you upload products, Snooth tries to work out if it has these already listed in its product database. If so, then it simply adds a pre-existing product ID to your listing so consumers can compare the same product from different retail stores. If not, it adds them to your account for you to edit (if you wish).

All Comparison Shopping Sites have hundreds of listings. It's why consumers visit them so they can compare prices and reviews. One way to get to the top of these listings is to pay the site. For some sites, you increase your bid price for a click, on others you pay a flat fee. With Snooth, you become a featured merchant and pay a commission on sale.

Featured merchants are the ones that appear at the top of the listings and get a yellow star with 'Featured' beside it. Many consumers don't go much further than the top 4-6 listings (that are 'above the fold'). So it is certainly worthwhile.

The downside is you have to pay a percentage (10%) of the purchase price. Snooth tracks this by asking (insisting) you install a small piece of code called tracking code in your website shopping cart. You'll probably need to get your eCommerce provider to do this if you aren't comfortable with html. This code tracks whether a customer came from Snooth (by using 'cookies'[65]), then tracks whether they actually purchase something by seeing if an order is completed (it looks for a success page, such as one headed 'Thank You' or 'Order Completed'). If it's successful then Snooth charges your credit card that percentage fee or 'commission'. If you go to your company setup in Your Account, you'll see a section called 'Featured Merchant Setup'. This is where you put in your details.

Most comparison shopping engines encourage you to provide more information in your listing by giving you a higher ranking for a richer description—especially reviews. So if you can do this once and do it well then you'll be rewarded many a time with more prominent and better rankings in shopping sites.

10.4 Wine-Searcher

Wine-Searcher is a large search engine of wine stores, wineries, wine auctions, price lists, and catalogues. According to Wine-Searcher, it has five and a half million products listed from about 38,000 wine shops. But its claim to fame is really the ability to compare wine prices.

Martin Brown created Wine-Searcher in 1999 having previously been involved in wine retail eCommerce. It provides two services to wine drinkers. The first one is free: consumers can search for wines but only see limited results. The paid or 'Pro' version costs the wine drinker $39.00 per year, and the drinker can see all the results.

In the free version, consumers only see sponsoring retailers—if they stock the wine. If they don't then other non-sponsoring retailers are shown. According to Wine-Searcher 97%, of the searches are free searches so becoming a sponsoring retailer may be a good idea. As well as always being listed on the free results page, merchants also have display ads.

Wine-Searcher takes a different approach from Snooth. While Snooth gets a commission for featured listings, Wine-Searcher gets a periodic fee from sponsoring merchants and 'Pro' version consumer buyers. Snooth is more oriented around wine consumers and the wine industry contributing ratings and reviews; whereas, Wine-Searcher is more about straight out price comparison. Both have significant free offerings for the wine consumer and the retailer.

A retailer can join Wine-Searcher by filling out a form[66], and they'll start the process from there. From experience Wine-Searcher, will often seed their database with your wines to help you get started.

But if they don't, the standard ways of uploading products apply as discussed above for Snooth.

Upload products by File. The file can be from many formats including: Excel spreadsheets, Word documents, and Text (CSV, Tab separated, etc.) files. You just need to be clear about your fields, e.g. name, price. Wine searcher seems much more relaxed about how you describe your wines—they require the name and the price but that's it, though they do encourage you to put in a lot more information.

Upload products by Feed. The data feed can also be either a XML file or a CSV Text file. So they're more relaxed about this as well, compared to Snooth. I'm guessing they have a manual process the first time in the background that maps the way the merchant defines a field to the way Wine-Searcher does.

A feed or text file that had the following fields would probably work well:

- name including varietal (up to 160 characters)
- price excluding sales tax
- vintage
- bottle size
- case or single bottle quoted price
- a product page URL

Wine-Searcher, like Snooth, suggests you add more information to your listing as this tends to get more referrals than less informative listings. So I'd also include as many of the following in their own fields as you can:

- Region
- Varietal
- Color
- Release Status
- UPC
- Organic
- Kosher
- Non-Alcoholic
- Biodynamic
- All-Natural
- Vegan
- Certified Sustainable
- Closure Type
- Sugar

- Alcohol
- pH
- Acidity
- Winery Notes
- Vineyard Notes
- Vintage Notes
- Tasting Notes
- Serving Suggestions
- Aging Details
- Review 1
- Review 2
- Review 3

10.5 Measurement

Tony has created feeds for Wine-Searcher and Snooth. They're comprehensive feeds full of valuable information. He's currently mulling over advertising on Wine-Searcher and paying commission on Snooth to be a featured listing. He may give them a test to see if they're worthwhile. Here are his CSE measurements in the context of his Business Plan.

Business Objective: Boost Margins and Volume by changing to a Higher Value Customer Mix.

Marketing Strategy >Promotion >Internet marketing: Increase CSE Traffic from Snooth and Wine-Searcher.

KPI: Conversion Average Order Value; Conversion Average Bottle Value. As measured in Google Analytics filtering for CSE referrals.

KPI Targets: For Year 2, see Table 10.2.

Segment	Conv.#	Ass. Conv.#	AOV	ABV
Luxury Enthusiasts:	2	1	$65	$25
Enthusiasts:	3	2	$33	$15
Image Seekers:	2	2	$26	$15
Luxury Image Seekers:	1	1	$65	$15

Table 10.2: KPI Targets: CSE (Year 2)

KPI Target Sources: Segment numbers come from the Internet Marketing spreadsheet *Segment Conversions Report.* For Conversion Average Order Value equations see SEO Measurement section.

CSE will add 14 more customers. Tony expects CSE to deliver three Luxury Enthusiasts. Along with the other marketing strategies this means he has 32 more to go before he reaches his target.

10.6 Summary

Comparison Shopping Engines (CSE) have higher conversion rates than most other internet marketing methods. Snooth and Wine-Searcher are excellent specialists. Both require either a manual upload by using a spreadsheet or automatically via a data feed. Each has various paid options to increase your presence and therefore sales.

10.7 Resources

- How well did you understand? Visit my website to discuss or ask questions about Wine CSE: `www.WineMarketingPros.com/csechap/`
- Google Merchant Center `google.com/merchants`

Part III

Engagement

With the explosion of Social Media, Mobile, and Local services, a business need not, and should not, rely just on Google. Your customers' time has been spent moving from Google to other web pages as well as other devices. Their attention has dispersed and an internet marketer's job has become more complex, more multi-faceted and, frankly, more interesting. Especially for a local business.

A local business is at the heart of the three changes we've seen in 2009-10: Social, Mobile, and Local. For example:

- Social—Facebook, Twitter
- Mobile—Apps, Foursquare
- Local—Yelp, Foursquare

This book partitions out the various internet marketing topics. But in reality they all intersect in a very human mishmash of the search, social, geographic, and technology worlds.

11 Social Media

Wine Social Media is big. Vintank, a wine social media tech firm, has measured over 300 million wine conversations and profiled 10 million wine consumers.[67] Many winery Facebook posts gets thousands of shares. The Wine Market Research Council in 2011[68] found 73% of core wine drinkers used Facebook and 24% used Twitter. Core wine drinkers are those people in the US who drink at least one glass of wine every week and make up more than 80% of the wine drunk in the US.

Some wine businesses feel that their target market is wealthy men aged between 45-54 years old and that these men do not use Facebook, but the facts suggest otherwise.

Facebook is used by 4.5 million men aged between 45-54 years old,[69] which is 46% of 26-34 year olds, but large nonetheless.

What's more, arguably the largest community of wine drinkers, CellarTracker's 236,000 members[70] show that 21% of its viewers are aged between 45-54 and 18% have incomes of $150,000+[71].

So why use social media? It's big, it's used by our target market, but there is also an element of common sense. Paul Mabray of Vintank described it this way[72]. When you go back to your office and you see you have voicemail messages on your phone you at least listen to them. If they ask you to call back then you are most likely to return the message, but you would never completely ignore them. It could be a customer placing a large order or perhaps a wine writer wanting an interview; it is just common business sense to regularly clear those message. Social media is the same. Rather than getting messages on your phone, you are getting them in the social media sphere. Sometimes those messages need to be returned, sometimes they can be just listened to, at other times a customer complaint needs to be diplomatically responded to. They are voicemail messages, but everyone can see them.

11.1 What is Social Media

Let's go back to the basics. Social Media is made up of two things: digital, the media part, and person-to-person interaction, the social part. If Jancis Robinson writes an article in the Financial Times then that is obviously old traditional media. If she writes the same article on her website but doesn't allow any sharing then that's digital media, but there is no ability for readers to interact with her so it's not social. If she then opens up the article to comments it becomes a blog post and one type of social media. Jancis Robinson's blog posts are behind a paywall, but a paid blog is still social media.

Truth be told, many famous newspapers and TV stations use the original blogging software, WordPress, as their website software. It is a highly optimized version of WordPress and used more as normal content management system website software than blogging, but it is inherently capable of being used as social media as more often than not readers are able to comment on news articles.

11.1.1 Paid vs Owned vs Earned Media

One way to think about social media is how Sean Corcoran from Forrester Research puts it:

- Owned media: a message delivered from a company to consumers through channels controlled by the company (such as corporate web sites and micro-sites)
- Paid media: a message delivered from a company to consumers by paying to leverage a channel not controlled by the company (mainly in the form of advertising)
- Earned media: a message about a company passed between consumers as a result of an experience with the brand (or social media).

However, there can also be overlaps[73] between these. When you publish a blog post, consumers can comment on it, or when your consumers use Facebook they could see your Paid Ad.

The idea is that Owned and Paid media are the foundation to achieve the much more valuable Earned media, in the same way that normal advertising aims to increase customers who hopefully promote your business via word of mouth endorsement.

I like the way this puts social media in context—it is just another form of media, that is publicity, at the end of the day.

11.1.2 The Wine Drinker Involvement

One of the best ways of describing how heavily people are involved in social media, as well as how people utilize it differently, is the Engagement Pyramid[74], see Figure 11.1.

Figure 11.1: The Engagement Pyramid

It can also be used to determine your own social media strategy as well as understand wine drinker usage.

Watching. Most of your potential customers almost certainly watch and read rather than actively engage in social media. Which is fine and worth keeping in mind when you feel like you're shouting into the void.

Sharing. Some of them will share. For example 'liking' or retweeting. So make sure they can do so easily with plugins like ShareThis or the Facebook 'Like'.

Commenting. Some will comment on your posts or retweet with a comment. Negative comments? Great. It helps you explain yourself better (and confirms you're not shouting into the void).

You can choose to write helpful and insightful comments on another blog or forum (the jargon is 'outposts'). This also shows your knowledge and piques potential customers' interest.

Producing. Some will produce their own blogs and forum discussions. These people are so involved in the topic they'll even produce their own blogs—fools like me for example and some talented wine bloggers I follow. If you choose to do this it will help you become recognized not only as the expert in (high margin) premium wines, but an expert who can also take the next step and supply them. You can also reduce customer purchase risk (a major wine industry issue) by providing reviews and ratings, as well as insightful stories about the wine (sales reps will help, I hope).

Curating. At the very top of the pyramid are 'curators'. They are like art gallery or museum curators who pull the best material together for a particular show. 'Wine curators' pull together the best information and/or moderate forums and blogs. They may or may not publish blogs or forums themselves.

11.1.3 Socialgraphics

Which social media technology you use depends on the behavior of your customers. This is basic marketing—but in this social media craze some commentators seem to be forgetting this. The co-creator of the Engagement Pyramid, Charlene Li, calls this 'Socialgraphics', which plays on the marketing term 'Psychographics'. *Demographics* provides statistical data on a particular group of people. *Psychographics* provides data on the psychology of particular groups of people buying brands. *Socialgraphics* is data on the social networks of particular groups of people. This is how she puts it[74],

1. Where are your customers online? Action: Don't aimlessly approach social networks without knowing if they are there, if they are in Hyves (competing Dutch version of Facebook), go there.
2. What are your customers' social behaviors online? Action: Which social features should we deploy? Example: if they are commenters, allow them to comment.
3. What social information or people do your customers rely on? Action: If they rely on their friends, facilitate a marketing program that encourages customers to share with friends.
4. What is your customers' social influence? Who trusts them? Action: If your customers are trusted by others, highlight your customers in front of their community. Example: Intercontinental Hotel features the photos created by top guests.
5. How do your customers use social in regards to your brand? Action: Understand how customers use these tools in researching new products, decision making, and support.

11.1.4 The Value of Influencers

The major difference between social media marketing and normal marketing is how we treat one particular group of customers—the influencers.

Normal marketing math is simple: a customer buys a certain amount of wine each year. Social Media math takes that customer and looks at how influential he or she is. This is dependent on the size of their social network and how likely the network will act on any recommendation that influential customer makes. If the influencer recommends your wine store on social media then their customer value is not just the wine they buy but the value of all the others in their social network that act on this recommendation. It is a concept I'll keep coming to back to in this part of the book.

There are a number of services that attempt to measure influence. It is controversial whether they do this well or not[75] but at least they provide an indication. These services include klout.com, peerindex.com, and kred.com. They all provide a score of some type and can be a useful way to search for influential people in the wine industry.

11.1.5 Social Media and the Marketing Funnel

Let's look at why you could be interested in wine social media, from a business objective perspective, not because it's the latest marketing buzz word. Here's a diagram I've compiled from my own general internet marketing knowledge combined with various social media experts, see Figure 11.2.

I've put some more traditional marketing and retail goals to the left, i.e. branding, engagement, information gathering, purchase, and customer service.[76] Then some ways to measure success or 'metrics', see the section *Social Media Metrics* below,[77] followed by various types of social media. Last comes a marketing funnel of Awareness >Consideration >Preference >Purchase >Loyalty to the right.[78]

Look at the Objectives column, choose the particular issue you face, and then check out what I recommend in terms of:

- how to measure success
- how it fits on the Paid : Owned : Earned continuum
- types of media (including traditional ones)
- the stage of the marketing funnel

Figure 11.2: Marketing Funnel overlaid with Objectives, Metrics, Media, Types

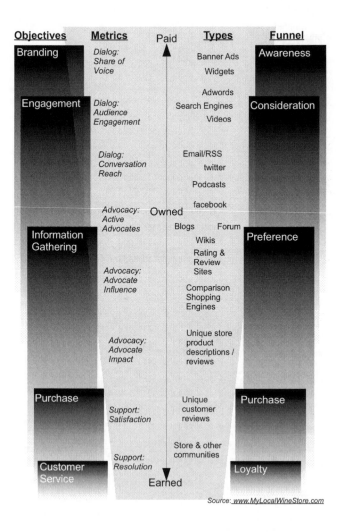

Source: www.MyLocalWineStore.com

If you have an awareness issue then perhaps social media is not the right place to start especially if you don't have many fans or followers. If you have lots of engagement but are failing to convert that into sales then perhaps you should be thinking more about changing the shopping cart to increase conversions. Most likely though, people are aware of you but just don't really consider or prefer your brand—in which case social media is a good solution to this problem.

Let's go through some objectives or problems you may face.

Awareness

Does Barefoot Wines and Bubbly or BevMo have an awareness problem— probably not. Does a local retailer on a side street in the suburbs have this issue—probably. So it's a valid business objective to increase the awareness of potential customers within 20 miles of your store by advertising on a local wine blog, for example.

Traffic

Does your local competitor drive a Mercedes while you drive an old Toyota? Could be he's doing something right on the internet. Do a Google search for his store name. Check each of the left hand side menu items to see if he comes up. It could be he's all over the web—and you're not. Your objective is to improve your position in the market when your customers are gathering information pre-purchase. Start your own blog, post comments on the Wine-Searcher Facebook page, or perhaps create your own video tastings.

Engagement

Those intense customers who have strong opinions—they're a god send. Would you refuse to talk to customers if they walked into your store? Likewise just watching and reading blogs or forums isn't enough either—you have an engagement issue. Take those discussions you have with your best customers face to face, to thousands more potential customers on your blog, others' blogs, Twitter, Facebook, and wine forums.

Conversion

Lots of traffic, no conversion? Your objective is to increase your conversion. Time to look at where you are spending your time—perhaps an industry blog is not the best place—building wine consumer trust on a consumer blog may be better (there is a good chance that Conversion is not related to social media but rather your website eCommerce process, see the eCommerce chapter).

Repeat

No one likes me? That is you have few repeat customers. Check it out—start to monitor what people are saying about you online. This is easily done with VinTank's Social Connect wine industry specialist social media software.

All my customers go where the price is lowest, there's no loyalty any more. According to wine research, only some customers do, some of the time. Many prefer the advice you give, and your range of premium wines. So start to include that advice to your email list rather than just a tasting note and a special promo. There is a very high level of consumer involvement in wine, so it's not hard to engage in this sophisticated and passionate community.

11.2 Measurement

This chapter was more of an overview of social media rather than looking at specific KPIs—I'll leave that for each individual chapter.

Tony's Wine Store social analytics strategy is deeply grounded in his business. You're already seen traffic measurements that can be tied back to the High Value Customer Mix business objective. We'll use social media specific tools to do this in the following chapters while not forgetting sales conversions.

11.3 Summary

Social Media is using web-based and mobile technologies to interact with others. Social Media can be looked at from the perspective of Earned vs Owned and Paid Media and the different levels of involvement of your customers and yourself. The value of influencers is significantly more important in social media marketing than normal marketing. What social media you use depends on the behavior of your customers, your business objectives, and your resulting social media strategies.

11.4 Resources

- How well did you understand? Visit my website to discuss or ask questions about Wine and Social Media: `www.WineMarketingPros.com/smchap/`
- Altimeter Group `www.altimetergroup.com/blog`

12 Blogging

12.1 What is a Blog

Blog is short for web log. It is a digital means to write your thoughts, opinions, ideas, and commentary and share them with the world via the internet. They allow visitors to comment and share and are usually information, commentary, or news about a subject. Indeed, the line between the online versions of well-known newspapers and magazines and a high quality blog has become very blurred.

12.2 Why Blog

I'm a strong proponent of wine retailers having blogs. A blog ties together many parts of the overall selling process. In some ways, it's the center of your online effort because the hardest part of selling online is creating content. A blog post is also easy to share with others and integrate with an eCommerce store. Below, I outline all of the benefits of blogs and a system to help get you started selling wine on the internet.

To see the first major benefit of a blog, let's review what the search engines want. The search engines (Google and Yahoo/Bing) are in a fierce, competitive battle. The better their search engine results, the more people use them, the more advertising they sell, and the higher their profits. People, or 'users', want the most relevant results for their search query. They want to type in a keyword phrase and see the solution to their search problem straight away. So if someone types in Napa Valley Merlot 2007 they may want to (a) buy it or (b) get information about it.

It's difficult to work out what a user wants from a simple phrase. So the search engines provide a list of possible answers feeling reasonably confident that one of them will solve the searcher's problem. When I searched Google for the 'Napa Valley Merlot' (see SEO chapter), Amuse Bouche winery headed the list, then a newspaper article, then

Hall Wines, a Yahoo wine shopping result, a Napa wine store, a wiki website, two more wineries, a price finder website, and lastly a gift company. A nice set of possible answers to an unclear query—and the reason why most people use Google. Google knows users want a list of different answers—not a list of the same answers from different websites. Which brings me to my first point.

1. Having the same standard product description is not good enough to do well with search engines

Top ranking websites have unique content. This is what Google's top search engine, Matt Cutts says on YouTube, answering the question, 'do I want to make the eCommerce site if I don't have a lot of original content?'

> What you should be asking yourself is... do I want to make the eCommerce site if I don't have a lot of original content, or value add, or if I have a lot of duplicate content... So I'd ask yourself, do you really want to jump into that and start optimizing that, or do you want to look for something a little more original or something more compelling... So my advice is... think about how you can move more towards that high value add, unique sort of site, not just... a page that looks just like 500 other pages that they've just seen on the web.

The best way to create unique content is to write down your thoughts daily via a wine blog.

2. Other websites want to link to relevant and useful pages they trust.

By writing your own useful posts about wine, you establish credibility with other websites who may link to your blog—those crucial external links. No sending emails asking for links, no dubious directories or paid links, just interesting blog posts that naturally attract readers.

3. Clearly show Google that you are a subject matter expert for target wine categories.

If you've read the SEO chapter you'll remember the SEO practice of 'theming' your website. It's the same for blogs. For example, a category, or what is also called a 'theme', might be merlot, with a sub-theme of Napa merlot, and the product Andrea's Vineyard Napa Merlot (2007). You clearly flag to Google your subject matter expertise by keeping your products in strict themes. You write unique content about each theme and sub theme. Now when Google looks at your site it sees that:

- the major theme is wine store and there are clearly some other (sub) themes
- one of them is merlot and there is some interesting unique content about your Merlot range that Google's users may find very useful
- there is clearly another sub theme in the merlot theme about Napa merlot with some more interesting content
- you can buy Napa merlot products
- and if the user is near the store then it flags that as well

4. Use social media to spread your word, your 'content'

Not all our time is spent searching for things. We also like to interact with others about things that we are passionate about, and wine is regarded as one of those things (the marketing term is 'high involvement'). We talk about wine to our friends on Facebook, tweet to our followers on Twitter, and present videos on YouTube. This interaction can drive lots of traffic to your website by diplomatically including your website address and all of your interesting, unique content (see Figure 12.1). Social media also includes blogs and forums. The classic example is Gary Vaynerchuk who created video content and interacted with his fans on his WineLibrary.tv forum. But first and foremost there is your blog.

12.2.1 Creating Content is a Real Pain

By now you've probably seen where I'm heading, let's review:

- Search engines want to list the most relevant sites for a user query
- They do this by looking for unique content that is linked to by other high authority websites
- Social media sites are awash with potential customers, but you need to provide them with a reason to visit your website

Figure 12.1: Re-using original content

Why you should Blog	Blog Content
Use the same content for:	
Search Engine - Organic	
Search Engine - Shopping	
Search Engine - Local	
Paid Search (e.g. Adwords)	
Social Media: Twitter	
Social Media: Facebook	
Social Media: Other Bloggers & Forums	
Social Media: Your product pages	
Social Media: YouTube	
Email Marketing (and RSS)	

You need to start creating content. Not just cut and paste winery reviews but create good content for search terms that are important to your business. The solution is to do what more than 14 million people have already done—start a blog. Rather than start with writing descriptions for 100s of products, do something that is a natural, which is the stress free way of creating useful and unique content. Every day or two you write a blog entry about whatever you want. I'd suggest that is firstly about varietals, but we want to make this easy, so just write whatever takes your fancy if that's the way it suits you.

It's like writing in a diary, or writing in your wine tasting notebook. Just a few notes regularly about wine. If you have a particularly good sales conversation with a customer in-store then use it by doing a quick blog. No need to worry too much about spelling and grammar, everyone knows that it's just your thoughts not War & Peace. Struggling to write? Try video blogging (preferably with a written transcript for SEO). Struggling for content? Then ask your staff, your friends and even your wine expert customers to write some blog posts.

12.2.2 The Software

If your eCommerce software doesn't have an integrated blog then ask your web developer to add WordPress to your website. WordPress has simple ways to 'post' (i.e. write and publish on the internet) your thoughts on wine. It's best to include the blog as part of your eCommerce website so you get the full SEO benefit of any traffic or links to your website. By this, I mean example.com/blog not exampleblog.com, i.e. a subpart of your existing website not a new website.

I prefer to use the most popular Content Management System and Blogging software in the world—WordPress.I use this because:

- it's simple to use
- it was originally made for naturally publishing content
- it's well set up for search engine optimization
- there are inexpensive design options (like a design for free or even less than $100)
- it is very flexible with lots of options
- it can integrate with other eCommerce systems
- it's open source, which means the software is free (though the installation and hosting usually isn't)

See the SEO chapter for what you should write about when it comes to important keyword phrases. Or just write from the heart about interesting and entertaining things going on in your wine business. You can post in any order you'd like, with as many paragraphs as you'd like. Write descriptions, reviews, or other content like the winery's history and personality. Add in some personality, trivia, fun, and humor—the aim with blogging as a social media tool is to encourage engagement with your readers.

Each time you create some content consider doing the following:

- Shall I tweet about the headline and link to my followers? Shall I tweet interesting sentences from the post?
- Is it time to combine the latest posts into an email newsletter?
- Shall I create an Adwords ad for the specific search term that drives traffic to this specific blog post page?
- Shall I take a three paragraph snippet with one of the photos and post it in Facebook or wine forums?

About a year later, you will be driving sales online and in-store, because now you have a system that has created and promoted 200 pieces of unique content. If you have taken the keyword approach then you may have 8 varietal theme pages * 5 regional sub themes * five product pages = 200 pages.

In fact you could argue the best way is to start with the blog, then once you have enough unique content attach an eCommerce system to it.

12.2.3 A Good Approach to Start with

Set up the wine retail blog, then start a cycle of Plan-Do-Analyze. Each cycle goes like this:

- Start blogging for themes you are interested in
- Implement local search optimization, i.e. Google Places, Yelp etc.
- Post part of the blog in your Facebook page
- Tweet key sentences
- Implement a local Adwords campaign (with location, phone, and product extensions)
- Refine web pages to boost conversions, especially through testing headlines and content
- Build repeat business through a regular email marketing program

You may choose also to comment on other people's blogs and engage in discussions on other people's forums.

Each Plan Do Analyze cycle lasts a month or two depending on factors such as content written, advertising budget, and your enthusiasm.

In the Conversion and Repeat Purchase parts of this book, we'll look at eCommerce and email marketing strategies. Below we'll cover Facebook and Twitter. Before we finish with blogs, let's look at the advantages of interacting with other people's wine blogs rather than just creating your own.

You don't have to write your own (although obviously I think you should). You can choose to just be a commenter on other people's blogs. However, if you are going to do this you want to make sure it is with the right type of wine blogs.

12.2.4 Local Wine Bloggers

Local wine retailers may choose to look to local wine bloggers. Sure they're not going to be as large as the top wine bloggers, but you have some overlapping interests not the least of which is a similar passion for wine.

First, contact the blogger, invite them for a coffee or wine, and see if there are ways you can work together. I'd keep it that general. Perhaps suggest some fool you've been reading (as in me) reckons that wine bloggers and retailers can help each other. At the end of the day this is just a friendly business arrangement between two people who care about the same thing—wine.

Maybe the blogger is thinking about:

- material to write about
- backlinks or reciprocal links
- store tasting opportunities
- tasting events that they run in your store
- paid writing work
- free or discounted wine
- advertising

Note you will want to ensure they stay independent and abide by FTC disclosure requirements. [79]

What you are after depends on your business objectives. Let's say you want to increase the engagement you have with customers. You could do this with:

- a blog post on their site about a particular niche range you stock with a link to your store's product page
- a blog post from you on their site linked back to a different post on the same topic on your site (you don't want duplicate content)
- a guest post on your blog
- ratings and reviews of some of your high margin wines
- tweets about some interesting wines you stock
- a tasting that they write about in a forum with a link back to your store as well as their blog

I have no doubt that over a bottle of good wine you'd come up with a great list of ideas!

A good way to assess a blogger's value is to regularly assign a blogger a low-volume, premium wine brand that they're interested in (no point in providing a big seller as you'll struggle to identify blogger related sales). Then measure sales in the month(s) of their activity. Try that every month (week?) for 3-6 months. If you see an increase in sales then start offering more cooperation and resources. Doesn't work? Then try another blogger or another marketing method (actually you should be doing this anyway).

The post may be on their blog or your blog/website. Note if they end up writing content on your site then make sure you avoid duplicate content issues (see the Duplicate content section in the SEO chapter) by ensuring it is unique, and not just a copy of one of their existing blog posts.

But it's a great example of the way two parties could both gain out of a business relationship.

Lastly watch the SEOmoz's Whiteboard Friday—Outsourcing Content Creation[80]. Rand Fish talks about outsourcing content creation and gives a 4 step process:

- Step 1: Requirements Gathering
- Step 2: Locating Potential Resources
- Step 3: Research Writing Quality & Voice Match
- Step 4: Scale, Evaluate, Track

Note I'm not saying this is the only way to work with wine bloggers— simple advertising is another way. It really depends on your social media objectives (or 'goals' as Rand puts it).

12.3 The Social Media Brief

So you know what your business objective is, and you believe social media can help you meet that objective. Let's write the brief. By writing a brief, I'm forcing myself to set some objectives and specific measures of success.

Here are some suggested sections of a social media brief:

- Background
- Business Objective
- Marketing Strategy
- Target Audience
- Success Metrics or KPIs
- Deliverables
- Budget and Timeline
- Mandatories

Background

Tony's Wine Store sells high quality wines and spirits in Notown. It has a wine eCommerce website, internet advertising campaign, and search optimized site but is failing to convert traffic to sales. Tony has spoken to a number of Luxury Enthusiast customers who say that the website needs more wine information, and they would like the chance to be more involved with the site. Tony is looking to use social media to engage with its customers in order to sell more wine.

Business Objective

Boost Margins and Volume by changing to a Higher Value Customer Mix.

Target Audience

Primary: Luxury Enthusiast wine drinkers are keen to receive advice, act on a knowledgeable sales person's recommendation, and try different wines. Given their enthusiasm they may be keen 'Commenters' if not 'Producers'. They are very likely to be 'Watchers' and 'Sharers'.
Secondary: Image Seekers search for information and will believe more expensive wines are better quality. They are very likely to be 'Watchers' and 'Sharers'.
Both: Wealthy consumers who will purchase their wine at your local wine store regularly. These two segments are likely to be male, tertiary educated, earning over $75,000 per year who seek advice and information about wine. The Luxury Enthusiasts know lots about wine, Image Seekers know only a little.
Geography: Notown and surrounding suburbs within 20 miles of the store.

Social Media Marketing Strategy

Social Media Strategy: Write interesting, informative, fun, and, sometimes, controversial blog posts that encourage commenting and sharing.

Success Metrics or KPIs

KPI: Conversion Average Order Value; Conversion Average Bottle Value; Increase Total Comments. As measured in Google Analytics using the 'Multi Channel Report'. Total Comments manually counted.

KPI Targets: For Year 2. See Table 12.1. Increase Total Comments for blog posts this month vs last month by two—each time the target is reached it is counted as one Assisted Conversion.

Segment	Conv.#	Ass. Conv.#	AOV	ABV
Luxury Enthusiasts:	1	4	$65	$25
Enthusiasts:	2	5	$33	$15
Image Seekers:	5	5	$26	$15
Luxury Image Seekers:	1	2	$65	$15

Table 12.1: KPI Targets: Blogging (Year 2)

Deliverables

- Attach a WordPress Blog to Tony's Wine Store website with the same look and feel and with the domain folder tonyswinestore.com/blog/. Categories to include Varietals, Regions, Vintage News.
- Create a Marketing Calendar for each week of Q1 2011 to help facilitate/regulate blogging process.
- Integrate Blog, Facebook, and Twitter buttons in website: Blog by email; Blog by RSS.
- Point of sale to include window stickers of website, blog, Facebook page, and Twitter account as well as signage to go behind and on counters.

Budget

To be discussed or Social media hours per day expected by Manager/Social Media rep/agency.

Timeline

Blog by: 15th March 2014
Marketing Calendar by: 15th March 2014
First Blog Post by: 21st March 2014

Mandatories

- Targeted audience must be 21 years or older with no sign of any underage marketing.
- No dubious associations, e.g. with pornography or gambling.
- Exact URL, anchor text, store name, and logo to be supplied.

This brief could then be handed to an agency, a staff member, or act as a plan to do it yourself.

12.4 Measurement

Tony has launched his blog, put aside 15 minutes every day to blog, and has created a blog calendar outlining the topics he'll write about. These topics are varietals, regions, and interviews with wineries that make ultra premium wines. He's had early success with a few Luxury Enthusiast customers commenting on his blog posts. Let's make sure we are using blogging to achieve our Higher Value Customer Mix objective.

Business Objective: Boost Margins and Volume by changing to a Higher Value Customer Mix

Marketing Strategy >Promotion >Internet marketing: Increase engagement with high value customers by blogging and encouraging commenting and sharing.

KPI: Conversion Average Order Value; Conversion Average Bottle Value; Increase Total Comments. As measured in Google Analytics using the 'Multi Channel Report'. Total Comments manually counted.

KPI Targets: see Social Media Brief KPI Targets above.

Tony expects blogging to deliver 23 customers of which five are Luxury Enthusiasts—27 more Luxury Enthusiasts to go before he reaches his target.

12.5 Summary

Blogs are an easy digital means to write wine commentary. They allow visitors to comment and share encouraging greater customer engagement. SEO is also helped by the unique content around important keywords and external links to your website if the posts are interesting enough. WordPress is excellent blogging software though not necessary if your eCommerce system allows content pages with commenting and sharing functionality. You can repurpose the same content for use in other social media. Local wine bloggers could be excellent partners in many ways, including good blogs for you to comment on if you don't feel you can create your own blog. Social Media math is all about referral value—the more influential the blogger the more likely their network will purchase your wine.

12.6 Resources

- How well did you understand? Visit my website to discuss or ask questions about Wine and blogging: `www.WineMarketingPros.com/blogchap/`
- WordPress blogging software `wordpress.org`
- Google Blog Search `blogsearch.google.com`

13 Facebook

13.1 What is Facebook

Facebook is huge—it has a billion users and is one of the most popular websites in the world.[81]

Facebook is huge with the wine community as well. Wine Market Council research shows that 38% of Core Wine Drinkers (the 75 million Americans who drink wine once or more per week) use Facebook.[9]

Facebook is a social networking service that was originally created by Mark Zukerburg for university students to find friends, catch up, and hang out—the 'social' in social media. In 2006, it was opened to everyone aged 13 and above and started the first major wave of social media. In 2007, Facebook announced Facebook Pages, which is how businesses can be represented on Facebook.

Unlike many internet services, people use their real name when signing up and using Facebook. Facebook users have various tabs, including your name and News Feed. If you click on your name then it takes you to a chronological list of all your activity on Facebook as well as snapshots of friends, photos, and Pages liked. This is known as the 'timeline'.

If you click on the News Feed tab (or Home tab) then it will take you to the 'News Feed' page. It has three columns: a navigation column on the left, a column on the right for short cuts and advertising, and most importantly a list of friend and business updates that you may find interesting in the middle. This middle column is also called the Wall, Wall Updates, or Home Page. This page is at the heart of Facebook marketing and is the key page for most Facebook users and Facebook marketers. Note that there is just the one column for a mobile or iPad.

Creating a business Facebook Page is a simple process. Sign into Facebook, go to the bottom of a Facebook page, and click on 'Create a Page'. You will then become an administrator of that Page. A key difference in between Personal and Business Facebook profiles is that a Facebook user *Adds Friends* for people but *Likes* brands or organizations. A person who likes a brand is known as a *Fan*.

A user can do various actions on Facebook, including Likes, posts, comments on others' posts, upload or view photos, play videos, answer or ask questions, and create or join events. Each of these actions is called an 'Edge' in Facebook parlance. These edges may be shared on friends' or fans' 'News Feed'.

Facebook also allows third-party websites and developers to integrate their applications with Facebook. This Facebook 'platform' (a code base developers can build on to) includes the:

- Graph API and Open Graph—this allows developers to integrate their software applications into Facebook.
- Authentication—the log on mechanism
- Social plugins—easy integration of Facebook into websites through the Like button, Recommendations and Activity Feed
- iFrames—is a way to create Facebook Pages by nesting a website inside Facebook.
- Facebook Connect—is a way to log in to third-party websites and applications using your Facebook identity.

Let's discuss Facebook's brain and heart: EdgeRank and News Feed, respectively.

13.2 EdgeRank and News Feed

Whether a person's or a brand's 'edges' or Facebook actions are shared on their friend's or fan's News Feed depends on a filtering algorithm called 'EdgeRank'. Facebook does not show all of your friends or fans your actions for if it did Facebook would be unusable. On average, users have 130 friends and have liked 80 pages or groups[82]. If everyone of those friends or pages performed some action on the same day then a Facebook user would have 210 edges to scroll through. Facebook wants the News Feed to be a good user experience so it filters out edges that it doesn't think you will want to see.

And it filters out a lot. The Facebook Chief Marketing Officer let it slip at one meeting that on average only 16% of Fans[83] will see a Page's action, such as a post. The rest of the edges are filtered out by a ranking algorithm, hence the name 'EdgeRank'.

Facebook has said that the filter algorithm is made up of three variables: *Affinity, Content Weight,* and *Time Decay.*[84]

13.2.1 Affinity

Affinity is best explained by using the example of a teenage girl and an older teenage boy who are friends on Facebook. The teenage girl really likes the older boy, she comments on all his posts, views his photos, and likes his comments on other friends posts. Facebook notes this and, as far as the girl is concerned, ranks anything the boy does highly. Therefore, Facebook will put most of the boy's activity into the girl's Facebook News Feed. The boy on the other hand hardly notices the girl and ignores her. Facebook notes this as well and so doesn't put any of the girl's Facebook activity on the boy's News Feed.

It is the same for wine retailer and winery Facebook Pages. If a Fan is actively engaged in your Facebook Page then Facebook will rank your Page's posts (and other edges) and more of them will get through the EdgeRank Filter on to the Fan's News Feed. Facebook doesn't care whether you view or Like the Fan's page—this is a one way measure that you cannot influence or game.

13.2.2 Content Weight

Content Weight is all about content types, e.g. photo posts, videos posts, questions, events, and text only posts. Facebook will, for example, note whether a user prefers photos or text-only posts and weight that content higher in EdgeRank.

Traditionally, it has been presumed that photos are more preferred by users, but evidence in late 2012 suggested that text only updates are making a come back[85]. Safe to say that Facebook will be continually changing the EdgeRank algorithm as it experiments with ways to increase Facebook usage by providing a good News Feed experience.

13.2.3 Time Decay

Last is the Time Decay variable. In essence, this says that the older the post the less interesting it will be to the user. Research suggests that posts appear on a News Feed for about 3 hours, with 50% of views being made within 90 minutes. Within 3 days the post has for intents and purposes disappeared from a Fan's News Feed.

Unfortunately, the research is mixed as to what is the best time of day or day of the week to post. What is clear is that you need to be posting most days as your previous day's post is most likely to have been swept away by the News Feed 'river'. My suggestion is you post after 3pm on weekdays and anytime on weekends on the assumption that your target market is more likely to view during this time.

The last thing to point out is that I believe a user who does not visit Facebook often is likely to see far fewer posts than someone who is checking their News Feed throughout the day. This is because Facebook will have a much larger backlog of potential posts to filter and will let fewer lowly-ranked posts get through.

Whether your posts are ever seen by your Fans comes down to your EdgeRank for that individual as per affinity, content weight, and time decay.

13.2.4 EdgeRank Makes Sense

There has been a fair amount of angst in the Facebook Marketing Community about why only a small percentage of Facebook Business Page posts make it onto fans' news feeds.[86] However if you take a step back and put it into a wider marketing perspective the varying intensity of fans liking brands is actually pretty normal.

In standard Usage and Attitude market research, we would see only a small part of our target market aware of us (awareness), a smaller part will buy from us (consideration set), and a smaller part still prefers us (preference). This last part, the loyal fans, is likely to be single percentage digits for most brands.

Let's convert that into Facebook world:

- Awareness: Facebook users interested in our category or 'Interests' (as Facebook describes it in Paid Ads).
- Consideration: Facebook Fans
- Preference: those who have affinity, interaction, and happen to see our Posts

EdgeRank is essentially an algorithmic assessment of Preference. It makes even more sense for the wine industry because about 20% of wine drinkers are brand loyal (see the Customer chapter). So, I believe, once we get fans then we in the wine industry should not expect to see more than 15-20% of them engaging with the brand.

Aliza Sherman lists six reasons[87] why people become fans of Facebook Pages in the first place, and suggests that most Fans don't really care. See Figure 13.1 showing how only the smallest number truly care. In descending order:

Figure 13.1: Why People Fan You on Facebook (based on Sherman's graph)

They're keeping up with a competitor (you).

They're just bookmarking.

It's (too) easy.

Someone asked them a favor.

Someone they know did it.

They really love you.

6. They want to keep up with a competitor or have a business reason to pay attention.
5. They are using the action of becoming a fan more like a bookmark for possible future reference.
4. Because it is easy to do (just click to become a fan) and then ignore.
3. They are doing it because someone they know asked them to do it as a favor.
2. They are doing it because someone they know did it.
1. They genuinely like or are interested in the object of the Page.

The only 'Fan' type that were true fans in her opinion was 'They genuinely like or are interested in the object of the Page', the other five reasons have little value other than the original fan broadcast on fan's friends' pages.

On my Facebook page some of my fans have nothing to do with the wine business or Facebook marketing. To be honest, I'm not really sure why they liked the page as I can't see anything in it for them. I call them 'random fans'.

Also many wine pages offer coupons on a custom Facebook advertising landing page if Facebook users will Like their pages. Add in the random fans above and you have a large number of Fans who may have no preference for your brand.

So I don't expect posts to be on all Fan's news feed—EdgeRank is rightly doing it's job for 3 reasons:
1. Preference is always low
2. The Winery Industry has low levels of Brand Loyalty
3. A large part of the Fan Base are not, well, fans but rather opportunistic or random

13.3 Facebook Page Marketing

Facebook encourages businesses to use it for marketing, as they put it,[88]

> Facebook's 4 Steps to Business Success. Your business can develop lasting relationships with customers and access the most powerful kind of word-of-mouth marketing— recommendations between friends.

They describe the steps as Build, Connect, Engage, and Influence. I'm going to use the same headings, even if I describe the steps a little differently.

13.3.1 Build

Building a Facebook page is easy. It changes regularly so I'm reluctant to nominate a process that could be out of date so quickly. However, there are many resources that show you how on Facebook or by doing just a simple Google search.

There is one recommendation I have for you and that is to choose a Place rather than a Brand. You want to be encouraging people to visit your Wine Shop or Wine Tasting room, and you can use Check-In deals as a promotional strategy—more on this below.

Note that once you reach 25 fans you are able to choose your own Facebook web address in the settings tab. Until then you'll have a convoluted alpha-numerical one.

13.3.2 Connect

Once you have a Page, you'll need to grow your Fan base. Without a Fan base, you'll have no method of communicating to them on Facebook. Unfortunately, even when you spend all your time growing the Fan base, you'll find only a minority are active Fans and even fewer are influential ones. Most of the rest are inactive or spam accounts (that will be deleted every once in a while by Facebook), or passive Fans who aren't really all that interested in your wine business.

First, the free methods of growing a Fan base. Put simply, make sure you have a Facebook icon with your Facebook URL everywhere. On every website page, emails, back of the wine label, stickers on the door of the wine shop or tasting room, shelf talkers, twitter background pic, event signage, cases, business cards, and invoices. Utilize all these free methods because the only other way is Facebook Paid Ads.

The harsh truth is that it is believed that most Pages build their Fan base through advertising. It also reflects some of the anger with businesses that they pay to grow their Facebook Fan base then pay to engage with them due to EdgeRank constraints.

Advertising: Connect

See the Internet Advertising chapter for more on Facebook Advertising, in short you have the following options:

- Ad
- Sponsored Story
- Promoted Post
- Offers
- Check-Ins
- Retargeting

A Facebook Page that is growing their Fan base will use standard Ads and Sponsored Stories. Retargeting is also a good option. The rest are better used for encouraging engagement with, and influence through, your Fan base.

13.4 Engage

As you can see from the previous sections, it is important to get Fan engagement. Facebook recognizes this in its EdgeRank algorithm and opens up communication between the Page and its Fans. But more importantly, more Engagement from Fans will lead to greater preference and purchase as the Fan works their way down the marketing funnel. Here are some general best practices that good Facebook marketers keep in mind.

13.4.1 Best Facebook Practices

Jeremiah Owyang, of tech research group Altimeter, outlines some ways, or principles, to evaluate Facebook pages and improve them based on his research[89]. Let's look at the key measures, italics are direct quotes.

Set Community Expectations

Clearly Articulate Expectations to Reduce Confusion and Abuse.
What should users who 'Like' you expect from this Facebook Page—discounts, information, discussion, etc? What is inappropriate behavior, or 'why we will delete your comments if we need to':

- Purpose of Facebook Page
- Community Guidelines
- Consistent Feedback

Provide Cohesive Branding

Create a Holistic Experience that Matches the Brand.
Keep your Facebook page familiar, don't deter potential customers with a page that looks inconsistent with your brand.

- Uploaded a logo, completed info page, and built out profile
- Custom tabs
- Branded landing page

Be Up To Date

Keep Interaction High with Fresh, Timely Content. Is this page 'alive'? Or just a passing thought that the company has since forgotten?

- Post regularity: 1 per day vs. 1 per month
- Best if 80% is informational and 20% or less is promotional
- Not good if they are all automated from e.g. RSS blog plugins

Live Authenticity

Build Trust by Personalizing Interactions with a 'Human Touch.'
Facebook purposely forces people to reveal their real names, it's a
unique part of Facebook, and one that you should respect by being
authentic yourself—not hide nameless behind a brand.

- First person
- Conversational
- Give a name (and photo) behind the company post
- A tab all about the company person(s) who comment on the
  Facebook page on behalf of the company

Participate in Dialog

Connect with Customers by Fostering Two-Way Dialog.

- You want to engage with users who 'Like' your page to build
  up trust and the spreading of information
- Initiate dialog
- Respond to most comments
- Further discussions, answer questions
- Comment on users' photos

Enable Peer-To-Peer Interactions

Be Efficient and Enable the Crowd's Help.
Customers are already talking to each other, so help them do it on
your part of Facebook and the social media world.

- Actively encourage peer to peer discussion
- Active Discussion board
- Q and A
- Active community
- Moderator
- Recognition—showcase, highlight, encourage user's contribu-
  tions

Foster Advocacy

Foster Word of Mouth—the Holy Grail of Marketing.
Your customers' recommendations mean a lot to their friends and
family, probably a lot more than your own.

- Specific requests to spread the word or share, entice users to
  share/interact on their own walls
- Requests to like, vote, sound off, share photos, contests, submissions
- Possibly use apps and custom tabs that promote this

Solicit A Call To Action

Bring it Back to Business and Provide a Succinct Next Step.
You've done all that hard work—now where's the Buy Now button!?

- Sign up for emails, Facebook only discount coupon
- Best of all, a selected catalog with Buy Now buttons that redirect to the relevant website eCommerce page
- Best of the best, have an actual Facebook eCommerce store,
  e.g. ecwid, Shopify

So those are the principles. Let's look at some best practices.

13.5 Pragmatic Recommendations for a Wine Retailer's Facebook Page

I'm a big fan of the 80/20 Rule also known as the Pareto Principle or 'the vital few and trivial many'. In general it means a few
people/products/customers/stocks/tasks etc are vital and many are
trivial. For example, about 80% of your volume will probably come
from about 20% of your products. I, and many other professional
marketers, also use it for prioritizing marketing effort. The idea is
that you should maximize your effort by using a marketing activity
just enough to get 80% of the benefit. That can often mean that you
don't do something perfectly but just well enough, which could mean
only doing 20% of 'perfect'.

It's also a pragmatic approach, as no matter how big or small you
are you never seem to have enough time to get all the things funded
or completed that you'd like. I am a strong proponent of writing content on your blog and then reusing that in other internet marketing

tools: the eCommerce product page, Twitter, email, review websites, comparison shopping sites, and a comment plus link in wine forums. It's the informative conversation (what I'd call a 'respectful sales pitch') you have with a customer that we want to replicate—from one-to-one in-store to one-to-many on the internet.

I'd also extend that to Facebook. It seems to me that few Facebook discussions are in-depth—but quick and fleeting. A 'quick comment in the hallway' (Facebook update) not 'an hour long in-depth meeting in an office' (blog post and comments). So I wouldn't spend much time on Facebook Updates. I'd make short personal comments about a user's choice in wine or respond quickly to their question. Perhaps even a regular Wall Update with simple questions like, 'what's your favorite Pinot?', or 'Burgundy vs. Oregon Pinot Noir, what do you prefer??' Actually the phrase 'nice but shallow' springs to mind—is that being unkind? I don't mean it in a negative way, perhaps 'nice but efficient' is better.

Next are some key tabs to set up to encourage greater engagement with your customers. This is the easy part.

13.5.1 The Tabs

Store

Have an integrated Facebook eCommerce store. I cover this one in depth in the Conversion part of this book.

Blog

A tab with republished content from your blog.

Info and Wall

Fill in as much as you can. Upload your logo and fill out the *Detailed Info* section of the *Info* tab. Include your name, a little bit about you, any staff members who comment on the page, store website, hours, parking, product range overview, contact details (telephone and physical address), and photos of your store (which are likely to be placed at the top of your Page). I think you should also include community guidelines a bit like Chevron does.

Here's how I do it on our Facebook page:

COMMUNITY GUIDELINES:
I encourage open, lively conversation with a few simple rules:
–I reserve the right to address factual errors.
–I will reply to comments when appropriate.
–If I disagree with other opinions, I will do so respectfully.
–You may not post anything that is spam or that is abusive, profane, or defamatory toward a person, entity, belief, or symbol.
–All posts must be in English. Sorry.
–While I support lively, open discussion, I reserve the right to delete comments at my discretion.
I support the Facebook Statement of Rights and Responsibilities and related Facebook policies and, within reason, I expect visitors to my page to do the same.
I look forward to the conversation!

Sign Up and/or Like

Have a prominent prompt to 'Like' your Page. This may be a tab all of its own as per Landing Page below. Also have a tab that has a sign up form or links to an email newsletter.

Landing Page

When a user who has not yet clicked 'Like' arrives at your page they can be directed to a Landing Page with a simple custom Facebook page. If you have a friendly web designer then perhaps ask them to put one together. Google can index a Facebook business Page (though not a personal Page), so make sure you follow good SEO practice.

13.5.2 Content Calendar

Setting up tabs is relatively easy. If you can't do it then you can get a web developer to do it for you. The hardest part is making Facebook (and all social media) a regular part of someone's job. The best way to do this is to create a weekly calendar that gives them tasks to do each day.

13.5.3 The Practices

Every day check for User comments

Make a quick friendly comment back, it should only take a sec. That's the engagement part of social media, it doesn't take much time, and is strongly appreciated by the users (who are, after all, like you - however mild that feeling might be). Note you can also set up email notifications of comments in *Your Settings*.

Always give your name

Sign it off formally or informally e.g Bruce McGechan—Wine Store Founder, or Bruce@WineStore. On your Info tab (or create a new Staff tab) ensure that every staff member who comments on the Page is introduced. Yes, a little privacy has died for your staff while they represent you.

Have a regular simple question

For example on Thursday ask what about favorite varietals e.g. 'What's your favorite Pinot Noir?'. On Friday update the wall with a simple 'What are you drinking?'. On Saturday, 'Anyone been to *trade customer's* restaurant? If so what did they drink?'. In theory you would do this every day. In practice, it is going to depend on how many engaged Likers you have.

Have trivia questions

For example, 'What is the name of the wine country valley in Sideways?'. Or 'Who owns Chateau d'Yquem?' Perhaps add a poll and ask 'Which makes the best Pinot Noir—California or Oregon?'.

Add photos and video

Photos and videos are much more easily digestible than words. Show photos of wine tasting events, visiting winemakers, staff having fun or being silly, and occasionally new products (though be careful about the promotional nature of these). If you feel comfortable doing videos then this can be a very quick way to post content where you may interview these people and, of course, review wines.

Add wine news

How are important harvests going? Wine bloggers as well as traditional media will give you a feel for this. Other news such as the
controversial or the silly.

Promote your wine tasting events

Have regular posts counting down to your next wine tasting. This
counts as true time-sensitive news and may garner more interest with
Facebook's algorithm as well as customers.

Promo messages

Not explicit unless it really-honestly-truthfully is a good deal—this is
social media not a newspaper ad. You'll lose your customer's interest
if you go all promo on them. So a tasting note with a price for
example—if there is only a case then point that out. If you have in-
store tastings then do a wall update on this as well. If you'd tell your
wine friends in the real world then it passes the 'Live Authentically'
test. If it's just sales hype then it doesn't. The rule of thumb is fewer
than 10-20% of your updates in social media should be promotional.

Creative Ideas

We are constantly tracking the best wine retailer and winery Facebook users. Here is the list of different creative ideas we see work
well:

- Vineyard Photos
- Winery Photos
- Company People Photos
- Tasting Room Customer Photos
- Event Customer Photos
- Entertaining or Informative Illustrations
- Question: What should we do?
- Sneak Peak at new release
- Twitter handle sharing
- Question: What are you drinking?
- Asking for Fan Photos
- Asking for then sharing Fan photos
- Pop quizzes and competitions

13.5.4 Advertising: Engage

Promoted Posts, Offers, and Check-Ins are all ways to boost the engagement with your Fan base. However, Promoted Posts stand out as the best method of all. Anytime you have particularly good content then it is best to spend $20 or so to ensure your Fans don't forget you and come back to your Page.

13.6 Influence

Remember way back in the Social Media chapter I mentioned the power of influencers? Well this is where the rubber meets the road. Facebook allows Fans' interactions to be seen by Fans' friends. If the Fan has a large network of friends who show strong EdgeRank type affinity for that Fan then that Fan's endorsement is going to significant referral traffic, engagement, and sales by that Fan's friends.

This is where Solicit a Call to Action can really assist your attempts to Influence Fans' friends. The Call to Action should be encouraging photo uploads or running contests and asking them to ask their friends to vote. Anything that has them directly uploading or sharing something on your Page or asking their friends to do something on your Page.

13.6.1 Advertising: Influence

Sponsored Story, Promoted Post, Offers, and Check-Ins are all good advertising choices to have your Fans endorse your wine business on their friends News Feeds. Indeed, Sponsored Stories are purposely made to influence others and can be very prominent especially on a mobile or iPad device where there is only a single column page.

13.7 Who Will do This

I think social media campaigns can be a bit like dieting or exercise. You start out highly enthusiastic in the first week, then find convenient excuses to avoid doing anything on some days in the following week, and by the third week your campaign has for all intents and purposes finished. The practices above need to be part of someone's job. It may be a sales assistant or yourself, but it needs to be part of their daily routine. That person needs to be accountable for doing the tasks each day and to clearly understand the measurements of success which is where the content calendar comes in.

If you have limited resources (don't we all?) then it's difficult to find the time to write posts, tweet, comment on other posts, moderate comments on your own forum and blog, monitor Yelp and Foursquare reviews, make sure your products are up to date for Snooth and Wine Searcher, manage your Adwords and Facebook campaigns, split test, send out emails to your list, write tasting notes and reviews for your own site and other sites... if it makes you feel any better the big guys are also struggling.

13.8 Like and Other Social Plugins

A simple and very effective way to harness Social Media traffic is to install Facebook social media plugins into your webpage (as well as Twitter's tweet and Google's +1).

For example, Levis added Like buttons to its website and received a 40X increase in traffic which resulted in 40% of it's overall traffic coming from Facebook.[90]

To increase numbers even further, Facebook recommends using versions, that[90]

> Show thumbnails of friends are used. They allow people to add comments. If they appear at both the top and bottom of articles. If they appear near visual content like videos or graphics.

Although this part of the book is about Engagement, social media is becoming more and more important in generating traffic and higher search engine ranking. The simple addition of the Like button shows why.

13.9 Measurement

Tony has set up his Facebook Place Page with tabs that include a landing page for new users encouraging them to 'Like' the Page, an info tab with lots of information about the store and wine range, and a store that remains in Facebook during purchase yet is integrated into the normal eCommerce store. He regularly posts questions, wine news, photos, tasting event dates, and occasionally a promotion he's running. Initially, there was little response, but now he's starting to get a few responses. He has also added 'Like' buttons on all his web pages including his eCommerce store product pages. Here are his Facebook measurements in the context of his Business Plan.

Business Objective: Boost Margins and Volume by changing to a Higher Value Customer Mix.

Marketing Strategy >Promotion >Internet marketing: Increase engagement with high value customers through the Facebook Place Page by encouraging Wall Post comments or users themselves posting on the Wall.

KPI: Conversion Average Order Value; Conversion Average Bottle Value; User Wall Post comments or user posting. As measured in Google Analytics filtering for Facebook referrals (excluding Facebook advertising and Facebook integrated store). Facebook Wall user comments and posts manually calculated.

KPI Targets: For Year 2. Increase user Wall Post comments or user posting vs last month by four—each time the target is reached it is counted as one Assisted Conversion. For other KPIs see Table 14.1.

Segment	Conv.#	Ass. Conv.#	AOV	ABV
Luxury Enthusiasts:	1	4	$65	$25
Enthusiasts:	2	5	$33	$15
Image Seekers:	5	5	$26	$15
Luxury Image Seekers:	1	2	$65	$15

Table 13.1: KPI Targets: Facebook (Year 2)

KPI Target Sources: Segment numbers come from the Internet Marketing spreadsheet *Segment Conversions Report*. For Conversion Average Order Value equations see SEO Measurement section.

Facebook will add 25 more customers, most of them indirectly. The greater engagement on Facebook is the biggest media influence on why they purchase from Tony's Wine Store. Tony expects Facebook to deliver five Luxury Enthusiasts. Along with the other marketing strategies, this means he has 22 more to go before he reaches his target of 44 Luxury Enthusiasts in Year 2.

13.10 Summary

Facebook is huge and many of these users are wine lovers. The way to build a Facebook community includes boosting interaction, and being authentic and up to date. Your Facebook Page should have a store, sign up tab, and customized landing page. Having a large number of users who 'Like' is important, but you also need to ensure that you have the quality practices and the ability to purchase your products inside Facebook.

13.11 Resources

- How well did you understand? Visit my website to discuss or ask questions about Wine and Facebook: `www.WineMarketingPros.com/fbchap/`
- Best Practice Guide, Marketing on Facebook `www.facebook.com/marketing`
- Inside Facebook blog `www.insidefacebook.com`
- Mari Smith `www.facebook.com/marismith`

14 Twitter

14.1 What is Twitter

Twitter has been called the SMS of the internet. However, unlike SMS, your Twitter messages are viewable by all, which also makes it a bit like a blog so is sometimes called a 'microblogging service'. It is also not just about communication but also sharing information and humor. These 140 character long messages, or 'tweets', are sent by at least 100 million (perhaps double that) active Twitter users worldwide.[91]

The process of subscribing to people is known as 'following'. When you follow someone their tweets appear on your Twitter Page. There is no equivalent to the Facebook EdgeRank so the home page can quickly become a 'firehose' of uninteresting tweets from people you are only mildly interested in. This can be frustrating when you are looking for only friends, industry experts, or perhaps suppliers and customers. So you can create lists which allows you to view only a particular category of users' tweets.

Twitter search provides a way to find out about *wine* related tweets. You simply type your *wine* into the search box on the main Twitter page. The ability to search becomes an important means of monitoring tweets about your business, local customers, and the wine industry in general.

Some other key features are:

- to create group followable posts by using the hash tag, e.g. #wine
- using the @ sign for replying to or mentioning other 'tweeters' (Twitter users)
- using RT to 'retweet' or forward another person's tweet to your followers
- you can send private tweets to a follower, called direct messages
- adding photos and your location
- you can create lists of Twitter users

- you can 'favourite' tweets

14.2 Why Twitter?

You should use Twitter for the same reason as you should use Facebook—fish where the fish are. If your (potential) customers prefer to engage with your store on Twitter then you need to be there. Wine Market Council research shows that 24% of Core Wine Drinkers use Twitter.[9]

When you compose a tweet, Twitter prompts you with the question, 'What's Happening?', which perhaps reflects how Twitter is more about what you are doing now. Certainly the tweet will only be in a person's twitter stream for a very short period of time as their is no filter applied to the home page.

Here's how Social Media expert Chris Brogan[92] put it:

> Online community is a tricky thing, and it's getting even trickier. We used to worry about building 'a place' for people to come and communicate and share with us. But that led to 'place' being all over the web. Think about how community has changed. We used to want people to come to our website, to our forum, to our blog. Now, even if they do go to those places, they also talk about you on LinkedIn, on Facebook, on Twitter, and elsewhere. Conversation and community is disparate and distant, and that's just the 'location-less' web. Think about when we add location-based products like Foursquare and Facebook Places. Suddenly, community is a tricky beast indeed.

Twitter is also starting to influence the search engine algorithms, though less than Facebook[41].

14.3 Twitter Marketing

The steps in using Twitter for business is similar to Facebook: (1) Listen, (2) Connect, (3) Engage, (4) Influence. The difference is that we will do a lot more listening and more sharing in Twitter than we do with Facebook.

14.3.1 Step 1. Listen

Or Research and Monitor. This is where you use Advanced Twitter search and other tools to research what the wine community is saying.

Start with Twitter Advanced Search `twitter.com/search-advanced`. Put in different search terms such as wine and #wine, different varietals and wine regions, and your own brand name (see the SEO chapter for the top wine keywords). Refine the search by filtering for geography to see what people in your target geographical market is saying. Follow these people and, where appropriate, put them into your own Twitter lists, for example the lists may be called Local Wine Tweeters, Wine Bloggers, Top Wine Tweeters, Pinot Noir Lovers, and Wine Journalists. Or valuable search terms can be saved and monitored using the 'Save search' Twitter function.

Next, search for influential people in the wine community. Search for wine writers and journalists, bloggers, and wine social media personalities. You might choose to use influence measurement companies like Klout.com, PeerIndex.com, and Kred.com. Follow and list these people as well. Remember that these influence measurement companies are often gamed—meaning that people change their behavior to get a higher influence measurement score. I recommend you don't use the companies to measure your own efforts (I describe simple methods below), but they are good for research as long as you cast a critical eye over the results.

Unlike Facebook or Google, there is no Twitter EdgeRank or PageRank. When you login to Twitter you see a stream of tweets from tweeters you are following, completely unfiltered. After a time many of those people you follow will turn out to be less interesting or relevant, to yourself and you'll find that this general twitter stream is an unmanageable firehose of messages you don't care about. This is where your Twitter Lists are helpful. Rather than being exposed to all your followers you can filter the stream of tweets to a manageable level. You'll start to see some Twitter users who you honestly find interesting.

In the Social Media Monitoring chapter, I'll show you how wineries can use an internet software application called Social Connect that can help you track your own brand name.

14.3.2 Step 2. Connect

Unlike Facebook it is not hard to have Twitter users follow you. Many of the users you follow, will follow you back if your Twitter Bio looks relevant to their interests. Some follow back automatically. Note I do not recommend this practice as you'll end up following people who do not share the same interests as you and could well be more spammer than tweeter. Best to follow back only if there bio looks relevant to your interests.

You can advertise on Twitter, though I'm not convinced this is needed for Connecting with followers. The harder part is to build a relationship with a Tweeter, which is the Engage part of Twitter.

14.3.3 Step 3. Engage

This is where you build real relationships with real people. By now you've identified relevant Twitters users. They may be influential tweeters or bloggers, they may be target market wine drinkers, or they may be locals who occasionally talk about wine. Regardless, it's time to use Twitter to build a relationship in an authentic way; we ain't stalking here!

For a start, share their tweets. If you have an insight or genuine praise then add that comment on. After awhile, feel free to mention them in your tweet, which will sometimes lead to positive engagement.

Another way to engage is to ask questions. You may be doing research or want advice; for example, what pinot noir brands should I stock, what varietal should I plant, which wine events are the best, etc.

14.3.4 Step 4. Create and Influence

By now you should have a feel for your wine community, in general, and by Twitter Lists. You've connected with many and engaged with quite a few. Time to start creating your own Twitter content. Possible content includes:

- Sharing other people's tweets
- Break news
- Provide the bizarre (pics)
- Introduce people to other people

- Design tweetable moments e.g. events #tag

In the Facebook chapter we looked at Altimeter's Facebook Page marketing principles. Many of those same principles[89] apply to Twitter Marketing.

We'll use these principles to go through Twitter best practices (italics are direct Altimeter quotes).

Provide Cohesive Branding

Make sure your Twitter background has a familiar look and feel. Don't deter potential customers with a page that looks inconsistent with your brand.

- Upload a logo, complete info page, and build out profile

Be Up To Date

Keep Interaction High with Fresh, Timely Content. Is this page 'alive'? Or just a passing thought that the company has since forgotten?

- Tweet regularity: 2+ per day vs 1 per month
- Tweet at times people are most likely to read, definitely 4PM local time for a wine retailer but also worth testing 9AM, 1PM, 5PM, and 6PM
- Best if 90% is informational and 10% or less is promotional

Live Authenticity

Build Trust by Personalizing Interactions with a 'Human Touch'. Unlike Facebook, Twitter does not force people to reveal their real names. Remember, we're trying to build trust here, so you need to remain authentic yourself—not hide nameless behind a brand. However, I do believe you should have separate business and personal twitter accounts—your customers are interested in your personal views on wine, not your personal life.

- First person
- Conversational
- Give a name behind the company tweet
- A link to your website

Participate in Dialog

Connect with Customers by Fostering Two-Way Dialog. You want to engage with followers to build up trust and the spreading of information.

- Initiates dialog (see 'What do I Tweet?!' below)
- Responds to most mentions and helps people out
- Furthers tweet discussions, answers questions
- Comments on followers' Twitter photos

Enable Peer-To-Peer Interactions

Be Efficient and Enable the Crowd's Help. Customers are already talking to each other, so be part of that Twitter conversation.

- Actively encourages peer-to-peer discussion
- Active Twitter stream board
- Q and A
- Active followers
- Recognition—RT interesting and relevant followers' tweets

Foster Advocacy

Foster Word of Mouth—the Holy Grail of Marketing. Your customers' recommendations mean a lot to their friends and family, certainly a lot more than your own!

- Specific requests to spread the word or retweet (RT)
- Requests to vote, sound off, share photos, contests, submissions
- Try to keep tweets to 100 characters or less—RTs often need up to 40 characters for Twitter names and a RT comment

Solicit A Call To Action

Bring it Back to Business and Provide a Succinct Next Step. You've done all that hard work—now where's the Buy Now button!?

- Sign up for emails, Twitter-only prizes
- Feature selected wines on your background page as teasers (note hyperlinks will not link on backgrounds)

14.4 What to tweet

Send out very short headlines on topics of interest to your customer base with website links for more info back to your website.

For example, your blog may have a post on, 'Latest Bordeaux Releases: Some Real Surprises'. The blog then goes on to say that the whole vintage is poor except for this area and these brands (of which you happen to have in stock). Your Twitter message would say 'Latest Bordeaux Releases: Some Real Surprises www.url.com'. Here are some ideas.

Information: News (preferably breaking news)

- Just rated by Wine Spectator
- New Arrivals
- New from vineyard
- Just awarded gold at
- The King of
- Once every 30 years
- A Discovery at
- Adventure in
- Share your love with
- Sure to Surprise
- Crisis in
- No Justice in

Information: Attention Seeking

- Alert
- Top rated
- 94 point rating
- Private Selection of
- Action required
- The best of
- Top 40
- Best selling wines under $15
- Deal Alert
- Vintage of the Decade
- Pay Dirt at
- Merlot Heaven
- The Merlot Insider
- Pinot Wine Guide
- Wine 101—how to

- Wines from
- Wines of
- Wine and Food, e.g. Salmon
- Wine and Climate, e.g. Summer
- One of the greatest
- Cult like

Promotional:

- Last call
- Last chance
- While they last
- Final chance
- 3 days only
- Ends at midnight
- Ends tomorrow
- Today only
- Rush shipping on us
- 50% off end of vintage clearance
- First Buyer Special
- A great offer from vineyard

14.4.1 The Mensch versus The Smore

Guy Kawasaki is one of the thought leaders in Twitter marketing. He has listed various types of tweeters which also illustrates best and worst Twitter marketing practice:[93]

- *The Newbie*—just signed up to Twitter, will be boring or will progress to another type
- *The Brand*—'balances the tension between using Twitter as a marketing tool and socially engaging people so as not to appear to be using Twitter as a marketing tool'
- *The Smore*—(social media whore) sees Twitter as a self-promotional tool to make a buck only
- *The Bitch*—complains, abuses, and shocks, is unhelpful with little to add to dialogue
- *The Maven*—an expert in their field, has lots to share in that field and is very interesting
- *The Mensch*—helpful, knowledgeable, and very useful

He believes that a successful business is a bit of the *Brand, Maven,* and *Mensch.*

14.5 Twitter Math—ROI

In the local wine blogger section, we looked at why and how you should partner with these talented folk. The strategy is to boost referrals with the aim of increasing purchases from those referrals. Likewise with Twitter.

You can find local Tweeters by conducting an Advanced Search on your city. Given you're both locals, perhaps try to contact the Tweeter, invite them for a coffee or wine, and see if there are ways you can work together. I'd keep it that general. At the end of the day, this is just a friendly business arrangement between two people who care about the same thing—wine.

Like the blogger perhaps the tweeter is thinking about:

- material to tweet about
- store tasting opportunities
- tasting events that they run in your store
- paid tweets, what Klout calls *Promoted Products*
- free or discounted wine

Note you will want to ensure they stay independent and abide by FTC disclosure requirements[79].

What you are after depends on your business objectives. Let's say you want to increase the engagement you have with customers. You could do this with:

- tweets about a particular niche range you stock with a link to your store's niche range page
- ratings and reviews of some of your high margin wines
- tweets about some interesting wines you stock
- a tasting and then tweeting about it

A good way to assess a tweeter's value is to regularly assign a tweeter a low-volume, premium wine brand that they're interested in (no point in providing a big seller as you'll struggle to identify tweeter related sales). Then measure sales in the month(s) of their activity. Try that every month (week?) for 3-6 months. If you see an increase in sales then start offering more cooperation and resources. Doesn't work? Then try another tweeter.

14.6 Measurement

The key measurement with twitter is retweets. Brian Solis[94] calls this Resonance—does the conversation start, are you retweeted, and how long does it last? Given tweets do not appear on a the general twitter home page for long you're looking to see how long they bounce around the wine community.

Tony has created a Twitter Background Page, he is tweeting regularly according to his marketing Twitter calendar, he's doing his best to initiate dialog with the twitterverse, he RTs any followers' tweets he finds interesting. He's is very aware of who are the most influential tweeters in his industry and locally and aims to engage with them when it seems natural. Good progress so far. Here are his Twitter measurements in the context of his Business Plan.

Business Objective: Boost Margins and Volume by changing to a Higher Value Customer Mix.

Marketing Strategy >Promotion >Internet marketing: Increase engagement with high value customers and influencers through Twitter.

KPI: Conversion Average Order Value; Conversion Average Bottle Value; Replies, Mentions, Retweets; Replies, Mentions, Retweets from Influencers. As measured in Google Analytics filtering for Twitter referrals.

KPI Targets: For Year 2.

Increase general Replies, Mentions, Retweets by 10 this month vs last month. Increase Influencer Replies, Mentions, Retweets by two this month vs last month. Each time the target is reached it is counted as one Assisted Conversion.

For other KPIs see Table 14.1.

Segment	Conv.#	Ass. Conv.#	AOV	ABV
Luxury Enthusiasts:	0	3	$65	$25
Enthusiasts:	1	3	$33	$15
Image Seekers:	3	3	$26	$15
Luxury Image Seekers:	0	1	$65	$15

Table 14.1: KPI Targets: Facebook (Year 2)

KPI Target Sources: Segment numbers come from the Internet Marketing spreadsheet *Segment Conversions Report*. For Conversion Average Order Value equations see SEO Measurement section.

Twitter will add 14 more customers, most of them indirectly. The greater engagement with influencers will provide great 'digital word of mouth' to Luxury Enthusiasts. Tony expects Twitter to deliver three Luxury Enthusiasts. Along with the other marketing strategies this means he has 19 more to go before he reaches his target of 44 Luxury Enthusiasts.

14.7 Summary

Twitter marketing best practices are similar to Facebook's. You want to build a community of followers, be authentic, interactive, and informative. You should follow and interact with the influential active users who will hopefully retweet you to their own followers. Try partnering with local wine tweeters to see if you can boost sales through their referrals. The best content to tweet is informative with links back to your blog, product page, and other interesting websites.

14.8 Resources

- How well did you understand? Visit my website to discuss or ask questions about Wine and Twitter: `www.WineMarketingPros.com/twchap/`
- Klout `klout.com`, PeerIndex `peerindex.com`, and Kred `kred.com`

15 Mobile Apps and Websites

Other chapters of this book cover mobile advertising, mobile eCommerce, Location Based Services, and local SEO. In this chapter, we focus on mobile applications, mobile websites, QR codes, and in-store Customer mobile usage.

In this chapter mobile means any smartphones (e.g. iPhone, Android phones) and tablets (e.g. the iPad).

15.1 Why Mobile

Wine Market Council research shows that 39% of Core Wine Drinkers use 'Wine, Food, Restaurant, or Bar Apps'.[9]

A Google study[4] found only 10% of our media interactions is via radio, newspaper, and magazines, the other 90% is through digital screens of one sort or another. Specifically, 38% of our media interactions was via a mobile, 9% via tablets, 24% via PC/Laptops, and 19% via TV screens.

In total, we spent 4.4 hours in front of these digital screens. On average, the time spent for a mobile interaction was 17 minutes, tablet 30 minutes, PC/Laptop 39 minutes, and TV 43 minutes.

Of the traditional media, only TV remains a major force. Small and medium business never really used TV advertising. They did, and do, still use newspapers, magazines, and radio, yet these are being consumed by a small minority of wine drinkers (at least in their traditional media format).

Just what digital screen a person uses depends on the amount of time we have (lots or little), what we are trying to do (research, social media, entertainment), our physical location (home, car, office), and our attitude (intense, relaxed).

So, for example, if we are at the doctors waiting room, we have little time, are hopefully relaxed, and so may open up a wine blog. The doctors' waiting room is an example of where a wine consumer has 'found time' and has spontaneously decided to read a wine blog.

The study found 80% of mobile usage is spontaneous not planned whereas about half of a PC/laptop usage is spontaneous.

Of all the PC/laptop and mobile shopping events, this study observed, about one-third was on a mobile. Of this one-third, two-fifths of mobile usage was out of the home. The study found people used whatever device was closest to them for many of their media interactions, regardless of their location. Of mobile shopping events, 81% were spur of the moment. There is nothing planned about using a mobile, it is convenient and can be used anywhere.

Google found that 67% of people used multiple devices to complete a purchase. Of the 65% who started shopping on a mobile, 61% moved to a PC/Laptop—no surprise. But what about the 25% of people who started shopping on a PC/Laptop, 19% moved to a mobile!

The study authors finished the study report by saying,

> Consumers shop differently across devices, so businesses should tailor the experience to each channel. It's also important to optimize the shopping experience across all devices For example, consumers need to find what they are looking for quickly and need a streamlined path to conversion, on smartphones... Smartphones are the backbone of our daily media use. They are the devices used most throughout the day and serve as the most common starting point for activities across multiple screens. Going mobile has become a business imperative.

15.2 What are Mobile Apps & Websites

A *mobile website* is a normal website that has been optimized for a small mobile screen (e.g. iPhone, Android phones) and the poorer cellular internet speeds.

A *mobile app* is a software application that resides on the mobile device, and is usually called an 'app'. These apps are either preinstalled on a mobile (e.g. email inbox, photo gallery apps) or are downloaded from mobile application software distribution platforms, usually called an 'App Store'. Apps can be downloaded via a PC and 'synched' with the mobile phone, or downloaded directly using the mobile phone. The two major app stores are Apple's iTunes *App Store* and Google's *GooglePlay*. Other ones that have much less market penetration include Windows and Blackberry and will be ignored in this chapter.

15.3 Mobile Websites vs. Mobile Apps

Here are the key differences[95] between a mobile website and a mobile app.

Apps must be downloaded

The most obvious difference is that an app is usually downloaded from iTunes App Store or the Google Play; whereas, a mobile website can simply run on your mobile's internet browser. There are pros and cons to downloading. Having to download an app is probably too much of a hurdle to ask a first-time customer who plans to make one purchase. Whereas, a regular customer could well find an app very convenient versus typing in your website address on a tiny keyboard. A definite upside of mobile websites is that they update independently of the mobile phone, so do not require the customer to download the latest update if you come out with a new version— unlike apps.

Mobile websites are available to all

A mobile website is usually just a distilled and very bandwidth-efficient version of your normal website. It can run on any phone with a browser. This means people who don't like downloading apps (or don't understand how) can access your website. Likewise, any smartphone customer can access your website—not just iPhone or Android phone customers. If you just have an app then only those who are able to download the app have access.

Mobile websites are easier

A mobile website is relatively easy to create. This is mainly due to 'device detection software'. This software can detect the mobile phone handset type and deliver a mobile browsing experience suited to the screen size and resolution. There is no need to create separate apps for Apples, Androids, and Blackberrys etc.

No authority needed for mobile websites

You have to meet Apple's (hard) or Google's (easier) app store requirements before they'll allow you to offer an app through iTunes App Store or Google Play. There are ways to do this from your website, but in the case of Apple you may face legal issues.

Apps can assess native handset functionality

Apps, on the other hand, can make better use of the handset's native applications, such as the camera, gyroscope, offline usage, and push notifications. It's also more convenient for regular users to just touch an icon rather than type in a URL. iPhone apps can also boost distribution due to the immense popularity of iTunes, especially if you get on the app top 10 charts.

Note there is one view that apps and mobile website functionality will converge, so this comparison should hopefully become dated in the coming years.

15.3.1 Case Study: CostCo's Mobile Website

Let's look at why CostCo developed a mobile website.

Here's how CostCo[96] explained their mobile website program,

> Costco.com has seen a greater than 100% increase in
> mobile-device traffic to the website. Obviously there is
> an interest in shopping or browsing the site with those
> devices. We've seen most mobile traffic coming from
> iPhones but also from iPads, Androids and BlackBerrys.
> Mobile access is a channel for which there is significant de-
> mand and going forward the growth in mobile access will
> be huge. We need to develop something simpler, faster
> to load and easier to navigate. So we've created a more
> distilled version of the website with smaller graphics that
> load faster and navigation that you can move through
> easier with a finger. Costco.com will recognize the device
> you're using to contact the site. It will be an automatic
> shift to the mobile platform when it senses you're using a
> phone. Beyond that the experience will only be different
> in terms of the navigation being simpler. Ordering from
> your mobile devices is just as secure as ordering from your

computer... the same levels of encryption are used. The warehouse (store) locator will be totally interactive with your web-enabled phone. You can enter a zip code or depending on your phone your location could be used to generate a custom map showing the warehouses near you.

So, mobile is important. Here is what mobile websites need to:

- Have easy 'finger touch' navigation
- Keep it Simple—reduce all screen clutter and offer a distilled version of your website
- Keep it Fast—due to mobile phone network speed
- Easy to use forms—'finger touch' again
- Device detection software so you don't need to worry about handsets (mobile websites only)
- Have a Geolocation or Zip Code Store Locator for local customers to take advantage of

15.3.2 How to Create a Mobile Website

Your web designer will need to add some special code to the design files to show a simplified version of your website. It is not terribly difficult to do and should probably be included in all new websites. The jargon is 'responsive web design', as in the design is responsive to the size of screen it is being shown on.

Once you've optimized the mobile website experience, you can use your mobile website to graduate regular users to a more robust native app. Apple will prompt users to download your app if the users are browsing your website on their mobile phones.

How to create an App? This is harder. Some eCommerce software solutions have ready made Apps that you can purchase for an extra fee. Alternatively, you will probably hire a contractor or an agency, I outline a requirements list below.

15.4 How to Create a Wine App

First, you need to decide how an app delivers your marketing strategy, then decide on the features, and finally write a developer brief.

15.4.1 Marketing Strategy

This book is about Tony's Wine Store focusing on higher value customers in order to boost profits. These customers are Enthusiasts and Image Seekers both of whom prefer lots of wine information. In previous chapters, we've also outlined how important Facebook and Twitter is to Tony so we want to make sure we integrate these marketing channels as well. In this chapter, we've seen how customers jump between mobiles, tablets, and PC/laptops as well as using them at home and in-store so perhaps a mobile Commerce shopping cart is necessary.

On the other hand, a winery might choose to focus on its loyal customers, this is likely to be the brand loyal segment called Traditionalists who are keen to spontaneously buy wine from their preferred wineries. Facebook and Twitter are important as is the different mobile, tablet, and PC/laptop usage, but they are less likely to be coming into the tasting room to buy. Therefore, a mobile Commerce shopping cart will be important.

15.4.2 Features

Winery Features

A winery's marketing strategy is for the app to (1) allow Traditionalist to buy wine and (2) maintain a good relationship by showing the latest information about the winery:

- Wines with a Shopping Cart—buy
- About—the brand story of the winery
- Location—how to get to the tasting room if they are nearby to buy more wine
- Tasting Room—when the tasting room is open so they can buy wine
- Wine Club—ways a loyal customer can buy wine without needing to remember
- Retailer Stockists—ways to buy wine nearby
- Facebook, Twitter, Blog integration—maintain engagement with the customer

If your focus was on the Enthusiast then perhaps you would show much more information about terroir with maps and ongoing news and updates. If it was Image Seeker perhaps you would show more information about the fancy events your winery was sponsoring or attending.

Wine Retailer Features

Tony's Wine Store marketing strategy is about increasing Enthusiast customers. From the Customer chapter, we know Enthusiasts hunger for wine information. They are passionate about wine and often have a personal relationship with particular wine shop staff. Whether they buy online or in-store, they want to explore different wines, they want to see what others think and how they rate the wine, and they want to get the technical specifics—what's the pH, the terrior, elevage, brix at harvest? You're happy explaining these things (where you can) face to face so with some effort you should be able to transfer this sales information to your website and app.

Your information is a great start but the aim of this mobile app is to provide as much information as you can for each wine, winery, varietal, and region. So you also want to include the wine blogs and magazines and various wine community notes, the wine writers books, and appellation association information. This information will need to be grouped together under a wine or topic and presented in the app.

Now, when these high-margin customers want information about your wines you can show them your iPad app with just your wines and your prices—as well as expert wine reviews and winery information.

If there is a wine review video they can look at this. If it is a single vineyard wine we can show them the location on a map. If there is a story about the vineyard from a wine blogger we can let them read this. They get all the information they need to make a purchase decision—not walk out of the store frustrated that they couldn't be comfortable with buying expensive wines.

It is probably best presented via an iPad or iPad Mini, so you can hold an iPad yourself, securely attach them to the wall, a shelf or a stand, or give trusted customers an iPad to go through the wines at their leisure. You will be even be able to offer your wine retail app to your customers to download from the internet. (In fact, I like this idea so much I'm making an app that does just this).

App Front End Features:

- Find winery information—accurate product data

- Fine other wine information (bloggers, magazines)—automated or manual system
- Browsable wines section—by type, varietal, region, vintage, rating
- Wine product page—with all accumulated wine information
- Winery page—with all accumulated winery information
- Wine Region, Varietal Category pages with all relevant information
- Social Media—allow sharing from any page via Facebook or Twitter (integrated with iOS app)

Management Back End Features:

- Upload own wine tasting notes information—easy to use
- Wine eCommerce—integrate with eCommerce solution
- Integrated QR code system—links wines on the shelf to iPad app
- Website app management—manage wines, choose whether to show only in-stock wines, price management

Two other possible inclusions may be Wine Journaling, which is recording your own tasting notes and possibly integrating with a system like CellarTracker. This would be for the customer more than the retailer. The other part is wine and food pairing recommendations.

Note what I haven't included is price comparison but a Consumer-focused App like HelloVino, Cork.kz, or Drync may integrate Wine-Searcher or Snooth data in order to do this.

15.4.3 Quick Response (QR) Codes

If you have a QR code reader then feel free to check out the mobile version of my blog by scanning the QR code in Figure 15.1.

Quick Response (QR) codes are a 2D barcode that when scanned brings up a smallish amount of information—a few thousand characters. QR codes have historically been used extensively by logistics and manufacturing companies for tracking inventory. The technology is mature even if consumers aren't quite aware of it as yet. For our purposes the information will be a website address that a smartphone can read.

In a retail store, a QR code sticker could be put on the shelf edge, shelf talker, on the bottle itself, or on some sort of neck tag. The customer takes a photo using a QR reader, which is just another

Figure 15.1: A QR code—links to www.MyLocalWineStore.com

app that is downloaded from iTunes App Store or the Google Play (depending on your phone). I use the QR reader, QRReader which:

- automatically scans for QR codes
- finds one and asks you if you want to go to the web site
- opens a browser and takes you to a web page

Simple—no using a touch keypad, it's an intuitive process, and takes you directly to a relevant page (which is hopefully optimized for a mobile). Let's look at how you can use these in your own store.

15.4.4 8 Ways a Wine Store Can Use QR Codes

Here's my list of how you can use mobile technology to sell more wine.

1. Provide Online Information

These codes can link the screeds of information on your (mobile optimized) website to the customer who wants to buy something in your store—including video, maps or competition links. And you can help direct them to information about your store rather than price checking or looking at competing websites.

2. Share with Social Media

Once they're at your website, give them every opportunity to share your products with their friends by providing Facebook Like and Tweet buttons optimized for mobile phones. This helps them get product recommendations from friends as well.

3. 24/7: Customer turns up after hours?

No problem—place a QR code in storefront windows to enable customers to purchase on their mobile for later delivery.

4. Share with 'Check In'

Another way to promote sharing is to have a Foursquare, or Facebook Places, etc. QR code sticker at the entrance to your store—this allows easy check-ins (see the Local Social Media & LBS chapter) at your store. Google actually mailed out over 100,000 QR code window stickers to local US businesses, the QR code was linked to the business' Google Places page. A great example of linking the physical store to online information.

5. Cross Sell / Up Sell

Provide cross-sell opportunities by suggesting similar wines or snacks.

6. Inventory Availability

Linking to inventory information—do you have a case? Can you get access to more?

7. Loyalty Programs and Tracking

What's more you can track the behavior of customers—see which codes they're scanning and what they do with that information (hopefully buy!). For customers that belong to your loyalty program, you could tie that in with your mobile app to make their in-store visit better and the data you collect even more insightful.

8. Advertising and Direct Mail

Include a QR code in your advertising so consumers can be directed with a simple app click right then and there, rather than having to type on a tiny keyboard.

15.5 Mobile Payments

When I was doing new product development for a mobile company back in 2001, this was the next big thing. A decade later it's still—the next big thing. The idea is you can use your mobile phone like you do a credit or debit card—SMS payment, pay online in-store, swipe against something. The good news it is starting to take hold. Here are some mobile related payment services you could use.

15.5.1 Credit Card Processing Services

Businesses traditionally have a merchant account to process credit cards. Merchant accounts fee structures are confusing and, therefore, difficult to compare to the new services, but here's one example.

Merchant accounts will have different fee structures depending on average transaction size and total monthly revenue processed. The lower the size and revenue, the higher the transaction fees. An example, for a $1.2 million turnover business with a $30 average transaction, is a 1.7% percentage fee made up of interchange fee, assessment fee and processor markup. Plus $0.20 per transaction made up of interchange fee, NABU/APF fee and processor markup. Plus a monthly fee of $9. Plus a terminal monthly cost of about $32. Confused?[97]

Square, squareup.com, an iOS and Android credit card processing app costs 2.75% period. It allows anyone to accept credit card payments by downloading an app that is loaded on an iPad, iPhone, or Android device. The app has an easy to use interface and emails receipts. It also has a credit card reader to allow you to scan credit cards. Pay Here is PayPal's competing offer and it charges 2.7%.

Although a retail store has monthly fees, the percentage fees are still significantly lower. So these new payment systems may be sexy, but they will add, perhaps, $300 per month on credit card processing fees for the above example.

15.5.2 Retail Point Of Sale Systems

Another area of related innovation is internet-based point of sale systems, called cloud or web apps, that work on any internet browser including Safari on the iPad. A leader in this area is Vend, vendhq.com, that offers not just payment processing but also inventory management, customer tracking, and accounting and eCommerce integration. It charges a monthly fee usually less then $100. It can process payments through merchant accounts or the likes of Pay Here.

15.5.3 Apple iOS PassBook

Apple's only app offering is Passbook. This simply organizes various items like movie or sporting event tickets, store membership cards, and airplane boarding passes into an app. Good for loyalty cards but no real mobile payment system is behind it, perhaps something will come out in 2013-14.

15.5.4 Google Wallet

US mobile companies have finally agreed on a standard for something called Near Field Communication (NFC). NFC allows consumers with a NFC chip in their mobile phones to make purchases with a merchant who has a NFC point of sale device using a short-range, high-frequency wireless connection. When the consumer waves his smart phone near the POS device, payment account information is shared and the purchase is completed. Google championed NFC chips in the Android range of mobiles under the Google Wallet brand name. Another group of mobile operators have launched a competing system called Isis. Momentum seems to be gathering with NFC, though Apple will probably need to join the NFC movement for it to really take off.

15.6 Measurement

Tony has noticed how many of his wealthier customers have smartphones, so with the help of an agency he has created a Tony's Wine Store mobile app. His eCommerce store already had a mobile website. It not only provides wine information from his website but is also integrated with the shelf talkers by using QR codes. He has noticed that mobile is taking up an increasing share of the devices used to access his wine store, and Luxury Enthusiast customers tell him they use it while commuting, or in restaurants and have been showing all their friends. Here are his mobile measurements in the context of his Business Plan.

Business Objective: Boost Margins and Volume by changing to a Higher Value Customer Mix.

Marketing Strategy >Promotion >Internet marketing: Increase engagement and traffic with high value customers through usage of the Tony's Wine Store mobile app.

KPI: Conversion Average Order Value; Conversion Average Bottle Value. As measured in Google Analytics filtering for mobile Website, and mobile App Devices.

KPI Targets: For Year 2, see Table 15.1.

Segment	Conv.#	Ass. Conv.#	AOV	ABV
Luxury Enthusiasts:	1	3	$65	$25
Enthusiasts:	2	3	$33	$15
Image Seekers:	3	3	$26	$15
Luxury Image Seekers:	1	1	$65	$15

Table 15.1: KPI Targets: mobile (Year 2)

KPI Target Sources: Segment numbers come from the Internet Marketing spreadsheet *Segment Conversions Report*. For Conversion Average Order Value equations see SEO Measurement section.

Mobile will add 17 more customers as a result of offering access to the store wherever the customers happen to be. Tony expects mobile to add four Luxury Enthusiasts. Along with the other marketing strategies mentioned above it means he has 15 more to go before he reaches his Luxury Enthusiasts target.

15.7 Summary

Mobile and Tablets are often used for shopping sometimes in conjunction with a laptop. Mobile apps are downloadable smartphone software applications. Mobile websites are just normal websites distilled into a smaller and very efficient mobile version. Wine mobile and tablet app functionality depend on marketing strategy but will often be delivering information and eCommerce functionality. QR codes bring all the information on your website into the store. You can then encourage sharing, check-in, up-sell, and purchase.

15.8 Resources

- How well did you understand? Visit my website to discuss or ask questions about Wine and Mobiles: `www.WineMarketingPros.com/mobchap/`
- Vintank's report on wine mobile apps (and wine social media) `vintank.com`

16 Local Social Media and Location-Based Services

The internet world has seen a number of waves of technology that have fundamentally shifted the way we sell wine on the internet. The 1990s was about wine businesses utilizing websites and eCommerce to drive sales and marketing. The start of the millennium saw the acceptance of Search (Google) as a crucial driver of internet traffic. In 2006, Social Media started to gain traction with the opening of Facebook. In 2007, Apple changed the Mobile landscape with the iPhone, and last but not least Yelp and FourSquare signaled the arrival of Local in 2009.

Each wave has taken a few years to take hold. Some of the services have dropped out such as MySpace, Digg, AltaVista, and Google Buzz. Recently others have found some traction, such as Pinterest and Google+. However, the general trend seems clear—more mobile, more social, and more local. Kleiner Perkins' John Doerr identified and named SoMoLo in 2010. [98]

This book partitions out Local, Social, and Mobile, but in reality they intersect in a very human mishmash of the search, social, geographic, and technology worlds. In the Traffic part of this book, we covered search; in the previous chapters of this part, we've covered Social Media and then Mobile. Here we look at the 'mishmash' of all of three.

This chapter is an overview of which Social, Mobile, and Local services you can use to boost your local internet marketing results. Figure 16.1 uses a Venn diagram to show the intersection: [99]

It is almost as though the internet started out as being the whole world then became,

>the world where your friends are
>>the world where your friends are nearby
>>>the world where your friends are nearby, on their mobile

A customer shopping near your store may use their mobile to check

Figure 16.1: Intersection of Social Media, Local, and Mobile

for availability, proximity, and/or prices. Then they may enter your store and use mobile apps to see their friends' recommendations and reviews, as well as unlocking potential rewards (discounts or 'badges') by 'Checking-In' with Location Based Services.

sectionWhat are Location-Based Services (LBS)

There are three types of Location-Based Services:[100]

- Match unmet demand with unused supply, e.g. Groupon, Facebook Offers, OpenTable
- Location-Based Social Network, e.g. FourSquare, Facebook local group, Facebook Check-Ins
- Local information, search and listings, e.g. Yelp, FourSquare, Google+ Local

A Location-Based Service (LBS) often is a mobile app that uses the GPS Geolocation (the pop-up message that says, 'would like to use your current location') functionality to offer deals, information, reviews, and ratings relevant to your physical location. The newer ones also:

- allow you to 'check-in'
- share your check-in with your friends
- provide rewards/coupons for checking in
- offer deals and discounts

LBS used to be about SMS and location (based on cell tower triangulation)—it never really took off. But the mobile world has moved on and smartphone apps and GPS functionality has made this an intensely competitive part of the mobile world.

At its simplest, it allows you to tell your friends you're at such and such a place. The location is calculated by the phone's GPS system (it's not as accurate as a tomahawk missile but close enough), and you can post via the app or Twitter to let people know. This process is known as 'check-in'.

There are different ways the LBS app can notify your friends whether that be by Facebook, Twitter, or a custom app messaging service. Some apps allow this check-in to be published for all to see or allow you to restrict it to just your friends. Most apps allow you to search your Contacts, Twitter, and Facebook friends in order to pre-load your friends contact details.

The LBS apps usually allow you to leave a note about the place. They might be friendly tips... or rants about rude service. So, for a retailer, it is the social media dilemma of making sure you are part of the conversation because you can't stop it.

LBS apps can also have a gaming component. This is where a customer completes some (trivial) challenge at your store using their mobile phone, which unlocks some reward, such as a badge or a discount. Gaming encourages engagement with your store and the sharing of this gaming with their friends (including by Facebook or Twitter).

16.1 Location-Based Services

Now before you get too cynical about LBS (yes I've gone down that road too) think back to when you were in your teens and twenties when your life revolved around your friends. Perhaps it now revolves around work, partner, and children (and occasionally yourself and friends). Back when you were younger it was important to know what your group was up to. You didn't want to miss out on a party or free drinks or that hot women you've been trying to pick up... you get the idea.

Yelp

I guess strictly speaking this started as a local business review website accessed via a PC that helps people find local places to 'eat, shop, drink, and play', to use Yelp's slogan, but it wasn't long before the mobile version came. Then they added a check-in feature after seeing the success of FourSquare in January 2010, and in November 2010

introduced rewards for check-ins. I have covered Yelp in the Local
SEO chapter: in short, it's worthwhile to use. It also has some
great advertising possibilities. So its strength, in a mobile context, is
helping customers read reviews about places they may be about to
go to when they're out and about.

Facebook

Facebook seems very aware of the merger of social, local, and mobile.
In 2012, it upgraded its iPhone and Android mobile apps, it very
successfully integrated mobile advertising, including the ability to
offer Check-In deals, and as the year drew to a close relaunched its
'Nearby' feature in mobiles. Nearby shows where your friends have
checked-in but also local business nearby—including yours? If not,
check your Facebook Page address and category details. See the
Internet Advertising and Facebook chapters for more about using
Facebook to promote your location.

Google

Google has a number of products that are part of this area, which
it has incorporated in a new Search, Social, and Local service called
Google+ Local. It also has apps for iPhone and of course Android
to give it mobile functionality. Google is the biggest player in Local
with Maps, +Local ratings and reviews (care of the purchase of Zagat
reviews service), and local Adwords, but it is acutely aware it needs
Google+ to be much stronger so it is not left behind in the social
arena.

FourSquare

FourSquare is one of the more popular LBS apps. When you check-
in you rack up points. These points can lead to 'badges', which are
symbols on your FourSquare profile page and a type of 'gaming'. If
you're the person who checks in the most then you become Mayor.
Some businesses reward you for being the Mayor, a regular check-in
customer, or special badge deals. Badges seems to cater to people's
competitive instincts as well as being a (trivial) status symbol. Whatever the actual psychological reason, they certainly seem to work for
a certain type of customer.

FourSquare also allows users to includes 'Tips' and 'To-Dos'. Tips are recommendations to others that are shared when FourSquare friends check-in the same business. To-Dos are notes to yourself that aren't shared. This is a greater level of engagement with the store that we'll use below in the Measurement section.

SCVNGR

The app that seems to have taken gaming to the extreme is SCVNGR (scavenger). This app presents users with trivial but fun things to do at places called 'Challenges'. This may be combined with 'Treks', which connects the various locations with challenges and then rewards people who complete the Challenges (and Treks). The idea is to attract people, engage with them in fun ways, and grow your loyal customer base. There may be something to this idea for wine stores as there are all sorts of wine challenges I can think of that would make a tasting evening much more fun. You could also partner up with restaurant and bar trade customers to offer something to consumers.

Groupon

Let's come back to Groupon. I regard discounting like I do taking heroin. Perhaps it gives you a short-term high, but it is deadly in the medium term (or probably the short term but you follow the analogy). Of course that's a sweeping generalization and many retailers successfully use discounting as part of their promotional strategy. My issue is that a small wine store just can't compete this way—the margin is not there. If they start training their customers to expect discounts then the slow death begins. Rant finished.

So it's with a large amount of skepticism that I've looked into Groupon. Here's how it works.

Consumers sign up to receive daily local deals from Groupon. If they like a deal they go ahead and enter their credit card details. Then here's the smart bit. The deal is only activated if enough people sign up. So you're encouraged to let all your friends know—which is where social networks step in. You let your Facebook friends and Twitter followers (and email list, SMS contacts etc) know in order to activate the deal. Groupon (the two words 'Group Coupon') calls this 'Collective Buying Power'. If it is activated, Groupon charges the consumer's credit card and sends the consumer a coupon. The consumer can print this out or download it to a mobile phone, and redeem the coupon at the store (so the store receives money from Groupon not the customer.)

Consumers can also search for nearby deals by using the Groupon mobile app that utilizes GPS. The same app allows you to also purchase deals.

On the merchant side the advantage is obvious—traffic and lots of it. But at a price. The rumor (but not official policy) is they want at least a 50% off deal. They then get half of the remainder. So you offer, say, $30 worth of wine for $15. The customer pays Groupon $15. You get a check from Groupon for $7.50, your share of the coupon purchased for your business. If the rumor is correct you will see what I mean by expensive!

Groupon justifies this by saying: [101]

- it encourages trial, and you get lots of repeat customers post promotion
- it is better than advertising because you can track customers and only 'pay' groupon for sales (via the discount)
- you get the benefits of exposure to a local audience
- Facebook Likes and Twitter Followers increase traffic overnight, there isn't a delay

This is great spin, as most internet marketing programs can claim the same sort of advantages. What I do accept is that they have a list of interested, active subscribers—so it's more of a direct marketing play than strictly LBS in my mind. Without the list, the service would not be successful. The list combined with the technology is what makes this a powerful promotional tool.

If you can track the number of repeat customers from a Groupon promotion you may find it is a worthwhile promo. Give it a test. I have seen Groupon used well with one wine store called NY Vintners, where they offered a 50% off deal for a wine tasting event. This makes sense to me as there is the gross margin to play with for an event, as contrasted with margin for wine bottles.

Groupon turned down a $6 billion offer from Google. [102] I have to admit I was surprised by the offer value but Google ain't stupid. It has been spending a lot of time and cash in developing local services and Groupon seemed to have adopted this strategy well. The rumor mill has it that Google got paranoid about Facebook working with merchants to offer consumers local business 'Deals'. Apparently something is going down in 'Mega Tech Company World' with location-based services and local stores. Mega Tech is either acting like Silicon Valley reef fish, darting this way and that after the Next Biggest Thing, or they are actually on to something.

My feeling is that they are on to something. Sure Location-Based Service penetration is low at about 4% of the US population, but so was Google's or Facebook's penetration in their early days.

16.2 Your LBS First Steps

The best start to LBS is making sure you've claimed your Google+ Local, Facebook Place, Yelp, and FourSquare listings, your details are correct, and you've started to monitor them for negative reviews (see below).

Next give FourSquare a trial. Ten million people actively use FourSquare[103], which sounds a lot but is still only a small percentage of the US market. However, those who do are passionate users, and you should be able to drag them your way, or at least encourage them to comment to their friends. The best way would be to reward loyalty by setting up a Competition for being Mayor (see the FourSquare instructions).[104] Make sure you ask for and have the FourSquare sticker prominently displayed. If the promo works well try creating a special for people who check-in X number of times a week or month. Perhaps make the rewards tastings, rather than product discounts. If that works well see if you can expand FourSquare but also add in a SCVNGR game as well as advertise on Yelp.

16.2.1 Negative Reviews

You need to monitor your LBS reviews and respond to any negative ones. I regard negative comments or reviews as an opportunity to show you at your best. By responding diplomatically, you take the sting out of these reviews. Most people know life isn't perfect and bad things happen, so with the right response you can sometimes turn a bad review in your favor. Have a look at this review for example (store name is Xed out),

> Don't Bother! Go to a friendlier place!!! I'm one starring this atrocious place. With as many places to purchase wine in Chicago, you are sure to find a place more deserving of your dollars, especially in this economy. I

talked to a miserable woman who was sarcastic, moody, and didn't care in the least bit to help me. She sighed and 'Ughed' every time I had a question or asked for a recommendation. She was especially frustrated that I inquired if they put bottles of wine in gift bags with notes (as most stores offer to wrap gifts), which after a final snarky comment, I decided to take my business elsewhere. Don't give XXX any more undeserving dollars! Until they post that the wench of a woman working there was fired!

It would be a nightmare to leave that up without a response. On the other hand, positive reviews should also get a friendly thanks, which helps make you look like a friendly grateful business.

I question whether Groupon deals work for wine stores as there is just not enough margin for discounting.

Your Local Blog

Blogging is such a big topic it has been covered in its own chapter. Blogs are 'local' when they are mostly about a certain region, or city, or suburb, or street (known as hyperlocal). I'd suggest suburbs in large cities are the way to go, or for smaller cities, choose the city name or zip code. It comes down to how your local customers refer to the general 2-20 mile area around your store.

To make your blog 'local' ensure you have location keywords in your posts' titles, headings, and text. The natural way to do this is to write about your industry in your town. Or at least give local examples. I'd also have your physical address in the footer of the blog and link it into your Google Places and Facebook Page—see the Local SEO chapter for more on this.

Only write informative posts and leave the sales talk to advertising. Perhaps if it's natural to include details about a promotion or a new service then that's okay, but if you go all commercial on your audience you won't get repeat traffic to your website. In effect, you'll come across as boring. And loud.

Other People's Blogs

Not everyone has to be a content creator. I kinda like writing, so I blog. Other people like talking, so they podcast. Most people just read blogs. However, there are other types of social media persona that Charlene Li (co-author of the 'Groundswell') calls curators and commenters.

Sharers find the best content about their industry on the internet, and then 'share' using Twitter, Facebook, and Google+. This is the easiest and quickest way to engage in social media. Commenters add insightful comments to the bottom of blog posts. But, 'Great post!' isn't going to be enough. You have to add a helpful and insightful comment or diplomatic criticism. This is a good halfway house between blogging and reading.

The key is to concentrate on local blogs. This way you get your name out there and build up credibility and personality with your blog posts. In fact, even comment politely on your competitors blogs (I'd be very diplomatic and complimentary if you did this). You can find local blogs through `google.com/blogsearch`.

Note that commenting doesn't directly help with building external links as links from comments have something called a 'nofollow' tag (see the SEO chapter above). But it will increase traffic to your site from wine enthusiasts if not from search engines. Best of all is to do all of the above! But who has that amount of time?

16.3 Measurement

Tony has claimed his Places, Yelp, and FourSquare listings. Most of the reviews are great but occasionally he needs to make a diplomatic reply to the odd negative one. He's giving FourSquare a try and check-ins seem to be done by a young but still wealthy crowd. He may give SCVNGR a try soon. He has made sure that he includes some local posts on his blog about upcoming wine events and is commenting on the Food and Wine section of a popular Notown blog. In fact, the Notown blogger has asked him to write a guest post about wine! Here are his LBS measurements in the context of his Business Plan.

Business Objective: Boost Margins and Volume by changing to a Higher Value Customer Mix.

Marketing Strategy >Promotion >Internet marketing: Increase engagement with high value customers through LBS by encouraging users to share 'Tips' of premium wines (using in-store posters).

KPI: Conversion Average Order Value; Conversion Average Bottle Value; FourSquare Tips. As measured in Google Analytics filtering

for FourSquare referrals, and by the FourSquare dashboard for Tips.
KPI Targets: See Table 16.1. Increase Total Tips this month vs
last month by 1—each time the target is reached it is counted as one
Assisted Conversion. For other KPIs see Table 16.1.

Segment	Conv.#	Ass. Conv.#	AOV	ABV
Luxury Enthusiasts:	0	1	$65	$25
Enthusiasts:	0	2	$33	$15
Image Seekers:	2	2	$26	$15
Luxury Image Seekers:	0	1	$65	$15

Table 16.1: KPI Targets: LBS (Year 2)

KPI Target Sources: Segment numbers come from the Internet Marketing spreadsheet *Segment Conversions Report*. For Conversion Average Order Value equations see SEO Measurement section.

LBS will add eight more customers, all bar two indirectly. The
two that do purchase use their smartphones to impress and can't but
help order some expensive wine at the same time. Tony expects LBS
to add just one more Luxury Enthusiasts. Along with the other marketing strategies this means he has 14 more to go before he reaches
his target of 44 Luxury Enthusiasts in Year 2.

16.4 Summary

Location-Based Services use mobile phones to provide local information, on a map, with social media sharing, and gaming. Some
well-known ones are FourSquare, Yelp, Google+ Local, and Facebook
Places. As a wine retailer, claim your listings and update them, then
monitor them for reviews and questions. Google+ Local, Facebook
Places, FourSquare, and Yelp are worth setting up and utilizing.

16.5 Resources

- How well did you understand? Visit my website to discuss or
  ask questions about Wine and LBS: `www.WineMarketingPros.com/lbschap/`

Part IV

Conversion

It's actually reasonably easy to get traffic to your website if you follow one or two of the strategies in the Traffic Part of this book. It's a little harder to keep people on your website and get them to regularly return but still very doable if you follow one or two of the strategies in the Engagement Part and Repeat Purchase parts of this book. Getting them to buy—now there is the challenge.

That's what this Part is all about—converting visitors into customers. To make the point let's compare two websites:

- Website A: 5,000 visitors per day, 0.5% conversion rate (conversion rate is percent of buyers / visitors)
- Website B: 1,000 visitors per day, 5% conversion rate

The number of buyers for A will be 5,000 * 0.5% = 25. The number of buyers for B will be 1,000 * 5.0% = 50.

A small increase in conversion rates has a disproportionate increase in sales. Note I'm not saying you should focus on conversion to the exclusion of all the other factors, but, rather, you should aim to increase the performance of every part of your internet marketing process. This should be a continuous process. Let's illustrate that again with some numbers in Table 16.2.

Website	Period 1	Period 2
Visitors at the start of the period	1000	1464
Traffic boost	10%	10%
Engagement boost	10%	10%
Conversion boost	10%	10%
Repeat boost	10%	10%
= Visitor #s at end of that period	1464	2143

Table 16.2: Compounding increase in visitor numbers throughout the funnel

It is just like compounding interest rates but with a stronger multiplier effect as there are parts of the process every month that increase the final result.

Conversion can be increased by improving website usability and reducing hurdles to purchase, as well as by the good old direct marketing strategy of testing. Conversion is mainly about eCommerce

(web, mobile, and social commerce) and conversion rate optimization. As with the rest of this book, many of these chapters could
fit into two or more parts but are here because their primary role is
conversion.

17 Introduction to Wine eCommerce

17.1 What is eCommerce

Put simply, websites have three elements:

- the content, e.g. a tasting note or a photo
- the design and presentation, e.g. colors, fonts, and columns
- the code, (or logic), e.g. software that says take this tasting note, use this font, and send it to the internet browser (Explorer or Firefox etc)

An eCommerce website uses these elements to add shopping cart software allowing website visitors to buy things.

Back in the nineties things were conceptually simpler. You just had one page with simple code called *html* that did all three things. So I would write *<p>Hello </p>* and this would create a paragraph with *Hello* in it. At the top of the page, invisible to the reader but visible to internet browsing software (e.g. Firefox or Internet Explorer), would be code that said any text that was between <p> and </p> should use, say, Verdana font 10 size. In other words, the content and how the content should look would be on the same page.

Things then got conceptually a little more difficult. You could say look in this special presentation file (called a 'cascading style sheet' or 'css' file) and that file will tell you how to present the data.

In the late nineties, I remember walking into a web development agency to find a very excited technical director. He explained to me a concept called 'database driven websites'. Whereas, previously you had the presentation file split out from the webpage, now you had the content split out too. This time it was put into a database, and the webpage would now say:

- get me this content from the database
- get me how it should look from the design file
- put it together and send it to the browser (as html code)

So that's a very short overview of web technology. That's why you can change the look and feel of websites so easily. It's why you can have millions of pieces of data and only a few webpages because all that's happening is the website (actually the web server) is pulling together the three sources into one page and sending (or serving) it to the internet browser (e.g. Internet Explorer) on your computer.

17.2 Wine Website Design

Although wine web design can be as artistic or as functional as you desire, the overall structure really comes down to a few simple components, see Figure 17.1.

- the header
- the body
- the footer

Figure 17.1: Website design basic structure

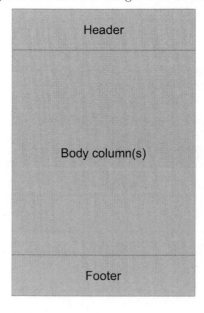

Wine Web Design Basic Structure

With the body you have four variations available for the body columns. You can have a single column, a left or right column, or three columns, see Figure 17.2.

There are many small variations of these, for example many blogs have two right columns and a large left column, some websites have banner images at the top of the body that seemingly splits a column into a box—but it is just a column with an image, others have 'floating' fourth columns to the left or right.

Different parts of a website can have different structures. Often you start with a home page and category with three columns and then move into left column product pages. Inside the columns you can have boxes or 'blocks'. These blocks often hold navigation bars, shopping cart summaries, recently viewed info, promo ads, 'widgets', images, or just plain text boxes, see Figure 17.3

So that's the basic overview of a wine store website design structure. Here are a few examples (it might be helpful to also view them on your internet browser at the same time as you're reading).

Wine Store Web Design Examples

Wine.com

Arguably the largest wine store online in the world. They probably have the biggest presence in wine drinkers' minds if not SEO and PPC. They offer a large range of selection, ratings, reviews, shipping deals, virtual cellars, recommendations, and wine guides. An impressive site indeed backed up by deep pockets.

The home page of wine.com uses a left column design with numerous blocks filling the main column. The product page is a standard left column design. Some other notable features:

- an expanding menu over all the ways people search for wine. Wine.com used to have a simpler design, so I'm guessing they've tested this and found that it converts better
- the split on shop, gifts, wine club, and wine accessories (probably based off keyword research)
- a busy page with lots of promo boxes and distraction (though less busy than a year ago)
- excellent product listing—succinct and to the point

Figure 17.2: Website column variations

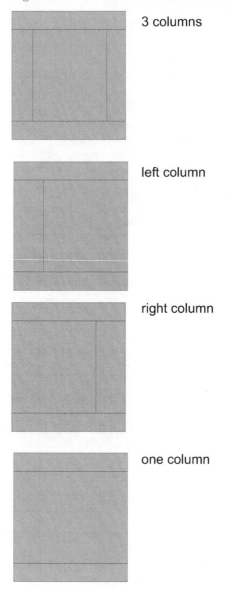

3 columns

left column

right column

one column

Figure 17.3: Website blocks

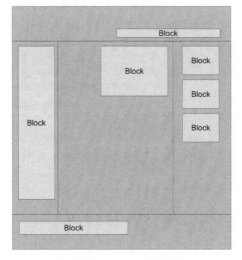

If you look at the product detail page they use winemakers notes, critical acclaim, drinker reviews, and lists. This is an excellent website from one of the big players.

KLwines.com

'1000s of Rare and Collectable Wines from around the globe...'. KLwines.com is based in Californian, has three large stores, and is a switched on state player.

Their home page is a left column design like their product pages. Other notable design features:

- nice, clean design with easy filterable navigation
- good, solid marketing with various web features clearly shown and not too much promotion going on
- the real time inventory is a big financial investment—these guys are serious players
- some really good reviews

The people behind this website put in some hard work, showing that it's often 99% perspiration and 1% inspiration to get these websites done well.

BevMo.com

Arguably the largest in the market because of its offline chain of stores in the western US. It boasts a huge selection of wines at cheap prices that can be picked up at the local BevMo. Also note the 'Pick Up Your Order In 1 Hour,' a great selling point for local wine retailers.

Their home page design is a left column structure. Their product page is a three column structure. Other notable design features include:

- very simple and draws you to the few deals they're offering
- navigation is easy, obvious, and 'filterable'
- the product detail page is very simple with some ratings
- BevMo is one of the top websites in the US despite its design being a little dated

Snooth.com

More of a portal or mall for wine stores and wineries than a direct competitor. Their home page is a three column design. The product page is essentially three column with a big box on top of the left two columns. Other notable features:

- easy search, ratings, and recommendation. They've focused on doing these things really well
- have had excellent SEO (though they may now be coming under pressure from other websites)
- offers the wine drinker the ability to get ratings and reviews from stores and drinkers all round the world
- you can compare prices and get recommendations
- they used to have too much noise with the wine consumer pulled in too many ways with ads and boxes, but they have since cleaned up the site

For more about Snooth, see the Comparison Shopping Engine chapter.

17.3 Web Development

Graphic Design Last

Unfortunately most people think of the 'design' first when they think eCommerce. If they mean 'usability' rather than color choice then that's fine but as a leading website designer, Ben Hunt, put it [105],

> No one really knows what design will work well. Good
> designers and clients can take the best guess and hope
> that it's the right one.

Ugly but true. The better way is to constantly test different components of design, copy, and headlines to see which combination best leads to conversion. In his words,

> In fact, graphic design appears to play a minor role
> in a site's success (although we like to think it's vitally
> important). The real keys to success are more basic, can
> take far less work, and are accessible to many more people
> who are not skilled in graphics.

Then he goes on to outline why measurable results are the best way to design a website,

> Whatever success is, the access to improving/optimizing
> it starts with a simple thing—measuring it! You cannot
> improve something you don't measure. Otherwise, how
> do you know it's improved? This really is the key to un-
> locking the secret to successful design. Measurable results
> open up the possibility of evolving your designs in order
> to make them more effective.

We'll look at measuring and testing in the Conversion Rate Optimization chapter.

17.4 eCommerce Requirements

17.4.1 Wine eCommerce Website: Custom Built or Off-the-Shelf?

Pretty much the only people nowadays commissioning true custom eCommerce websites are very large corporations and governments. Every other company uses pre-existing 'modules' or packages of code to make at least 80% of their website and customize the rest. Indeed 'Off-the-shelf' eCommerce websites can often provide 100% of what is needed requiring no code customization at all. The amount of customization is dependent on the expected extra sales or cost savings for a business—the larger the business, the bigger the benefits, and therefore, the larger the development budget. For a small company any customization may prove uneconomic and so a website that is 99-100% off the shelf is an option.

In a continuum based on purchase price, eCommerce options may look like this:
>Really honestly free (e.g. x.wordpress.com)
>>Simple software with simple built-in customization (e.g. Yahoo, Volusion, Joomla VirtueMart)
>>>Software that requires not so simple customization (e.g. Magento, specialist wine eCommerce software)
>>>>Software that requires a programmer to build your website out of various pre-existing modules (e.g. .NET, web developers)
>>>>>Custom-Built software.

What particular software you choose will depend on your 'requirements'. If your requirements are to post wine reviews and new releases for customers to see online, and buy in-store, then the x.wordpress.com may be sufficient. If you require:

- live integration with your stock, point of sale, accounting systems, suppliers for drop shipping, and CRM
- complex price promotions, loyalty schemes, truly heavy website traffic, trade and retail pricing
- plus all the normal eCommerce features, such as shopping cart and catalog,

. . . then you're likely to have some significant customization.

The trick is to decide what requirements are 'Must Have' vs 'Should Have' vs 'Nice to Have'. Then look at the software websites to see how many offer all your Must Haves and what's the price. Chances are you'll have to contact them with your list of requirements so you can get an accurate quote. Once you've collected the quotes, you'll have a minor heart attack as to how expensive your requirements are. Then you'll have a glass of wine and reconsider just how *must* your Must Haves really are. Here's a good way to do this.

17.4.2 Refine Your Requirements into Three or More Stages

Stage I

Must Haves are probably basic eCommerce catalog, content pages, shopping cart, shipping, email and payment processes. A key decision you'll need to make in Stage I is whether you can accept just your logo and brand colors on the website or whether you want a custom design. Sometimes there is a happy medium of being able to choose from a number of different designs (called 'templates') for no or little cost. In a corporate role, I've insisted on full custom design; in a small business, I've been happy with just the logo as long as the website looks professional.

Note, for a small business, integration with other systems will be *Nice to Have*. Instead of integration, you will probably upload inventory using a spreadsheet file, use PayPal not your own merchant account, and use simplified shipping quotes, e.g. flat rate or by the case. For a medium business, you'll probably save money by having this integration so it's a worthwhile *Must Have* assuming you have the budget.

Stage II

After a couple of months (or years) of use, experience confirms that you really do need some features you discarded in Stage I as too expensive. Perhaps the software restricts your online promotions and marketing, or you've had negative customer feedback about something. So add some of the *Should Have* and maybe even *Nice to Have* features to your website.

Stage III

Your online business has really taken off and can now increasingly justify *Should Haves* and *Nice to Haves*.

Controversial Alternative to Stage III

Frankly, when your online business has grown to Stage III, I think you should comprehensively redo your requirements list as you'll have a lot more experience with what you need. Also the eCommerce market is moving very swiftly so new solutions may now be available at more affordable prices than when you last checked.

You've done the hard yards of creating content for product listings, legal statements, shipping and return policies, so you can just upload this into the new system. There may be some Google issues, but these can be resolved (with something called a '301 redirect') with little effect on Google Ranking. You can now afford to have a web developer add in lots of payment and shipping options.

I used to think you should start with a clear roadmap. You would know what you were going to do to increase the functionality of your website, and how you would do it. Perhaps you would start with eCommerce 'bronze' edition knowing that you can upgrade to 'silver' then 'gold' in the future. But as the speed of eCommerce development picks up, with new or updated eCommerce software coming out every month, I reckon you should choose what software suits you now and then look to move to new software every 6-12 months.

This will be sacrilege to some—and would have been to me a couple of years ago. But two years ago there was no Magento; Word-Press was just a blog; Google shopping products were only just being launched, customer reviews were unlikely, and social media was for geeks and hippies. Outsourcing to India was for corporates, selling to China was for optimists or fools, and expecting a guy from Croatia to provide sensible comments on a technical forum in good English was ridiculous.

Since then the whole landscape, or 'webscape', has changed. All those things have happened plus much more. If your current provider isn't upgrading their software then you may be able to get a better eCommerce website at half the price with new functions which hadn't occurred to you 12 months ago.

So the key task is deciding what requirements are *Must Haves*, *Should Haves*, and *Nice to Haves*. The next is reconsidering, re-prioritizing and reviewing these every 6-12 months based on cumulative experience.

Let's look at those requirements in more detail. We'll first look at the requirements of a small versus large wine retailer, then look at a small-medium versus medium-large wine retailer.

17.5 The Requirements List for Different Wine eCommerce Websites

Firstly we'll look at the requirements list for four different size wine retailers, then we'll look at the requirements list for a small and medium sized winery.

The eCommerce Requirements document below [106] has *Must Have*, *Should Have*, *Nice to Have* columns on the left for a very small wine retailer, see Tables 17.1, 17.2, and 17.3. The columns on the right are for a very large wine retailer or winery company. Note, see the Resources section at the end of this chapter for where to download these files. You can see just how different each retailer's requirements are despite both being in the same business.

The two wine retailer decision makers are very different.

17.5.1 Very Small vs. Very Large Wine Retailers

The Very Small Wine Retailer

Is owner operated. He (I'll use a female example next) gets time off by having two or three retail assistants run the store one or two days a week, or just closes the store on a Monday. He has no specific promotional budget as any expenses directly reduce his income, so he's a reluctant spender. Any expenses, such as advertising and website development, must lead to more dollars in than out.

He is really busy just keeping the business running. If he has a way to keep costs down he'll take it, despite being really busy already. Most of his customers are local and repeat regardless of whether he has a website or not. He is happy with using the internet, but it is not his expertise. His expertise is wine and retailing.

The Large Wine Retailer Company

Has a 1000 staff with a sales and marketing team of 100 people, including an internet marketing team of five. The team is led by a young, smart marketing expert. She lobbies for part of a large marketing budget versus other sales and marketing managers. She is willing to try all sorts of marketing campaigns to boost sales, many of which will be handled by media agencies.

Her team is driven by two things (1) if they screw up, their career could be over in that company and, (2) if they do really well their

Table 17.1: Wine eCommerce Requirements: Small vs Large Wine Retailer (page 1)

eCommerce Requirements List	Must Have	Should Have	Nice to Have		Must Have	Should Have	Nice to Have
	For: Very Small Wine Retailer				For: Very Large Wine Retailer		
Set up:							
Design: Unique			x		x		
Design: Blog theme integration			x				x
Design: Extensive Range of Themes		x					x
Design: Limited Selection + Logo	x						x
Design: Mobile responsive design		x			x		
Ease of use: Text Editor (html not required)	x				x		
Hosted (Software as a Service)	x					x	
Open Source with no "vendor lock-in"			x		x		
Price Tiers: Retail and Trade		x			x		
Sales Tax	x				x		
Legal Compliance: age	x				x		
Legal Compliance: interstate shipping			x		x		
International: Currencies			x		x		
International: Languages			x		x		
Search Engine Optimization (SEO):							
Custom title and meta description tags	x				x		
Custom URL	x				x		
xml sitemap		x			x		
Comparison Shopping Engine feeds		x			x		
Load time speed		x			x		
Robots file		x			x		
Canonical page links		x			x		
User Experience:							
Navigation: Drill down menus		x			x		
Navigation: Breadcrumbs		x			x		
Usability: Function over 'Art'		x			x		
Advanced Search capabilities		x			x		
Reviews (Customer and Retailer)		x			x		
Ratings		x			x		
Recommendations		x			x		
Up-sell / Cross Sell		x			x		
Content Pages (CMS): text	x				x		
Social Media:							
Video functionality (e.g. youtube)			x		x		
Audio functionality (e.g. podcasts)			x		x		
Facebook integration			x		x		
Local Review Site Links		x			x		
Blog		x			x		
Social media sharing buttons		x			x		
Catalog:							
Category Management	x				x		
Product Management	x				x		
Product in multiple categories	x				x		
Custom Attribute Creation (e.g. vintage)	x				x		
Bulk Product Upload/Download	x				x		
Bulk Inventory Upload/Download	x				x		
Live Inventory			x		x		
Inventory: Global and Product Specific		x			x		
Inventory: Low/No Inventory Notification	x				x		
Inventory: Display Out of Stock, or Remove	x				x		
Inventory: Back orders (show out of stock as in stock)		x			x		
API / RSS integration			x		x		
Grid and list views		x			x		
Media Manager with automatic image resizing		x			x		
Product number limit minimum	500		None		None		
Category limit minimum	25		None		None		

Table 17.2: Wine eCommerce Requirements: Small vs Large Wine Retailer (page 2)

eCommerce Requirements List	Must Have	Should Have	Nice to Have	Must Have	Should Have	Nice to Have
	For: Very Small Wine Retailer			*For: Very Large Wine Retailer*		
Shopping Cart:						
Upfront shipping and tax cost estimation		x		x		
Guest no-registration		x		x		
Confirm Age at Checkout	x			x		
Promo: Coupons		x		x		
Promo: Gift Wrapping, Messages		x		x		
Promo: Discounts $ or %		x		x		
Promo: free shipping	x			x		
Promo: Buy X get Y		x		x		
Promo: discount by product or category		x		x		
Promo: discount by volume		x		x		
Payment methods: merchant account credit card		x		x		
Payment methods: PayPal Standard	x			x		
Payment methods: Google Checkout		x		x		
Payment methods: Pick up & Pay	x			x		
Payment methods: Internet banking & Invoicing		x		x		
Security: secure check out (SSL)	x			x		
Security: credit card rule compliance (PCI)	x			x		
Security: expert server administration	x			x		
Security: regular eCommerce software upgrades	x			x		
Order Management:						
Dashboard Overview			x	x		
Shipping: Pre setup UPS, Fedex, USPS		x		x		
Shipping: Pick up	x			x		
Shipping: Multiple Addresses			x	x		
Shipping: Third Party Fulfillment House			x	x		
Shipping: Packing fee			x	x		
Good Invoice / Credit process	x			x		
Phone order entry			x	x		
Flat rate shipping	x			x		
Table rate shipping	x			x		
Weight rate shipping	x			x		
Email System for Customer Support	x			x		
Email notifications of orders	x			x		
Print invoices and packing slips		x		x		
Tax rates per location	x			x		
Export: orders and customers into CSV formats	x			x		
Export: import orders into accounting system		x				
Live Integration: POS system			x	x		
Live Integration: Inventory system			x	x		
Live Integration: Accounting system			x	x		
Live Integration: CRM			na	x		
Live Integration: ERP			na	x		
Live Integration: Shipping Compliance			x	x		
Reporting:						
Google Analytics		x		x		
Google Webmaster Tools		x		x		
Sales by product and customer		x		x		
Repeat Purchase:						
Email Marketing: Pro Service		x		x		
Email Marketing: Autoresponder		x		x		
Clubs			x	x		
Allocation			x	x		
Support:						
Email (business hours)	x			x		
Forum		x		x		
FAQs, Documentation	x			x		
Tutorials		x		x		
Phone			x	x		
24/7			x	x		

Table 17.3: Wine eCommerce Requirements: Small vs Large Wine Retailer (page 3)

eCommerce Requirements List	Must Have	Should Have	Nice to Have	Must Have	Should Have	Nice to Have
	For: Very Small Wine Retailer			For: Very Large Wine Retailer		
Custom Coding:						
User Experience			x	x		
Catalog			x	x		
Shipping			x	x		
Order Management			x	x		
Reporting			x	x		
Repeat Purchase			x	x		
Price:						
Price: per month	Low			High		
Price: Set up	Low			High		
Price: Sales Commission charges			None	None		
Price: Support Normal (e.g. < 2 business days)	Low			Med.		
Price: Support Priority (e.g. < 1 day)		Med.		Med.		
Price: Support Urgent (on demand)			None	High		
Contract term (if any)			None			
Domain name included			x			na
Hosting Included	x					x
SSL included	x					x
Notes:						
"na" = not applicable						
"Med. = Medium						

career could skyrocket. So they minimize risks and maximize chances to achieve marketing success.

Their customers are national, and their shipping is from numerous (distributor) warehouses around the country. They have to communicate and cooperate with other teams throughout the company (including a very risk averse IT team). They need to integrate with all sorts of systems from the sales and customer services team's 'CRM' through to the accounting department's software and operation's 'ERP' shipping and supply software. Any eCommerce project is likely to be decided by recommendation from a committee made up of all the departments. A vice president will sign off on the committee recommendation.

The difference being the small retailer's key requirement is to have more cash come in versus out. The large company's key requirement is to not screw up. The small retailer's *Must Haves* are based on a simple calculation of net margin, i.e. sales margin less expenses. If a requirement's expense does not outweigh its cost then it's not needed. The *Must Haves* of large companies are all of these plus more to do with the technical specification of integrating systems. Although I may seem overly cynical about large companies, the fact is they have the budget to allow them to be more careful.

Some web developers may think the very small retailer needs a few more *Must Haves*, and the large company needs a few less but I think that's probably splitting hairs. The bigger question is for those retailers in between the very small and the very large. What do they really need? What are the *Must Haves* versus *Should Haves* versus *Nice to Haves*? Let's look at that next.

17.5.2 Medium Wine Retailers

The small-medium wine retailer

Is owned by a number of people only one of whom actually works in the retail store full time. This person, the general manager, works hard, perhaps 60 hours per week, much of that time in his office as he has retail assistants to man the store and even a store-man to manage stock and delivery.

He has a significant promotional budget that is mainly spent in newspapers. He has a website and is very aware of the importance of the internet, but he has yet to get his head around what he should be doing (his website developer seems to speak a different language). He also runs public tastings when he can and sends out a newsletter email to a list of customers. His ideal advertising results in measurable sales; however, he reluctantly accepts the famous John Wanamaker saying, 'I know that half of my advertising dollars are wasted. . . I just don't know which half'.

Most of his customers are local and repeat. He has a significant trade and corporate clientele. His best customers are wealthy doctors or lawyers who like to try high margin wines and/or have a favorite they always buy. He is happy with using the internet, but it is not his expertise. His expertise is wine and retailing.

The Medium-Large Wine Retailer Company

Is a multi-store company. It may be a state chain store, or perhaps it just has a few stores spread strategically over the county. Let's say the company has 100 staff members with a dedicated marketing team led by a hardened marketing pro.

Her marketing team of three has a large promotional budget much
of which is spent on price promotions. Before the last recession,
this was mainly newspapers with a little local TV. Now it is rapidly
becoming internet focused, and the team is now almost completely focused on professional internet marketing. Everything is measured—
each advertising campaign has to show better results than other campaigns or it's dropped. This team is driven by sales results, specifically if $1 is spent on ads then at least $1.01 is made in profit. She
despises as old school the saying, 'I know that half of my advertising
dollars are wasted... I just don't know which half'.

The customers are state wide, the shipping is by Fedex from their
large retail stores, and a number of payment systems are offered from
PayPal to Authorize.net.

The eCommerce requirements document [107], see Tables 17.4, 17.5,
and 17.6 below has *Must Have*, *Should Have*, *Nice to Have* columns.
The ones on the left are for a small-medium wine retailer. The
columns on the right are for a medium-large wine retailer[1].

Unlike the previous comparison, the retailers' requirements are
similar. The difference is in live integration, custom coding, price,
and options for shipping and payment, as well as the promotional
tools of social media, email marketing, and testing. This reflects the
bigger budget as well as the desire for more marketing tools. There
are of course many different combinations for each individual retailer,
but these requirements are a good indication dependent on store size.

17.5.3 Winery eCommerce Websites

Winery websites are different in that they have only a few products,
and therefore search and filtering is not as important as a store with
hundreds. Below I cover the requirements for a small vs a medium
sized winery, see Tables 17.7, 17.8, and 17.9.

17.6 eCommerce Solutions

Now that you have created your Requirements Document, you can
confidently look for an eCommerce solution. Here are your options:

- Specialist wine eCommerce providers (see list below)

---

[1]See the Resources section for how to download this file

Table 17.4: Wine eCommerce Requirements: Small-Medium vs Medium-Large Wine Retailer (page 1)

eCommerce Requirements List	For: Small-Med. Wine Retailer			For: Med.-Large Wine Retailer		
	Must Have	Should Have	Nice to Have	Must Have	Should Have	Nice to Have
Set up:						
Design: Unique			x		x	
Design: Blog theme integration		x		x		
Design: Extensive Range of Themes		x		x		
Design: Limited Selection + Logo	x					x
Design: Mobile responsive design	x			x		
Ease of use: Text Editor (html not required)	x				x	
Hosted (Software as a Service)	x			x		
Open Source with no "vendor lock-in"			x		x	
Price Tiers: Retail and Trade	x			x		
Sales Tax	x			x		
Legal Compliance: age	x			x		
Legal Compliance: interstate shipping			x	x		
International: Currencies			x	x		
International: Languages			x	x		
Search Engine Optimization (SEO):						
Custom title and meta description tags	x			x		
Custom URL	x			x		
xml sitemap	x			x		
Comparison Shopping Engine feeds	x			x		
Load time speed	x			x		
Robots file	x			x		
Canonical page links	x			x		
User Experience:						
Navigation: Drill down menus	x			x		
Navigation: Breadcrumbs	x			x		
Usability: Function over 'Art'	x			x		
Advanced Search capabilities	x			x		
Reviews (Customer and Retailer)	x			x		
Ratings	x			x		
Recommendations	x			x		
Up-sell / Cross Sell	x			x		
Content Pages (CMS): text	x			x		
Social Media:						
Video functionality (e.g. youtube)		x		x		
Audio functionality (e.g. podcasts)			x	x		
Facebook integration			x	x		
Local Review Site Links	x			x		
Blog	x			x		
Social media sharing buttons		x		x		
Catalog:						
Category Management	x			x		
Product Management	x			x		
Product in multiple categories	x			x		
Custom Attribute Creation (e.g. vintage)	x			x		
Bulk Product Upload/Download	x			x		
Bulk Inventory Upload/Download	x			x		
Live Inventory			x	x		
Inventory: Global and Product Specific		x		x		
Inventory: Low/No Inventory Notification	x			x		
Inventory: Display Out of Stock, or Remove	x			x		
Inventory: Back orders (show out of stock as in stock)	x			x		
API / RSS integration		x		x		
Grid and list views		x		x		
Media Manager with automatic image resizing		x		x		
Product number limit minimum	2000	None		None		
Category limit minimum	100	None		None		

Table 17.5: Wine eCommerce Requirements: Small-Medium vs Medium-Large Wine Retailer (page 2)

eCommerce Requirements List	Must Have	Should Have	Nice to Have		Must Have	Should Have	Nice to Have
	For: Small-Med. Wine Retailer				*For: Med.-Large Wine Retailer*		
Shopping Cart:							
Upfront shipping and tax cost estimation	x				x		
Guest no-registration	x				x		
Confirm Age at Checkout	x				x		
Promo: Coupons	x				x		
Promo: Gift Wrapping, Messages	x				x		
Promo: Discounts $ or %	x				x		
Promo: free shipping	x				x		
Promo: Buy X get Y	x				x		
Promo: discount by product or category	x				x		
Promo: discount by volume	x				x		
Payment methods: merchant account credit card	x				x		
Payment methods: PayPal Standard	x				x		
Payment methods: Google Checkout	x				x		
Payment methods: Pick up & Pay	x				x		
Payment methods: Internet banking & Invoicing			x		x		
Security: secure check out (SSL)	x				x		
Security: credit card rule compliance (PCI)	x				x		
Security: expert server administration	x				x		
Security: regular eCommerce software upgrades	x				x		
Order Management:							
Dashboard Overview		x			x		
Shipping: Pre setup UPS, Fedex, USPS	x				x		
Shipping: Pick up	x				x		
Shipping: Multiple Addresses			x		x		
Shipping: Third Party Fulfillment House			x		x		
Shipping: Packing fee			x		x		
Good Invoice / Credit process	x				x		
Phone order entry		x			x		
Flat rate shipping	x				x		
Table rate shipping	x				x		
Weight rate shipping	x				x		
Email System for Customer Support	x				x		
Email notifications of orders	x				x		
Print invoices and packing slips		x			x		
Tax rates per location	x				x		
Export: orders and customers into CSV formats	x				x		
Export: import orders into accounting system		x				x	
Live Integration: POS system			x			x	
Live Integration: Inventory system			x			x	
Live Integration: Accounting system			x			x	
Live Integration: CRM			na				x
Live Integration: ERP			na				x
Live Integration: Shipping Compliance			x				x
Reporting:							
Google Analytics	x				x		
Google Webmaster Tools		x			x		
Sales by product and customer	x				x		
Repeat Purchase:							
Email Marketing: Pro Service	x				x		
Email Marketing: Autoresponder		x			x		
Clubs			x		x		
Allocation			x		x		
Support:							
Email (business hours)	x				x		
Forum		x			x		
FAQs, Documentation	x				x		
Tutorials		x			x		
Phone			x		x		
24/7			x		x		

Table 17.6: Wine eCommerce Requirements: Small-Medium vs Medium-Large Wine Retailer (page 3)

eCommerce Requirements List	Must Have	Should Have	Nice to Have	Must Have	Should Have	Nice to Have
		For: Small-Med. Wine Retailer			*For: Med.-Large Wine Retailer*	
Custom Coding:						
User Experience			x	x		
Catalog			x	x		
Shipping			x	x		
Order Management			x	x		
Reporting			x	x		
Repeat Purchase			x	x		
Price:						
Price: per month	Low			Med.		
Price: Set up	Med.			Med.		
Price: Sales Commission charges	None			None		
Price: Support Normal (e.g. < 2 business days)	Low			Med.		
Price: Support Priority (e.g. < 1 day)		Med.		Med.		
Price: Support Urgent (on demand)			High	High		
Contract term (if any)			None			None
Domain name included			x			na
Hosting Included	x					x
SSL included	x					x
Notes:						
"na" = not applicable						
"Med. = Medium						

- Small business eCommerce providers, of which there are hundreds, e.g. Volusion, Yahoo
- Wine shopping comparison websites Snooth.com, Wine-Searcher.com, and a few others
- Local web developers
- Large eCommerce brands, e.g. IBM
- Do it yourself for free with MagentoeCommerce.com (Community Edition) or WordPress (with the WP-eCommerce plug-in)

One of the central tenets of this book is that the website is just one part of the process of selling wine online. You also have to generate traffic, engagement, and repeat purchase. So let's also look at the options to do this. I'm including search engine optimization (SEO), internet advertising, wine shopping comparison engines, and social media (Facebook, wine blogs, Twitter).

- large SEM agencies
- local SEM services
- eCommerce providers who offer this as an add-on service sometimes with their own marketplace

Table 17.7: Wine eCommerce Requirements: Wineries (page 1)

eCommerce Requirements List	Must Have	Should Have	Nice to Have		Must Have	Should Have	Nice to Have
	For: Small Winery				*For: Medium Winery*		
Set up:							
Design: Unique			x			x	
Design: Blog theme integration			x			x	
Design: Extensive Range of Themes		x				x	
Design: Limited Selection + Logo	x					x	
Design: Mobile responsive design			x		x		
Ease of use: Text Editor (html not required)	x				x		
Hosted (Software as a Service)	x					x	
Open Source with no "vendor lock-in"			x		x		
Price Tiers: Retail and Trade		x			x		
Sales Tax	x				x		
Legal Compliance: age	x				x		
Legal Compliance: interstate shipping			x		x		
International: Currencies			x		x		
International: Languages			x		x		
Search Engine Optimization (SEO):							
Custom title and meta description tags	x				x		
Custom URL	x				x		
xml sitemap		x			x		
Comparison Shopping Engine feeds		x			x		
Load time speed		x			x		
Robots file		x			x		
Canonical page links		x			x		
User Experience:							
Navigation: Breadcrumbs		x			x		
Usability: Function over 'Art'		x			x		
Up-sell / Cross Sell		x			x		
Content Pages (CMS): text	x				x		
Social Media:							
Video functionality (e.g. youtube)			x			x	
Audio functionality (e.g. podcasts)			x			x	
Facebook integration			x		x		
Local Review Site Links		x			x		
Blog		x			x		
Social media sharing buttons		x			x		
Catalog:							
Category Management			x			x	
Product Management			x			x	
Product in multiple categories			x			x	
Custom Attribute Creation (e.g. vintage)			x			x	
Bulk Product Upload/Download			x			x	
Bulk Inventory Upload/Download			x			x	
Live Inventory			x			x	
Inventory: Global and Product Specific		x				x	
Inventory: Low/No Inventory Notification	x				x		
Inventory: Display Out of Stock, or Remove	x				x		
Inventory: Back orders (show out of stock as in stock)		x				x	
API / RSS integration			x			x	
Grid and list views		x				x	
Media Manager with automatic image resizing		x				x	
Product number limit minimum	50		None		500		
Category limit minimum	10		None		25		

Table 17.8: Wine eCommerce Requirements: Wineries (page 2)

eCommerce Requirements List	Must Have	Should Have	Nice to Have	Must Have	Should Have	Nice to Have
	For: Small Winery			*For: Medium Winery*		
Shopping Cart:						
Upfront shipping and tax cost estimation		x			x	
Guest no-registration		x			x	
Confirm Age at Checkout	x			x		
Promo: Coupons			x			x
Promo: Gift Wrapping, Messages			x			x
Promo: Discounts $ or %			x			x
Promo: free shipping		x			x	
Promo: Buy X get Y		x			x	
Promo: discount by product or category			x			x
Promo: discount by volume		x			x	
Payment methods: merchant account credit card		x		x		
Payment methods: PayPal Standard			x		x	
Payment methods: Google Checkout			x		x	
Payment methods: Internet banking & Invoicing			x		x	
Security: secure check out (SSL)	x			x		
Security: credit card rule compliance (PCI)	x			x		
Security: expert server administration	x			x		
Security: regular eCommerce software upgrades	x			x		
Order Management:						
Dashboard Overview			x		x	
Shipping: Pre setup UPS, Fedex, USPS		x			x	
Shipping: Multiple Addresses			x		x	
Shipping: Third Party Fulfillment House			x		x	
Shipping: Packing fee			x		x	
Good Invoice / Credit process	x				x	
Phone order entry			x		x	
Flat rate shipping	x			x		
Table rate shipping	x			x		
Weight rate shipping	x			x		
Email System for Customer Support	x			x		
Email notifications of orders	x			x		
Print invoices and packing slips		x			x	
Tax rates per location	x			x		
Export: orders and customers into CSV formats	x			x		
Export: import orders into accounting system		x				
Live Integration: POS system			x		x	
Live Integration: Inventory system			x		x	
Live Integration: Accounting system			x		x	
Live Integration: CRM			na		x	
Live Integration: ERP			na		x	
Live Integration: Shipping Compliance			x		x	
Reporting:						
Google Analytics		x		x		
Google Webmaster Tools		x		x		
Sales by product and customer		x		x		
Repeat Purchase:						
Email Marketing: Pro Service		x		x		
Email Marketing: Autoresponder		x		x		
Clubs			x	x		
Allocation			x	x		
Support:						
Email (business hours)	x			x		
Forum		x		x		
FAQs, Documentation	x			x		
Tutorials		x		x		
Phone			x	x		
24/7			x	x		

Table 17.9: Wine eCommerce Requirements: Wineries (page 3)

eCommerce Requirements List	Must Have	Should Have	Nice to Have		Must Have	Should Have	Nice to Have
	For: Small Winery				*For: Medium Winery*		
Custom Coding:							
User Experience			x			x	
Catalog			x			x	
Shipping			x			x	
Order Management			x			x	
Reporting			x			x	
Repeat Purchase			x			x	
Price:							
Price: per month	Low				Med.		
Price: Set up	Low				Med.		
Price: Sales Commission charges			None			None	
Price: Support Normal (e.g. < 2 business days)	Low				Med.		
Price: Support Priority (e.g. < 1 day)		Med.			Med.		
Price: Support Urgent (on demand)			None		High		
Contract term (if any)			None				
Domain name included			x		na		
Hosting Included	x						x
SSL included	x						x
Notes:							
"na" = not applicable							
"Med. = Medium							

- specialist wine online marketing consultants or Digital Marketing Agencies
- a plethora of services found on the internet, sometimes of dubious nature
- media agencies
- direct marketing agencies
- ad agencies
- do it yourself

Before we can go any further, let's not forget that the liquor industry is a legal minefield. As you no doubt know, the legal environment for selling wine online is a complex and dynamic area including:

- Complying with laws as to minimum age to purchase liquor
- Complying with US inter-state liquor shipping law or 'shipping compliance'. Many US states legally restrict the distribution of wine from out of state (and in-state) suppliers

This book purposely does not cover the legal issues of selling wine on the internet. Every US state (and indeed country) has different legal requirements. You need to refer to a lawyer for such advice.

17.6.1 The End to End Cost of Selling Wine Online

eCommerce Cost

Traditional wine eCommerce websites cost about $5-20,000+ depending on your local website developer. For that price, it should look good, have a catalog, and a shopping cart. Payment probably is by PayPal and hopefully not unsecured credit card payment systems.

There is absolutely nothing wrong with using your local website developer. Indeed, you didn't have many options until recently, and a decade ago you were probably paying $50,000 for a website. The website industry changed after the internet stock-market bubble burst in 2001 as it left many extremely talented web developers without capital. With developers forced to find ways to make websites cheaply, various innovative ways sprung up. We're seeing the fruits of that now. For example,

- Cloud computing—the software resides in a hosted web server not on your PC
- Open Source—a large community of programmers make the core of a particular software program available free to everyone
- IBM might have dropped the hardware crown in the 1990s, but they become experts at pulling together disparate IT systems, many of which were based on cloud computing & Open Source software, in the new millennium
- Others continued with developing proprietary software successfully. Most of them now offer that software via cloud computing so you don't need to purchase a CD and install it yourself

Another big thing that changed the internet was Google. Google dominated many of the previous chapter topics, and most of their superb tools are free but highly effective.

So with pricing we have parts of the solution that can cost $0—or $10,000! Yet I'd suggest that in many cases the free tools are worth immensely more than the expensive tools, such as good SEO practice on your website that includes Google Analytics and Webmaster tools. Let's focus on the wine eCommerce website. Note, prices are accurate as at 1 December 2012 and depend on the exact product you choose.

There are some basic small business eCommerce systems that work just fine, for example Yahoo (plus scores of others). Yahoo was waiving its set-up ($50) and charging a promo of $29.96 to $75.96 per month for the first 12 months (usually $39.95) plus 1.5% to 1% of sales respectively to run. The hosted version of Magento, called Magento Go, costs \$15 to \$125 per month to use. Shopify cost \$29 to \$179 plus 2% to 0% of sales respectively to run.

Most expensively, and more for medium to large businesses, there is IBM's WebSphere (about \$30,000+) or Magento Enterprise. Indeed, there are hundreds of different eCommerce systems, so this is just illustrative of pricing levels for the eCommerce site alone.

There are a number of specialist (or specialist version) wine eCommerce development systems. These include Vin 65, eWinerySolutions, Nexternal, Beverage Media Group, Bottlenose, WineZap, WineWeb, Fort Systems, Easy Wine Shopper, and Vineyard2Door. The only publicly available wine eCommerce prices (correct as at December 2012) are Vin65's system and charges at least \$250 per month[108], and the WineWeb which charge's \$450 set-up fee and a 0.5%-2% transaction fee (or \$295 per month).

Internet Marketing Cost

Internet marketing development costs include:

- internet advertising (Google, Facebook, and other networks) including creating banner ads
- SEO on-page optimization, local SEO optimization
- blog development
- Facebook Page development
- Twitter background development
- landing page optimization and development
- comparison shopping engine optimization
- social monitoring tool creation

Internet marketing management costs include:

- advertising management, creative and optimization
- SEO content creation (if outsourced) and editing
- website analytics reporting
- social media monitoring and measurement
- active social media engagement on Facebook, Twitter, and other social media and location-based services
- integration of mobile marketing into store, e.g. QR codes and point of sale
- landing page optimization testing and measurement program

There is an overlap between what an eCommerce company will provide and what an internet marketing agency will do. Some agencies do both eCommerce and internet marketing.

The cost can be based on development or management hours, a percentage of advertising cost (10-20%), a retainer, and/or a performance basis. Each method of payment has its own problems and so a hybrid approach might be best where cost-based pricing is used, with an additional performance based bonus if agreed upon when measurements are met[109].

17.6.2 Ranking Solutions

As discussed throughout this book, the process of selling wine online is only partly eCommerce. This can be seen by weighting the different parts of the process as follows:

- Traffic (SEO, advertising, CSE): 20%
- Engagement (blogs, Facebook, Twitter, Mobiles, and LBS): 20%
- Conversion (various eCommerce systems and Optimization): 20%
- Repeat Purchase (email marketing and remarketing) 20%
- Pricing (Set-up, monthly fee, transaction fee, SEM fee): 10%
- Support (forum, email, FAQs, phone call center) 10%

This equals 100%, and reflects the importance of a process rather than concentrating on just one part of it.

I've then reviewed each of the ranking solutions providers as a group as follows, see Table 17.10. SME stands for Small and Medium Enterprise and SEM stands for Search Engine Marketing (also known as internet marketing or digital marketing agency).

In essence, if the company is a wine specialist or has strong marketing ability then it's ranked high. If it provides general eCommerce first and then SEM as an extra, then it ranks lower. I may be a little too skeptical about local web developers and local SEM (Search Engine Marketing consultants)—perhaps your local one is much better than average. All of them could do better in parts with the large SEM agencies probably being too expensive for small retailers.

Table 17.10: Wine eCommerce Solution Rankings

Selling Wine Online Solution Ranking							
Criteria: 1=poor, 5=great, 0=n/a	Weight %	SME Basic Generalist	Winery Specialist	Local web dev.	Large web dev.	Large SEM	Local SEM
Traffic:	20%	2	3	2	2	5	4
Engagement:	20%	1	2	2	2	5	4
Conversion:	20%	3	4	3	5	4	0
Repeat Purchase:	20%	3	5	3	3	4	2
Pricing:	10%	5	3	2	2	2	1
Support:	10%	4	4	4	4	4	2
Simple Total		18	21	16	18	24	13
Simple Total Ranking		3	2	5	3	1	6
Weighted Total		2.7	3.5	2.6	3.0	4.2	2.3
Weighted Total Ranking		**4**	**2**	**5**	**3**	**1**	**6**

Notes/Key:
SME (Small Medium Enterprise) Basic Generalist – e.g. Volusion or Yahoo
Winery Specialist – e.g. eWinerySolutions, vin65
shopping comparison site – e.g. snooth or winezap
large web dev. (developer) – e.g. IBM Webscope or Varien Magento Enterprise
large SEM (Search Engine Marketing) – a big PPC and SEO agency with min spend of $20,000 per month on adwords
local SEM – a small PPC or SEO agency that charges an hourly rate

17.7 Social or Facebook Commerce

In the Engagement part of this book, I discuss how a Facebook Page is an excellent way to increase your relationship, trust, and authority with (potential) customers, as well as generate traffic to your website. The presumption was that your eCommerce website was off-Facebook—it didn't have a website address that started with facebook.com but rather was your own domain, e.g. examplestore.com. What these (partially integrated) Facebook stores do is list products with a simple Buy Now button that directs the customer off Facebook onto the normal wine eCommerce site.

There is a growing body of thought that this is not ideal. Facebook users arguably don't wish to move out of their social environment and do wish to take advantage of being able to converse with their friends while they shop. Practical eCommerce puts it this way,[110]

> Think of it like when you were a teenager going to the mall to hang out with friends. You're there to socialize, if you walk into the store and find yourself a mile down the street then it's very disruptive. Point being to stay where they want to stay—on Facebook, not on your website.

Here's what social media commentator Paul Marsden[111] says in support of staying on Facebook:

There are essentially two social commerce strategies— 'putting water coolers next to tills' (helping people connect where they buy), and 'putting tills next to water coolers' (helping people buy where they connect).

Needing to stay within Facebook to complete transactions is controversial because there is no research to date that seems to prove the above opinion. However, until it is decided one way or the other, I tend to agree with this approach as,

- clicking off Facebook is a serious interruption
- it means you will lose the conversation between users
- having a Facebook Page enables impulse purchases

It's a social environment—we want to be part of conversation, not to interrupt it.

Similarly, a business that has a Facebook presence is in a social environment and should be part of the consumer's conversation not overtly selling. For ideas on conversation prompters, see the Twitter and Email Marketing chapters. This conversing approach may also put your business into their friends news stream generating more traffic.

Ideally, shopping should be personalized given that Facebook gives you age, gender, and location plus their interests. So perhaps wine retailers could use the interest data to present different varietals, regions, and price points. I've yet to see this data available, however. Perhaps it will become available in the future.

17.7.1 Social Commerce Requirements and Vendors

The requirements for a Social Commerce Store are similar to an eCommerce store except the store needs to stay within the Facebook environment and 'Liking' of products and categories is a *Must Have*. See the eCommerce chapter for a comprehensive list of requirements for wine retailers.

There are two ways to create an integrated Facebook Store and iframe and an app. The first is to create a window in Facebook that looks into your website, called an 'iframe'. It is a bit like a window, the 'window frame' is the Facebook Page, the 'window pane' is actually your webpage, which fits into the window frame. The advantage is you only need to do a few design changes for whenever that page is shown on Facebook, a relatively simple job for a web designer. The disadvantage is you can only use the central column, which restricts width to 520 pixels (about 10 cm) [112].

The advantage of apps is they take up the left most 720 pixels but require additional administration and the app fee. Facebook eCommerce is undergoing rapid development by many very talented companies. I'm not brave enough to recommend software when I know the recommendation will be out of date so quickly (though I see good things with Ecwid).

17.8 Measurement

Many companies would consider eCommerce to be the natural place to put eCommerce measurements, such as Average Order Value and Average Bottle Value. In this book, we won't be measuring eCommerce itself but rather how effectively traffic sources and devices convert in the eCommerce website. This has been done in each marketing strategy chapter's Measurement section. In the Landing Page Optimization chapter, we look at optimizing the eCommerce shopping cart process through testing it's different components, which is perhaps more the natural home for an eCommerce Measurement section.

17.9 Summary

Web development is a process of deciding what your Must-Have requirements are and then deciding whether you do it yourself or will hire a web developer or digital marketing agency. These requirements will be different for different sized retailers. Having built the eCommerce website you have completed only one part of the selling wine online process—you then need to then market it. There are various agencies who can help you with this from marketing specialists to local web developers.

17.10 Resources

- How well did you understand? Visit my website to discuss or ask questions about Wine eCommerce: `www.WineMarketingPros.com/ecomchap/`

- Wine eCommerce Requirements Document—see the Wine eCommerce webpage: `www.WineMarketingPros.com/ecomchap/`

18 Conversion Rate Optimization

18.1 What is Conversion Rate Optimization

Conversion Rate Optimization, one part of which is called Landing Page Optimization (LPO), is all about testing what works and what doesn't with the aim of selling more wine. You may remember this quote from the eCommerce chapter from a leading website designer, Ben Hunt,[105]

> Whatever success is, the access to improving/optimizing it starts with a simple thing—measuring it! You cannot improve something you don't measure. Otherwise, how do you know it's improved? This really is the key to unlocking the secret to successful design. Measurable results open up the possibility of evolving your designs in order to make them more effective.

One particular issue is losing people in the selling process. If you run an eCommerce website check out the number of shopping carts started versus the number of shopping carts completed. This metric is known as the *shopping cart abandonment rate* and is often very dispiriting. One LPO specialist says that[113],

> the shopping cart abandonment rate averaged 73 percent in the first two weeks of January (2010), some 12 percent higher than the low of 61 percent recorded on December 16 (2009). While the abandonment rate usually falls during the Christmas period, these are still huge swings, reflecting the impact of Black Friday/Cyber Monday deals, public holidays, and January sales.

There are some things you can do that are regarded as best practice, such as allowing guest registration and showing estimated shipping costs upfront rather than at the end of the checkout process.

These should help, but what you really want to do on your checkout pages and every other important page is have a conversion rate optimization process.

Let's put Conversion Rate Optimization in context. Remember when you were developing your website? Perhaps you hired the best web developer in town. He had more acronyms than a medical professor - expert in SEO, PPC, PHP, ASP, and SEM. He makes an eCommerce website look like something from NASA and Picasso; he even integrated it with social media. You're impressed and have every right to be.

Your website is launched. Nothing happens but he prepared you for this. He told you that it needed some traffic from Google Adwords in the first few weeks and then slowly search engines would start to send traffic. It made sense, was confirmed to be true by your geek brother-in-law, and it turns out they were right. They had also installed tracking software (Google Analytics) that tells you how many visitors you are getting. And slowly but surely you started to get more and more traffic. Before long you are happy with traffic.

But not with sales. Sales in fact seem minuscule versus the number of visitors to your site. Thousands come into the site and immediately fly out the other end without doing much at all. The fact is that only a tiny percent of visitors buy anything (use 1-2% as a rough guideline).

Truth be told, you may have hired a very good web developer or purchased a system from one of any number of good wine eCommerce companies. You may even have hired an excellent internet advertising person who is ensuring you get lots of traffic to your great website. The problem is that no one knows why the website has a low conversion rate. They are all experts at what they do - web design and internet advertising - they have well-considered opinions, and you're not dumb either. But you really need some facts, not speculation, on your dime.

Finding out what no one knows is done through something called Conversion Rate Optimization.

18.2 Conversion Rate Optimization

The experts I follow in this subject area are Conversion Rate Experts[114] and Tim Ash who owns the San Francisco firm SiteTuners[115], literally wrote the book[116] on this area. Essentially what Tim says is that it's unlikely you'll ever find out why your visitors aren't buying, even if you're a so-called Internet Marketing expert. So if no one knows, then leave it up to your customers' vote, albeit unconsciously but seamlessly, on your website pages. Do this by offering two or more versions of the same webpage and see which one converts the best.

Direct marketers have been doing this since Claude Hopkins[117] in Chicago in the early 1900s. He used newspaper adverts with coupons. He had two ads with differences in various elements, like the headline or picture, with a different coupon for each. The housewife cut one out and took it down to the local store. The more coupons redeemed the more successful that particular ad.

Exactly the same principle applies to the internet and is being used extensively today. This is not some obscure science, it's very mainstream. It is a warp speed version of the old coupon method and is made possible because websites allow you to track large (and therefore statistically valid) numbers of visitors to see which particular webpage variants convert better than others.

Some simple examples are:

- Two web pages that are exactly the same but with two different headlines. One says, 'Featured Napa Valley Merlot', the other says, 'Napa Valley Merlot - the heart of Wine Country, the Marquis of Grapes, but at Everyday prices'.
- Or perhaps on a product page you have a Buy Now button versus and Add to Cart button. Or the button is at the top, or at the bottom, or both.

You could have experts giving you their opinions on what is best— or just find out yourself. The easiest way to do this is by using Google Analytics Content Experiments—'usually' because it's free vs other expensive options. This puts code on the two variants of the page and you nominate what Google Analytics Goal you want to achieve. This Goal could be a specific shopping cart success page or other simpler goals you can nominate in Google Analytics. Google Analytics then randomly presents the different variant pages to different visitors. The page that gets the most visitors to the Goal page, e.g. purchases/conversions, is pronounced the winner—eventually.

The more volume and sales you have the quicker the process. Google Analytics Content Experiments has some complex statistical math working in the background, and it will only call a winner when there are enough completion pages to be statistically valid. To speed up this testing process, you often will use an indicator of success like email newsletter sign-ups or even change the success page to shopping cart entry rather than checkout completion. Frankly, sometimes I've decided not to wait until Google Analytics Content Experiments says it's statistically valid but make a call after about 30-40 sales. In effect, I'm trading off speed to market vs statistical confidence levels.

The Japanese call this 'kaizen'. That is incremental improvements that, over time, equal large improvements. This is what we're doing here. Rarely are there large improvements from one test; it is more likely that there are a series of small improvements from many tests over many parts of the 'Funnel'.

I think most people understand the sales funnel. It is described in different ways, and I've used it too with social media measurement, and my general overview of selling wine online. Tim Ash uses it for Landing Page Optimization. He uses the Acquisition >Conversion >Retention terminology.

Figure 18.1: LPO and The Marketing Funnel

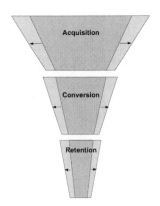

Acquisition—what I call Traffic. It's the top of the funnel. Visitors may come from your efforts in SEO, Banner Ads, Adwords, Affiliates, Blogs, Social Media in the online world and advertising, word of mouth etc. in the off line world.

Conversion—what I likewise call conversion. Tim says this is when a visitor to a landing page takes a desired action. So he's including signing up to a newsletter as a conversion; whereas, for a high traffic eCommerce store, I would only count sales.

Retention—what I call Repeat Business or the number of repeat purchases by a unique customer. This is where you build on the initial sale to further develop the customer relationship especially through engagement.

The aim is to improve each part of these processes incrementally. Improve parts of your landing page headlines, buttons, cart layout, email newsletter sequence etc. So rather than expecting growth of 100% immediately you expect a little every month from every part of the business as Table 18.1 shows.

Website	Period 1	Period 2
Visitors at the start of the period	1000	1464
Traffic boost	10%	10%
Engagement boost	10%	10%
Conversion boost	10%	10%
Repeat boost	10%	10%
= Customer #s at end of that period	1464	2143

Table 18.1: Conversions Compounding

Each part of the process improves by 10% every month for 24 months, compounding like interest rates.

The Myth of the Perfect Conversion

Lastly, let's cover what Tim calls the myth of the 100% conversion. There is no 100% conversion rather visitors can be split into Noes, Maybes, and Yeses. The aim is to concentrate on the Maybes. Firstly, the more Yes-Maybes, then the Maybe-Maybes and then the No-Maybes. There are many good reasons why visitors to your website may not purchase, not the least being they got a poor search result and immediately leave your page. They may also not be in a purchasing frame of mind - just researching. Figure 18.2 is based off one in Tim's book which shows making the marketing funnel bigger allowing more sales to come through the bottom.

Figure 18.2: The Myth of the Perfect Conversion

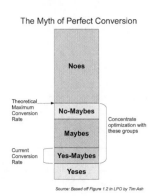

The Noes aren't going to buy no matter what you do. The Yeses have decided to buy so leave them to it. The Maybes are where you'll make a difference in your website.

18.3 Six Steps in Wine Conversion Rate Optimization

Google Analytics Content Experiments is the best software to start with and is free. There are better paid systems, such as Visual Website Optimizer, which provide better tracking of eCommerce shopping carts yet still integrate well with Google Analytics. Here we assume you are using Google Analytics.

Step 1 Set up Google Analytics

Ensure that Google Analytics is installed, this is an easy process that any web developer can help you with.

Step 2 Set a Baseline

You need to set a baseline, or a benchmark, of your current results. The aim will be to attempt to beat this benchmark time and again with the better test becoming the new benchmark, thereby ratcheting up the performance of your page. You may also find your new tests don't do as well as the benchmark, so you end up discarding them and stay with the benchmark. In the direct marketing industry, this is called 'beating the control'. In order of preference, your benchmark should be:

- Profit per visitor
- Revenue per visitor
- Conversion rate
- Shopping cart abandonment rate

Here are some definitions:

- Profit per visitor = average profit per sale per annum / total number of visitors pa
- Revenue per visitor = average revenue per sale pa / total number of visitors pa
- Conversion rate = visitors who purchase pa / total number of visitors pa
- Average revenue per sale = (price * quantity * % first time purchases) + (price * quantity * % repeat purchases) Note repeat customers tend to buy more at higher prices.
- Average profit per sale = (price - product cost) * quantity - credit card fee - average net freight cost

In order to take out seasonality influences, you usually use time periods, such as per annum (pa), or versus the same period last year.

You should use Profit Per Visitor. This requires Google to have data on the margins of your wines, which may be technically challenging. It's usually easier to provide access to prices. If that's the case then Revenue Per Visitor will do. The problem is you want to increase profit not revenue—you could increase revenue but reduce profit by cannibalizing high margin wine sales with low margin wine sales.

If you're unable to access prices then fall back on conversion rates and shopping cart abandonment. Benchmark these as follows[118]:

- Visit to product page Ratio (60%)
- Product page to Cart Ratio (30%)

- Cart to Checkout Ratio (60%)
- Checkout to Order Ratio (75%)

Basic measurements of success all set up? Let's move on to testing.

Step 3 Decide What to Test

Just choose two simple things to get started and then get more sophisticated over time. The usual suspects are:

- Headlines
- Images
- Product description copy
- Offers (e.g. free shipping, 1 case only)
- The 'call to action' (e.g. Buy Now vs Add to Cart, button at top or bottom or middle, high contrast, different colors, 'Register' vs 'Delivery Details')
- Clean design - get rid of as many links and other distractions as possible, focus on the the key action for the page usually the product purchase

Other possibilities:

- Ratings and medals (have them or not; hint: have them)
- Reviews (have them or not; hint: have them)
- Prices (test price points)
- Single Page Checkout vs. Multi Page (hint: go single)
- Guest checkout option vs. forced registration (hint: Guest is Best)

Gather testing feedback, conjecture, insults, and opinions by:

- 5 or 10 sec test - informal (show your mother/acquaintance your website for 5 seconds and ask them what the page is about)
- Usability tests - paid see SEOmoz's CRO list[119], to which I would add Clicktale.com
- Online and Email Surveys
- Feedback requests on website, like Feedback boxes you see on the side of pages (like mine!)
- Team brainstorming
- Look at your competitors' sites

If you use surveys here are some questions[120] you might ask:

- 'How likely is it that you would recommend us to a friend or colleague?'

- 'Which other options did you consider before choosing our shop, and why did you decide to use us?'
- 'If you were in charge of our company, how would you persuade people like yourself to use us?'
- 'If you were in charge of our company, how would you 'spread the word' about us?'

Another way Tim Ash comes up with ideas is by using these 'scales' to look for ideas.

Anxiety vs. Trust. Guarantee safety and security. Privacy Policy, shipping, returns, testimonials, certificates, and trust symbols. Indeed, I would have all these things regardless and test their prominence. Not convinced that trust symbols like BBB and GeoTrust are worth it? Then give them a test.

Confusion vs. Clarity. By emphasizing too many things we destroy visitors' ability to find key information. This paralyzes their decision making. The best way to test this is through things like the 5 sec test or Clicktale.

Alienation vs. Affinity. Your tone and manner makes them feel understood and valued, part of my 'tribe'. For example, I follow two expert SEO firms: SEOmoz and Bruce Clay Inc. I like the way Rand Fish in SEOmoz approaches his readership - friendly, slightly tongue in cheek, self deprecating, and humorous in a geeky way. Bruce Clay Inc, one of their biggest competitors, on the other hand is more formal and professional. I identify much more with the Rand Fishes of the world than the Bruce Clays, so I tend to turn to SEOmoz first for advice.

It's not just single pages, the sales funnel is a multi-page process— from landing page to cart to checkout to order to follow up to repeat business. Tim Ash uses an analogy of a rickety rope bridge with missing pieces. The aim is to fill in the missing pieces to ensure that the customer is satisfied as they go from one end of the bridge, the landing page, to the other, the order. You fix one plank at a time, then turn it into a concrete footbridge, then a highway, then... okay I'm getting carried away with the analogy.

Alcohol beverage marketers say that brand building is all about the right people drinking the right products at the right places. Tim Ash has a variant he calls the 'matrix' where he says you ensure the right people go through the right activities in the right order.

The normal practice of doing this in eCommerce is fixing the pages closer to the checkout, including the checkout itself. This tends to have a greater effect on increased sales compared to say the home page. So test variants of:

- Headlines, probably sub-headings on the product page
- Image - clear and present
- Product description copy - e.g. taste, terroir, people, reviews, ratings, humorous, conservative, shorter, longer
- Action block - with all the key info highlighted, price, quantity, add to cart button. Perhaps do a simple 1-2-3 step to show just what a person needs to do to buy
- The shopping cart - upfront shipping, guest checkout, single page checkout

I would just start with one experiment with sub-headlines on your product page (the headline probably being the actual product name). As you start to get a feel for it, try a few more experiments until you're testing all the high traffic landing pages on your website.

Step 4 Start a Content Experiment

Most web developers and/or eCommerce software integrate directly with Google Analytics Content Experiments. You need to create two webpages: the control and the challenger. You also nominate what the Google Analytics Goal is. You may now find that Content Experiments is too limited and you need to purchase Visual Website Optimizer, Otimizely, or such like to better track financial conversions.

The cost and time of setting up and running experiments varies greatly. It depends on whether you have decided exactly what you want to test, whether you need assistance on choosing test elements, and how long you need to wait while enough conversions occur for Content Experiments to make a call as to the winner of the test.

Step 5 'Beat the Control'

This book is for small wine retailers. However, it's read by all sorts of companies so here are some rules of thumb.

Your conversion page:

- If you have more than 10 sales per day, then make this your eCommerce 'thank you' or 'payment confirmed' page
- If you have less than 10 sales then I (controversially) recommend your shopping cart page. I say controversially because

I'm implicitly trading off time of testing for accuracy of testing. In the business world, we don't have the time that perfectionists would like us to have. You'll probably check every week or perhaps month to see if Google Analytics has made a call on a winner.

Your conversion measurement:

- To start out just use conversion rate % (conversion #s / unique visitors). It is preferable that you put dollar figures to this, but let's walk before you run
- If you're technically able and have many sales per day then you can use revenue per visitor. This assumes your margin is similar across wines: if not, then you risk increasing revenue but reducing profits as you replace more profitable orders with less profitable ones
- Best of all, use profit per visitor especially if your wine bottle margins are not similar across your product range

Apply the 80/20 rule to choosing the pages you test. Use Google Analytics, or your web logs to find the top product (or post) pages. If you're running Google Adwords then the ad's landing page is a good one to optimize. I suggest you just choose one at first, but aim to do this for the 20% of products that make up 80% of your sales.

Decide on your testing elements:

- I'm a big proponent of blogs in addition to (and sometimes instead of) eCommerce sites. The most important part of a blog post is the headline, so test headlines if you're blogging
- If you have an eCommerce site then you may be able to change a sub heading. Otherwise check out Step 3 for what to test. I suggest product description may be the easiest thing you can change.

Do it:

- Create the original page known as the 'control,' 'baseline,' or 'champion'
- Create the alternative page known as 'variant' or 'challenger'
- Follow the Content Experiment steps as per their Help page tutorials
- Try to manage your impatience as the days go by and Google Analytics still hasn't made a call

Have you beaten the control? If so, the challenger page becomes the new control. If not, one theory down, try something else. Record it in a testing document so we don't try the same test again in a years time. Then move on to the next test.

Step 6 The Plan

Most people would have this as Step 1, but I think the best way to learn is put your 'toe into the water' and then step back and plan. Time to look at the forest not the trees. Make a list of all the pages and all the elements you want to test. Prioritize them and knock 'em off. Do not just get lost in one simple test for one element on one page. You want to spend the next 12 months making lots of changes to lots of pages to get a big overall improvement. It becomes just another thing you do every week or month.

18.4 Measurement

Tony is a keen tester and user of Google Analytics and Visual Website Optimizer. In particular, he has focused on reducing the shopping cart abandonment rate as well as increasing the conversion rate of his Adwords campaigns. He has a plan in the form of a testing calendar of lots of things he wants to test. Here are his conversion measurements in the context of his Business Plan.

Note, that for this we will use the measure Revenue per Visitor. This is because we want to increase the number of visitors who purchase as a proportion of all visitors, as well as to increase the average order value. He also applies the same markup across his product range so feels he does not need to use Profit per Visitor. For the purposes of this book, we'll count each time he beats last month's Revenue per Visitor as a converted customer.

We'll also measure shopping cart abandonment as a secondary measure and call each month he reduces this as an Assisted Conversion in the table below.

Business Objective: Boost Margins and Volume by changing to a Higher Value Customer Mix.

Marketing Strategy >Promotion >Internet marketing: Increase Revenue per Visitor through using LPO to increase conversions and revenue.

KPI: Beat last month's Revenue per Visitor per annum (RPV, average order value / total number of visitors) by segment (as determined by price of bottles). Beat last month's Shopping Cart Abandonment % (SCA%) by segment. As measured by Visual Website Optimizer and Google Analytics.

KPI Targets: For Year 2, see Table 18.2.

Segment	Conv.#	Ass. Conv.#	RPV	SCA%
Luxury Enthusiasts:	2	3	$12+	<65%
Enthusiasts:	3	3	$33	<65%
Image Seekers:	3	3	$26	<65%
Luxury Image Seekers:	1	1	$65	<65%

Table 18.2: KPI Targets: LPO (Year 2)

KPI Target Sources: Segment numbers come from the Internet Marketing spreadsheet *Segment Conversions Report*. Note, Visitors is a hypothetical number based off 249 new customers divided by a conversion rate of 1% which equals 24,900 visitors pa; if the store eCommerce revenue is $300,000 (illustrative only) then a benchmark Revenue/Visitor pa equals $12. Likewise, the Shopping Cart Abandonment Rate is also hypothetical and will depend on the eCommerce software you use as well as sources of internet traffic.

LPO will add 19 more customers as a result of offering access to the store wherever the customers happen to be. Tony expects LPO to add five Luxury Enthusiasts. Along with the other marketing strategies mentioned above it means he has six more to go before he reaches his Luxury Enthusiasts target.

18.5 Summary

Conversion Rate Optimization is a way to test which ideas convert best. It's a process that aims to make continuous improvement to each part of the selling online process. Most small companies use the Google Analytics Content Experiments to help you test different webpage components. You should be doing this on your order pages, product and category pages, and advertising landing pages.

18.6 Resources

- How well did you understand? Visit my website to discuss or ask questions about Wine LPO: `www.WineMarketingPros.com/lpochap/`
- Landing Page Optimization specialist agency `SiteTuners.com`
- Visual Website Optimizer `visualwebsiteoptimizer.com/`

Part V

Repeat Purchase

Acquiring new customers is expensive. As you can see from the various parts of this book, a significant amount of work goes into a sale. Sometimes that is just through the amount of time to set up Search Engine Optimization, create Comparison Shopping Engine feeds, write blog posts, comment on Facebook and Twitter, monitor the blogosphere, manage your wine catalog, and undertake a testing program. Sometimes it is through time and money, such as internet advertising.

So turning new customers into profitable, long-term customers by building a relationship is vital. You can do this with blogs, Facebook, and Twitter, but email is still the proven method and many of the techniques outlined below also can be applied to social media. Note, however, the fact that there is only one marketing strategy chapter in this part. That is because of the division of topics into the marketing funnel is artificial. Most internet marketing strategies also are important for boosting repeat sales.

19 Email Marketing

19.1 What is Email Marketing

Email marketing is a well-known form of internet marketing where a business sends out emails to their customer base. Most often small retailers do this by sending out newsletters using Microsoft Outlook. In this chapter, we look at a more effective approach.

19.2 Email Best Practices

I'll outline the key elements of a successful wine email marketing campaign. We'll cover lists, double opt-in, Internet Service Providers (ISP), personalization, and content topics.

19.2.1 Responsive Lists are Better

To see why, let's illustrate this with some some math (* means multiply):
Value of one email mail out =
List size * Delivery rate % * Open rate % * Click through rate % * Conversion rate % * Order value $
Let's look at each part of that:

- List size: # of subscribers
- * Delivery rate: emails that still exist at time of sending
- * Open rate: emails opened and not immediately deleted or put in spam folder
- * Click through rate: readers actually click on link to your website
- * Conversion rate: readers who then buy something
- * Average order size: a case perhaps
- = Total Order Value: value of this mail out

Table 19.1 gives an example of how a smaller list is more effective than a larger list.

Element	Big List	Small but Responsive List
List size	10,000	1,000
* Delivery rate	80%	90%
* Open rate	20%	60%
* Click through rate	20%	60%
* Conversion rate	1%	3%
* Average order size	$80	$120
= Total Order Value	$256	$1,166

Table 19.1: Responsive Lists

Notice how the list that is 10 times smaller in Table 19.1 has an order value four times bigger! You could go further: if you send out 24 great emails to a responsive list then that's $27,000, vs six poor emails to an uninterested list of $1500 per annum.

But the math gets even worse. To get a customer using Adwords, it may cost, for example, $0.25 per click * 500 clicks = $125. Of which, 1% converts to sales = 5 customers. Each of whom buy two $10 bottles of wine = $100 of revenue. Less cost of goods of $66 = $34 of gross margin. So it has cost you $125 to acquire 5 customers for a total loss of $25. You are no further ahead unless you get repeat sales. If only one of those customers buys every month then you will have a profitable campaign. Without that repeat customer you are losing money.

What's more is, if you can get regular repeat sales then you can afford to spend more on your marketing than anyone else as your total customer value per annum for each customer acquired is higher than a competitor who does not get repeat business. So in this chapter I'm not going to look at list size but how to make your list more responsive.

19.2.2 Double Check with Double Opt-In

The Double Opt-in Process is where a subscriber is sent an email asking them to click on a link to confirm that they have subscribed. When they do this the link notifies your email system that the person has opted in twice ('double') and is therefore a valid email subscriber. If you do nothing else, force your subscribers to double opt-in to your emails. Subscribers who do this,

- are found to be more responsive
- cannot say to the authorities they did not opt-in as you have proof that they did
- cannot be subscribed by someone else
- confirm that email address is correct

All the big email marketing service providers (e.g. aweber, mailchimp, iContact, Vertical Response) have this process. I agree that it puts a barrier in front of a potential subscriber, but email has had such a checkered history of delivering spam that it is worth their inconvenience in order to get a responsive list.

19.2.3 How to Handle Email Unsubscribes and Paranoid ISPs

If you use a professional email marketing service (e.g. aweber or mailchimp), you can automatically process the regular unsubscribe requests you get from your email list. These services put a simple unsubscribe link at the bottom of each email they send out. At anytime your subscriber can automatically unsubscribe by clicking on the link. Mailchimp is free for smaller lists. Apart from being saved from the tedious job of manual unsubscribes, you also keep ISPs (e.g. Yahoo or AOL) happy. If these guys get a complaint and blacklist you then it's a long drawn-out process to get back in their good books and through their spam filters.

Similarly, the email marketing service providers automatically 'clean' your lists. If someone's email expires the email marketing software removes them from your list. Emails expire due to inactive use, moving companies, or ISPs. If you don't remove these then the ISPs may well find out and, you guessed it, assume you're spam (because you're sending to inactive email accounts) and blacklist you.

Are you using MS Outlook? If you have a small list you may be able to get away with this. But once you send 200 (and perhaps even 50) people an email the ISPs again start to get nervous and may tag your emails as spam. You also have the time consuming manual unsubscribe issue.

Most western countries now have anti-spam laws. In the US, this is called CANSPAM. To abide by this legislation you need to provide your physical address and the ability for recipients to unsubscribe. Some people put in a telephone number as well. There are various other constraints most of which are common sense.

Even once you've done all that you may find your recipients aren't even opening your emails. You may never really know. The traditional way of an email service working out whether an email is opened is through analyzing whether a tiny image in the email has been uploaded. However many recipients (e.g. Gmail users) have images turned off so this analysis can be very inaccurate. They could also be going straight into the Outlook spam folder or deleted by the subscriber without opening them. So use an email marketing service and you'll get a majority of your emails opened, depending on your content, which is next.

19.2.4 Personalize Everything

Have a customized Thank You or Subscription Confirmed page. Most companies just have something like 'Thank you for subscribing' and that's it. Instead, I recommend you immediately 'pounce' on this consumer interest and encourage sales with an offer. Perhaps a time-limited gift with purchase, perhaps with a popular wine brand and/or a super exclusive wine with an Add to Cart Button right beside it.

Always personalize your emails—both ways

- People are much more likely to respond to real people not computers
- your From field should be name@YourStore.com not do-not-reply@YourStore.com
- your email should start with Dear (or Hi, Hey, Howdy) first-name, easily done through email marketing software

Have a Plan B. Send out html emails by all means; however, keep them simple and make sure you have text as well as images. The classic email mistake is a fancy image-only email, the mistake being that the image will never be shown to people who block images in their email Inbox (e.g. Gmail users). It'll be a blank email—not the best way to get response! Also html emails can come out poorly formatted with silly backgrounds that show no text.

My preference is to use text for B2B emails, and limit html in B2C (to just product image shots and your logo). You then refer people to a web page to see a perfectly formatted landing page on your website.

Regularly send out emails. An email is an attempt at maintaining and building a customer relationship. If you don't regularly say or offer something interesting then that relationship will just wane away. If you're good at writing then start blogging (or podcasting or making short videos). Send out the blog post by email once a week, but no less than once a month. The rule of thumb is to not expect any action until you've contacted someone seven times (though this contact could be through other internet marketing strategies, such as social media or SEO).

Send a little bit of content a lot, rather than a long email a little. People normally hate long emails. You also want one message per email. So take each topic and send it out separately in a few paragraphs, if not just one. This promo one week, that tasting the next, a new release on the third sort of thing.

I used to get Gary Vaynerchuk WineLibraryTV emails everyday, and I didn't mind because I found his content entertaining and informative. Some lists send me emails I read just once and immediately unsubscribe—the content was just plain boring or irrelevant. So how often depends on your skill and the interest of the recipient.

19.2.5 Content is King (again), Some Suggested Topics

There are two types of emails:

- Information type emails
- Promotional emails

Information emails keep people interested and engaged but information emails will get less sales response. Promotional emails get great sales response, but if we send out too many promotional emails then customers will regard it as spam and will stop opening them or unsubscribe. So it's a mix, keep them interested yet responsive, perhaps an 80/20 or 90/10 split in favor of information emails.

We also want one message per email—do lots of information emails then a promotional one.

As with landing page optimization, make sure you test your emails. Randomly split the list into two, send out different emails, and find a winner after a longish period (rule of thumb is both lists have at least 30-40 sales). Then start another test.

I would also first test the subject line with different wording ('copy') as the subject (and headline in webpages) drives response the most. It is likely to be the only thing that all your lists see before making a decision as to whether to open your email.

No matter what content you write, always have a call to action that links to a relevant page on your website, preferably to a product page where they can buy a particular wine. The call to action might be something like Buy Now or Read More. It would be prominent and at the top, middle, and bottom of the email.

Below I've listed some prompters for emails. Your subject line would be the prompter in Title Case. Your content would then be a few paragraphs (or just one) on the subject line. You would always have a call to action. They would be part of a sentence. Where I use [brackets] then the word is just an example.

Information Email: Headlines (garner response by intriguing people like a newspaper does)

- The King of
- Once every 30 years
- A Discovery at
- Adventure in
- Share your love with
- Sure to Surprise
- Crisis in
- No Justice in

Check out all the titles on magazine cover pages at your local magazine stand, especially the womens magazines. They are the experts at catching attention through titles.

Promotional Email: Discount

- Free shipping
- 1 buck shipping
- Save an additional 15% on already reduced prices
- Rush shipping on Us
- Best Deals
- 50% off end of vintage clearance
- First Buyer Special
- A great offer from [vineyard]
- Half price
- Buy one get one free
- Save 33%

- 1 cent shipping

Free shipping has become a very popular promotion for online retailers, but for wine retailers, the product is heavy so this makes this an expensive promo.

Information Email: Attention Seeking Emails

- Alert
- Top rated
- 94 point rated
- Private Selection of
- Action required
- The best of
- Top 40
- Best selling wines under $15
- Deal Alert
- Vintage of the Decade
- Pay Dirt at
- Merlot Heaven
- The Merlot Insider
- Pinot Wine Guide
- Wine 101—how to
- Wines from
- Wines of
- Wine and Food, e.g. Salmon
- Wine and Climate, e.g. Summer
- One of the greatest
- Cult like

Promotional Email: Scarcity (of time)

- Last call
- Last chance
- While they last
- Final chance
- 3 days only
- Ends at midnight
- Ends tomorrow
- Today only

Information: News (preferably breaking news)

- Just rated by Wine Spectator
- New Arrivals

- New from abc vineyard
- Just awarded gold at

19.3 Measurement

Tony has abandoned his old email newsletters sent out by Microsoft Outlook. He is using professional email marketing software called MailChimp that he has integrated into his website as well as Google Analytics. Here are his Email measurements in the context of his Business Plan.

Business Objective: Boost Margins and Volume by changing to a Higher Value Customer Mix.

Marketing Strategy >Promotion >Internet marketing: Increase traffic with high value customers through Email Marketing that leads to conversions.

KPI: Conversion Average Order Value; Conversion Average Bottle Value. As measured by Google Analytics filtered for the traffic sources tagged 'email'.

KPI Targets: For Year 2, see Table 19.2.

Segment	Conv.#	Ass. Conv.#	AOV	ABV
Luxury Enthusiasts:	2	1	$65	$25
Enthusiasts:	5	2	$33	$15
Image Seekers:	2	2	$26	$15
Luxury Image Seekers:	2	1	$65	$15

Table 19.2: KPI Targets: Email (Year 2)

KPI Target Sources: Segment numbers come from the Internet Marketing spreadsheet *Segment Conversions Report*. For Conversion Average Order Value equations see SEO Measurement section.

Email Marketing will add 17 more customers. Tony expects Email Marketing to add three Luxury Enthusiasts. Along with the other marketing strategies mentioned above (and the spreadsheet rounding error of three) it means he has reached his Luxury Enthusiasts target!

19.4 Summary

In summary, make sure your list is responsive, use professional email marketing services, personalize your message, and keep your content information focused with the odd promotional message.

19.5 Resources

- How well did you understand? Visit my website to discuss or ask questions about Wine Email Marketing: `www.WineMarketingPros.com/emailchap/`
- There are many good email services, I use MailChimp `mailchimp.com`

20 Conclusion

This book has shown how a wine retailer or winery can take internet marketing strategies and reinvigorate a 'brick and mortar' store or tasting room into a 'clicks and mortar' store. How understanding the component parts of the selling wine online process is vital to building a profitable online business, and how selling wine online can help solve important business issues through using the correct strategy for the correct business problem.

As every business should, we looked at Customers first. Various types of customers were presented with the Project Genome study being used extensively throughout this book. In particular, the identification of a group of higher value customers who can afford the higher priced wines and have a desire for wine information that small wine retailers are well set up to provide.

We looked at the Competitors, which showed that other 'brick and mortar' wine stores could be as much of a concern, if not more, than the online variety. Indeed, Social Media research showed BevMo is a particularly strong competitor with its local stores and national eCommerce website. However, wine.com continues to perform strongly in many of the more traditional internet research measures, such as SEO ranking.

Not to be disheartened, we considered the Company advantages that a small wine store has. The local element is hugely important, and can be used to great effect, with many internet marketing strategies as well as providing a cost advantage when it comes to fulfillment and freight. We also looked in detail at the illustrative Tony's Wine Store and saw how internet marketing fitted into the Business Plan and contributed to profits.

We then took a winery perspective, which is more brand management focused than a wine retailer. We created a market model with consumer segments and wine competitors positioned on it, then decided where to position our brand. We then created a brand definition and ensured that everything the winery did, including internet marketing, helped to push the brand towards its ideal place in the wine market.

Internet marketing sometimes is associated with 'high tech hype', so a whole chapter was on how to measure the success. A key problem, multiple attribution, was introduced as were web analytics tools, such as Google Analytics.

Search Engine Optimization was the first internet marketing strategy to be covered. We looked at Google's algorithm for ranking websites and how to change your website to boost SEO driven traffic. The need for unique, interesting content was brought up from the perspective of building links from other relevant and high authority websites.

The first local advantage was comprehensively explained in the Local SEO chapter. Google+ Local has become increasingly crucial for a local business, as has tagging your website with local addresses and embracing local directories such as Yelp.

Internet Advertising, especially Adwords, was covered next. The basics, as well as wine tips and tricks and local advertising, were outlined. Banner, Mobile, and Facebook are all good sources of traffic, with the first two covered in concept and the latter one covered in practice.

Given their high conversion rates Comparison Shopping Engines are perhaps under appreciated by the wine industry. In the CSE chapter, I cover two of them – Snooth and Wine-Searcher. I explain what are feeds and what's best to put in them.

The sexy part of internet marketing is covered next – Social Media in Part III: Engagement. Sexy now, perhaps, but what is likely to be sexier in the future are services which incorporate social, local and mobile. These too are covered in Part III.

Exactly what social media covers, whether they're worth time and money, and how to measure them are explained and put into context.

Blogging is introduced as an excellent way to write content. The engagement comes from readers commenting, but there also are significant SEO benefits as well. This chapter finishes with a Social Media Brief.

Facebook is the new behemoth of the internet industry. We look at why you should have a Facebook Page, how to set it up, and the best practices for running it.

Twitter is perhaps Facebook's social media sister. We look at why, what, and who to tweet. We look at how to measure influence and why tweeting makes sense.

The rise of the smartphone and the 'mulit-screen world' is considered. In particular, what are the best apps, what is the best wine store app, and in-store usage through QR codes.

The new kid on the block, Location-Based Services, is reviewed with some suggestions on how to handle negative reviews and some first steps with FourSquare.

The next part is about the point at which the sale takes place – Conversion. Firstly we consider wine eCommerce: what is it, what a wine store wants from it, and who supplies it. In particular, we take a requirements approach based on the relative importance of each part of the selling wine online process.

Mobile and Social Commerce is ensuring that customers can buy how they want to, when they want to, and where they want to. If that's by staying in the Facebook environment, or in the train on the way home from work, then so be it. Although the technology is not as developed as normal eCommerce, there are still good options to increase sales from these particular sources.

Internet marketing success is generally a steady process of building, creating content, and testing what works. Landing Page Optimization is the process of testing and measuring which internet campaigns work best. It can be used in most of the marketing strategies above and aims to increase each one a little each month, the result being a large increase by the end of each year.

Last, let's not forget email marketing. Perhaps the original internet marketing strategy, it still is a very effective technique, though one that is more for boosting repeat business through building responsive lists.

Tony's Wine Store, this book's illustrative wine store, started with a significant financial loss from competing with a large discounting chain store. By the end of the book, he had a plan to boost his profits by focusing on high-value customers through using internet marketing strategies. Your wine store may face different issues, but the business strategy of selling more high-margin wine, more often, works for most wine retailers. It just requires the right plan and good execution.

For more resources, including wine internet marketing updates, forum support and the various files mentioned in this book visit www.WineMarketingPros.com. I hope to see you there, and that this book helps you enjoy financial success through selling wine online.

Bibliography

[1] "Nokia CEO Stephen Elop rallies troops in brutally honest 'burning platform' memo?."
www.engadget.com/2011/02/08/nokia-ceo-stephen-elop-rallies-troops-in-brutally-honest-burnin/.

[2] "Shoppers spent more online last year, but that trend won't last forever."
http://www.tampabay.com/news/business/retail/shoppers-spent-more-online-last-year-but-that-trend-wont-last-forever/1270433.

[3] Economist, "Retail v e-tail in america. bleak friday, bricks-and-mortar shops struggle to win customers back from virtual ones.," *The Economist*, Nov 26 2009.

[4] Google, "The new multi-screen world: Understanding cross-platform consuemr behaviour," August 2012.

[5] T. Ferriss, *The 4-Hour Workweek*. Crown Archetype, 2009.

[6] "What's Wrong With Wine on the Web."
online.wsj.com/article/SB123939668806909355.html.

[7] J. Lecinski, "ZMOT Winning the Zero Moment of Truth," tech. rep., Google, 2011.

[8] "Macy's chief addresses power of e-commerce.," Sept 23 2009.

[9] "Wine market council's 2010 consumer tracking study."
www.winemarketcouncil.com/research_slideview.asp?position=1.

[10] "LinkedIn Group: Vintage Wines."
www.linkedin.com/groups?home=gid=2105414.

[11] "Isabelle Lesschaeve." ilesschaeve.wordpress.com/.

[12] . B. J. Johnson, T, "An empirical confirmation of wine-related lifestyle segments.," *International Journal of Wine Marketing*, vol. 15, no. 1, 2003.

[13] . B. Johnson, T, "Generic consumer risk-reduction strategies (rrs) in wine-related lifestyle segments of the australian wine market," *International Journal of Wine Marketing*, vol. 16, no. 1, 2004.

[14] "Tony Spawton." www.linkedin.com/in/spawton19862009.

[15] Constellation-Wines, "Project Genome." www.cwinesus.com – see bit.ly/pt9wDz, 2010.

[16] "Constellation Sells Australian Wine Business." www.winemag.com/Wine-Enthusiast-Magazine/February-2011/Constellation-Sells-Australian-Wine-Business/, 2010.

[17] R. V. Kozinets, *Netnography: Doing Ethnographic Research Online*. Sage Publications Ltd, 2009.

[18] "Brand Passion Index: Piper's Bubbles Burst with Love." www.netbase.com/blog/sentiment/brand-passion-index-whose-bubbles-fell-flat/, 2011.

[19] "Survey Random Sample Calculator." www.custominsight.com/articles/random-sample-calculator.asp.

[20] "Consumer Base." www.netbase.com/consumer_insights/consumer_base.php.

[21] Economist, "ecommerce special report: Distribution dilemmas," *The Economist*, Feb 24 2000.

[22] Economist, "The lesson from online grocery," *The Economist*, June 25 2001.

[23] Economist, "Santa's helpers," *The Economist*, May 13 2004.

[24] B. Rosenbloom, *Marketing Channels: A Management View*. Thomson Southwestern, 2004.

[25] "Amazon stops selling wine before it ever starts; Wine blogs on Forbes.com." www.drvino.com/2009/10/25/amazon-wine-suspended-best-wine-blogs-on-forbes-com/,
2009.

[26] "Googles local search number." http://searchengineland.com/chitika-we-got-googles-local-search-number-wrong-135965.

[27] "Google: 50www.screenwerk.com/2012/10/01/google-50-of-mobile-search-is-local/.

[28] D. J. Gaiter and J. Brecher, "Wine Stores With Shtick." guides.wsj.com/wine/buying-and-storing-wine/wine-stores-with-shtick/,
2007.

[29] "Current Economic Trends in the California Wine Industry." giannini.ucop.edu/media/are-update/files/articles/v11n4_2.pdf.

[30] R. Hamlin, "Talking to our financial backers: The key role of financial 'offer models'." University of Otago.

[31] O. Wagner and Thach, *Wine Marketing and Sales*. Wine Appreciation Guild, 2007.

[32] R. Higham, "Deloittes, now kpmg."

[33] M. Gerber, *The E-Myth Revisited*. HarperCollins, 1995.

[34] D. Arnold, *The Handbook Of Brand Management*. Basic Books, 1 ed., 1993.

[35] "Maslow's hierarchy of needs." www.simplypsychology.org/maslow.html.

[36] A. Gourdie, "Brand management training." Company training.

[37] A. Kaushik, "Occam's Razor Blog." www.kaushik.net/.

[38] "Excellent Analytics Tip 13: Measure Macro AND Micro Conversions." www.kaushik.net/avinash/excellent-analytics-tip-13-measure-macro-and-micro-conversions/.

[39] "Wine directory."
http://www.vintank.com/our-sandbox/data-syndication/.

[40] S. S. on SEOmoz Blog, "Mission ImposSERPble: Establishing
Click-through Rates." www.seomoz.org/blog/mission-
imposserpble-establishing-clickthrough-rates,
2011.

[41] SEOmoz, "Search Engine Ranking Factors."
www.seomoz.org/article/search-ranking-factors, 2011.

[42] R. Fishkin, "The end of search without social."
www.seomoz.org/webinars/the-end-of-search-without-social,
Sept 2011.

[43] R. Fishkin, "Illustrating the long tail."
www.seomoz.org/blog/illustrating-the-long-tail, Nov 24 2009.

[44] B. Clay, "SEO Siloing: Building a Themed Website."
www.bruceclay.com/seo/silo.htm.

[45] R. Fishkin, "What separates a good outreach email from a
great one? - whiteboard friday."
www.seomoz.org/blog/what-separates-a-good-outreach-email-
from-a-great-one-whiteboard-friday, Dec 14
2012.

[46] M. Cutts, "How do I optimize an e-commerce site without rich
content?." www.youtube.com/watch?v=LI_NmnXn5A4, 2009.

[47] M. Blumenthal, "Ed parsons: 1 in 3 searches at google are
local." blumenthals.com/blog/2012/11/13/ed-parsons-1-
in-3-searches-at-google-are-local/.

[48] Google, "Google Places." www.google.com/places/.

[49] "Local search ranking factors."
www.davidmihm.com/local-search-ranking-factors.shtml.

[50] Google, "Google Places: Help customers find you on Google
Maps." www.google.com/placesforbusiness.

[51] "Best local citation sources by category."
getlisted.org/resources/local-citations-by-category.aspx.

[52] TechCrunch, "Google In Discussions To Acquire Yelp For A Half Billion Dollars Or More." techcrunch.com/2009/12/17/google-acquire-buy-yelp/, 2009.

[53] I. A. Bureau and P. W. Coopers, "Iab internet advertising revenue report," tech. rep., Internet Advertising Bureau, October 2012.

[54] Google, "Google 2011 Financial Tables." investor.google.com/financial/tables.html, 2011.

[55] "Adwords policy center - alcohol." support.google.com/adwordspolicy/answer/176005?hl= en&ref_topic=1310883&rd=2#.

[56] "What are keyword matching options? - Broad Match." support.google.com/adwords/answer/2497836?hl=en.

[57] G. A. Help, "How much do I pay for a click on my ad? ." support.google.com/adwords/answer/6297?rd=1.

[58] G. A. C. Support, "Ad approvals and policies." email to author, Nov 20 2012.

[59] "How does AdWords know where geographically to show my keyword-targeted ads?." support.google.com/adwords/answer/2453995?hl=en.

[60] eMarketer, "Unexpected growth from facebook, google lead to significant uptick in us mobile advertising." http://www.emarketer.com/newsroom/index.php/tag/mobile-advertising/, December 2012.

[61] eMarketer, "Google to become us display ad leader." http://www.emarketer.com/newsroom/index.php/google-display-ad-leader/, Sept 2012.

[62] TechCrunch, "Initial trials show facebook exchange retargeted ads deliver massive return on investment, up to 16x." techcrunch.com/2012/09/13/facebook-exchange-results/, Sept 2012.

[63] G. (et al), "Best Practices in Facebook Marketing," tech. rep., Search Marketing Now and Acquisio, 2011.

[64] Fireclick, "Fireclick Index - Speciality." index.fireclick.com/fireindex.php?segment=6.

[65] "The unofficial cookie faq." http://www.cookiecentral.com/.

[66] "Wine-Searcher contact." www.wine-searcher.com/contact.lml.

[67] P. Mabray, "Vintank connect: Powering social intelligence for the wine industry." Report pdf, 2012.

[68] "Highlights from wine market council's 2011 u.s. wine consumer trends and analysis report." winemarketcouncil.com/?page_id=35.

[69] "December data on facebook's us growth by age and gender: Beyond 100 million." www.insidefacebook.com/2010/01/04/december-data-on-facebook

[70] "Cellartracker website." CellarTracker.com.

[71] "Cellartracker network in quantcast." http://www.quantcast.com/cellartracker.com!demo.

[72] "Techsmart episode 5." Podcast, 2 Oct 2012.

[73] J. O. Rebecca Lieb, "The converged media imperative: How brands must combine paid, owned, and earned media." Altimeter Group.

[74] C. Li, "Understand Your Customers' Social Behaviors." www.altimetergroup.com/2010/01/socialgraphics-webinar-slides-and-recording-now-available.html, 2010.

[75] "The problem with measuring digital influence." techcrunch.com/2012/11/09/can-social-media-influence-really-be-measured/.

[76] S. Corcoran, ""no media should stand alone"," tech. rep., Forrester Research, December 2009.

[77] J. L. S. Jeremiah Owyang, "Social marketing analytics! a new framework for measuring results in social media!","," tech. rep., Altimeter Group, Web Analytics Demystified, April 2009.

[78] M. Greene, ""justifying social marketing spending"," tech. rep., Forrester Research, February 2009.

[79] "FTC Publishes Final Guides Governing Endorsements, Testimonials." www.ftc.gov/opa/2009/10/endortest.shtm, 2009.

[80] "Whiteboard Friday - Outsourcing Content Creation (at 5'.03")." www.seomoz.org/blog/whiteboard-friday-outsourcing-content-creation, 2009.

[81] "Facebook - Wikipedia." en.wikipedia.org/wiki/Facebook.

[82] "Facebook statistics." www.statisticbrain.com/facebook-statistics/.

[83] B. Bosker, "Facebook explains how often your posts actually get seen." www.huffingtonpost.com/2012/02/29/facebook-posts_n_1311330.html, 29 Feb 2012.

[84] "Edgerank: The secret sauce that makes facebook's news feed tick." techcrunch.com/2010/04/22/facebook-edgerank/.

[85] "Mari smith post." facebook.com/marismith, October 2012.

[86] "Facebook: I want my friends back." dangerousminds.net/comments/facebook_i_want_my_friends_back.

[87] "Mar 31, 2010 - 7:00am pt 5 things that don't work on facebook pages (and 5 that do)." gigaom.com/2010/03/31/5-things-that-dont-work-on-facebook-pages-and-5-that-do/.

[88] "Facebook marketing." facebook.com/marketing.

[89] J. Owyang, "Altimeter Report: The 8 Success Criteria For Facebook Page Marketing." www.altimetergroup.com/2010/07/altimeter-report-the-8-success-criteria-for-facebook-page-marketing.html, 2010.

[90] D. Sullivan, "By The Numbers: How Facebook Says Likes Social Plugins Help Websites." searchengineland.com/by-the-numbers-how-facebook-says-likes-social-plugins-help-websites-76061, 2011.

[91] "Twitter - Wikipedia." en.wikipedia.org/wiki/Twitter.

[92] C. Brogan, "The Future of Community." www.chrisbrogan.com/futureofcommunity/, 2011.

[93] G. Kawasaki, "The Six Twitter Types." www.openforum.com/articles/the-six-twitter-types-guy-kawasaki, 2010.

[94] B. Solis, "The rise of digital influence: A "how-to" guide for businesses to spark desirable effects and outcomes through social media influence." Altimeter Group Report, March 2012.

[95] K. Nakao, "Why You May Not Need a Mobile App." mashable.com/2010/06/10/why-you-may-not-need-a-mobile-app/, 2010.

[96] "Beaming up to CostCo (The CostCo Connection)." www.costcoconnection.com/connection/201011pg87, 2010.

[97] "Square calculator." feefighters.com/square-calculator.

[98] "Reconsidering john doerr's solomo internet boom." www.bizjournals.com/stlouis/blog/BizNext/2012/12/reconsidering-john-doerrs-solomo.html.

[99] "Dealmap Launches 'Exchange' for Deals." www.screenwerk.com/2010/12/07/dealmap-launches-exchange-for-deals/, 2010.

[100] P. Lane, "Special report: Technology and geography." The Economist, Dec 18 2012.

[101] "Grouponworks for Business." www.grouponworks.com/.

[102] "Groupon Turns Down Google's $6 Billion Offer."
       mashable.com/2010/12/03/groupon-google-no/.

[103] "10,000,000 Strong." foursquare.com/10million, 2011.

[104] "Foursquare Merchant Platform."
       foursquare.com/business/venues, 2011.

[105] B. Hunt, "Web Design is Dead."
       www.webdesignfromscratch.com/blog/web-design-is-
       dead/, 2010.

[106] B. McGechan, "Wine eCommerce Requirements: Small vs
       Large Wine Retailer." www.mylocalwinestore.com/wp-
       content/uploads/WineEcommerceRequirements.pdf,
       2010.

[107] B. McGechan, "Wine eCommerce Requirements:
       Small-Medium vs Medium-Large Wine Retailer."
       www.mylocalwinestore.com/ – pdf at bit.ly/qWrEcK, 2010.

[108] "Sell Wine Online. Open your Wine Shop Online for as little
       as $250/mo.."
       www.bevsites.com/index.php/category/sell-wine-online/,
       accessed 8 Sept 2011.

[109] A. G. Search Marketing Now (with Brad Geddes and
       A. Rimm-Kaufman), "Choosing a ppc management pricing
       model. structuring ppc agency contracts for long-term
       success," tech. rep., Third Door Media, Inc, 2010.

[110] P. eCommerce, "500 Million People and Growing: The
       Facebook Conversation Turns to Commerce."
       www.practicalecommerce.com/webinars/41-500-Million-
       People-and-Growing-The-Facebook-Conversation-Turns-to-
       Commerce,
       2010.

[111] P. Marsden, "Does My Butt Look Big in This? Emerging
       Trends in Social Commerce."
       www.slideshare.net/paulsmarsden/does-my-butt-look-big-in-
       this-emerging-trends-in-social-commerce,
       2010.

[112] Mashable, "The beginner's guide to facebook commerce."
     http://mashable.com/2011/07/14/facebook-commerce-guide/.

[113] SeeWhy, "What Conversion Rates from January 5 and 6 Can
     Tell Us." seewhy.com/blog/2010/01/25/what-conversion-
     rates-from-january-5-and-6-can-tell-us/,
     2010.

[114] "Conversion Rate Experts."
     www.conversion-rate-experts.com/.

[115] "SiteTuners." sitetuners.com/.

[116] T. Ash, *Landing Page Optimization: The Definitive Guide to
     Testing and Tuning for Conversions.* Wiley Publishing, 2008.

[117] C. Hopkins, "My life in advertising and scientific advertising."

[118] R. Vandenberg, "Show-Me-The-Money Conversion Ratios."
     www.practicalecommerce.com/articles/479-Show-Me-The-
     Money-Conversion-Ratios,
     2007.

[119] D. P. J. Meyers, "Priceless CRO Advice for $224."
     www.seomoz.org/blog/priceless-cro-advice-for-224, 2010.

[120] C. R. Experts, "15 tools that reveal why people abandon your
     website." www.conversion-rate-
     experts.com/articles/understanding-your-visitors/.

Index

59505562R00230

Made in the USA
Columbia, SC
04 June 2019